Eileen Ormsby is a Melbourn[...]n. Leaving school in her early teens [...], admin, serviced office managem[...]re getting an Arts/Law degree at Monash [...] 2003 as a mature-age student. After seven years as a corporate lawyer in top-tier firms in Melbourne and London, she threw it in to do a Diploma of Professional Writing and Editing at RMIT in 2012. Freelance journalism saw her investigative features appear regularly in *The Age* and a smattering of other publications. Her chick-lit novel is languishing in a drawer.

Eileen lives in St Kilda with her elderly dog, Zonker, where they enjoy the beach and live music venues. She blogs at allthingsvice.com.

SILK ROAD

EILEEN ORMSBY

MACMILLAN

Pan Macmillan Australia

To Matt. Because you have always been my hero.

First published 2014 in Macmillan by Pan Macmillan Australia Pty Ltd
1 Market Street, Sydney, New South Wales, Australia, 2000

Reprinted 2015

Copyright © Eileen Ormsby 2014

The moral right of the author has been asserted.

Cataloguing-in-Publication entry is available
from the National Library of Australia
http://catalogue.nla.gov.au

Typeset in Fairfield LH Light 12.5/17.5 pt by Post Pre-press Group
Printed by IVE

The author and the publisher have made every effort to contact copyright holders for material used in this book. Any person or organisation that may have been overlooked should contact the publisher.

Contents

A Word from the Dread Pirate Roberts

Greetings and welcome to Silk Road!

I know you can't wait to get to the good stuff, but please take a moment to read this message. It's been written to help keep you safe, make the most of your time here and let you know what this is all about.

Let's start with the name. The original Silk Road was an old-world trade network that connected Asia, Africa and Europe. It played a huge role in connecting the economies and cultures of these continents and promoted peace and prosperity through trade agreements. It is my hope that this modern Silk Road can do the same thing, by providing a framework for trading partners to come together for mutual gain in a safe and secure way.

You may be shocked to find listings here that are outlawed in your jurisdiction. That doesn't mean Silk Road is lawless. In fact, we have a very strict code of conduct that, if given a chance, most people I think would agree with. Our basic rules are to treat others as you would wish to be treated, mind your own business, and don't do anything to hurt or scam someone else. In the spirit of those rules, there are some things you will never see here, and if you do please report them. They include child pornography, stolen goods, assassinations and stolen personal information, just to name a few. We also hold our members to the highest standards of personal conduct and work tirelessly to prevent, root out and stop any scammers that may try to prey upon others.

However, the best way to stay safe and make sure your experiences here are enjoyable is to educate yourself on how Silk Road works, and take advantage of all the tools and guidelines we have made for you. A link to a complete guide can be found on your account page, but here are a few tips to get you started:

- Always use the escrow system! This can't be stressed enough. 99% per cent of scams are from people who set up fake vendor accounts and ask buyers to pay them directly or release payment before their order arrives. This behaviour should be reported immediately. If you do choose to do this, we will be completely unable to help you in the event of fraud.
- Read the forum and the wiki. They contain a wealth of information and many in our forum community are eager to help a new member with a respectful attitude.
- Start small. Do a few small trades until you are comfortable with the process before throwing all of your bitcoins at a big purchase.

The old saying 'With freedom comes responsibility' couldn't be more true here. You will find easy access to things that could get you in trouble with your authorities and are downright terrible for your health. So, just because you can doesn't mean you should. However, I'm not your daddy and it's your job to judge what is good and bad for you. No one else can do that.

Stay safe, have fun, and come say hi on the forums!

Your faithful servant,

Dread Pirate Roberts

'A Word from the Dread Pirate Roberts'
from the landing screen of the Silk Road website

Prologue

The computer screen displays a bewildering array of drugs. Colourful pictures of powders and pills in various quantities offer inducements to buy: *Border-proof delivery! Ten per cent extra on orders over 5 grams!* Underneath each picture is a price, using an unfamiliar currency symbol.

Scrolling down the green-and-white page, a potential customer might click on heroin from Canada, crystal meth from Australia or LSD from the Czech Republic. Once a choice is made, another click adds them to the checkout basket, ready to be shipped. Just like on Amazon.

In the top left-hand corner of the screen a strange symbol – like a capital B with two lines through it, reminiscent of an American dollar sign – displays the user's account balance in bitcoin.

A German seller calling himself 'Jurgen2000' is offering MDMA, the powder form of ecstasy. Clicking on the listing reveals

Jurgen has a great reputation. His feedback is full of praise for his prices, quality and delivery times.

A savvy Silk Road user uses PGP ('pretty good privacy') encryption to encrypt the delivery address to Jurgen. Once installed, with a couple of clicks PGP can change any block of text into a long paragraph of indecipherable gibberish that will be unreadable to all but Jurgen, who will have the private key to crack the code to return it to normal text. Anyone who managed to seize the Silk Road servers would not be able to get the buyer's name and address from that order. Not even the Silk Road administrators could unscramble the information.

Within a few hours of an order being placed, Jurgen marks the delivery as 'in transit' and sends the buyer a cheery message saying that the order is on its way.

'Please,' Jurgen writes, 'if there is any problem, send me a message before complaining to admin or in the forums. We should be able to work it out without the need to go to resolution.'

Depending on where you are in the world from Jurgen, a few days later a nondescript white envelope bearing a German postmark and the return address of a real estate agent arrives. Folded within a couple of pieces of paper that are blank except for '1M' typed on one of them, is a vacuum-sealed pack of a brown–white powder.

The buyer tests the ecstasy – either using a reagent purity-testing kit, or the old-fashioned way: ingesting it. Then it is a matter of logging in to the site through Tor, the program that provides anonymity, and finalising the order by releasing the funds from escrow into Jurgen's account. The site then ask the buyer for feedback, and Jurgen always gets five out of five.

He's a polite seller on the other side of the world, eager to provide good service to ensure he maintains his five-star rating and receives repeat custom.

Welcome to a new era of drug dealing.

Part One

Onionland

Silk Road Charter

Silk Road is a global enterprise whose purpose is to empower people to live as free individuals. We provide systems and platforms that allow our customers to defend their basic human rights and pursue their own ends, provided those ends do not infringe on the rights of others.

Our mission is to have voluntary interaction between individuals be the foundation of human civilization.

We conduct ourselves and our enterprise from the following fundamental values that are at the heart of who we are:

Self-ownership
Individuals own their bodies, thoughts and will. Anything they create with their property or obtain without coercion is also theirs.
Responsibility
People are responsible for their actions. If one infringes on another's rights, the victim has the right to defend themselves.

Equality

Property rights apply to all individuals equally, without exception.

Integrity

Honoring one's word as one's self. Word, thought, and action are aligned.

Virtue

Striving to improve one's self and the lives of others in all actions. To create value.

We promise to be true to our purpose, to accomplish our mission, to operate consistent with our values, and to run our enterprise in service of our customers.

    This is who we are.

    This is what you can count on.

Silk Road website

I began working on a project that had been in my mind for over a year. I was calling it Underground Brokers, but eventually settled on Silk Road. The idea was to create a website where people could buy anything anonymously, with no trail whatsoever that could lead back to them.

– Dread Pirate Roberts journal entry, 2010

Taking Drug Deals Off the Street

Drug deals can be problematic for recreational users. The pills may not contain the substances they are supposed to, the powders may be cut with toxic matter. The quality can vary wildly from purchase to purchase and there is no ombudsman to complain to in the case of being ripped off. The dealer might be a shady character who reacts violently when things go wrong.

Sam Tyler, a thirty-something Sydneysider, relayed a familiar story about his weekend. He'd wanted some ecstasy for a night out and visited a friend-of-a-friend dealer he'd used twice before. 'I arranged to pick up a couple of green mitzis [ecstasy tablets stamped with a Mitsubishi logo],' Sam said. 'But when I got there, they'd run out of them and gave me these other ones, yellow Russians, which they said were just as good.' Although he would have preferred to research the other pills before committing his $70, dealers could get pissed off when customers left empty-handed.

'When I got home, I checked them out on Pillreports [a website on which users provide feedback on pills available in their area],' Sam said. 'Flashed up red. Fuckin' pipes.' 'Pipes', or piperazines, are a family of drug with vaguely similar effects to ecstasy, but that are generally considered far less desirable and have more adverse side effects.

Ten years ago Sam would have swallowed them anyway – they could be a different batch. But at his age he wasn't prepared to risk the headaches and vomiting pipes gave him after a far less pleasurable experience than he enjoyed with MDMA. He knew it was pointless going back to the dealer. He also knew it was likely he would find himself there again if the local ecstasy scene stayed the way it was.

Despite the risks, recreational drug use continues to rise globally, with the illegal drug trade turning over hundreds of billions of dollars per year. Sam's story is a common one faced by recreational users – by the time they hit the street, drugs are so far removed from the manufacturing source that it is impossible to determine how often they have been cut with foreign substances or even whether they are what they are advertised to be. A few years ago people began to wonder if there wasn't an alternative to the traditional face-to-face drug deal. Where better to turn than the place where more and more people were spending the bulk of their time – the internet.

Online markets for illegal drugs were not a new phenomenon. The late 1990s saw the emergence of private mailing lists, such as The Hive (which developed cult status) and the Research Chemical Mailing List. Many of the participants were part of the Cypherpunk movement that had commenced in the early nineties, in which expert cryptographers combined computer skills with their interest in philosophy and politics. Privacy of information was at the heart of their cause.

In the early 2000s, there was a group of sites selling research chemicals that became known as the 'Web Tryp sites', named after the Drug Enforcement Administration (DEA) operation that eventually closed them down. There were also dozens of private email lists and web pages where information was traded clandestinely between members after trust was established. Although some information was available publicly to those who could find the sites, deals were made via private messages and emails between those in the loop. A drug user could access drugs this way only by word of mouth.

But the problem was always the same: money transfers over the web were traceable, and it was difficult to build trust with potential customers. Payment had to be made by credit card, cash in the mail or Western Union. There was no security for buyers or sellers from being scammed by each other, and anonymity could be easily compromised once the sites were discovered by the authorities.

The Silk Road story began at the end of 2010, when a young computer user and magic mushroom and marijuana aficionado imagined a market where willing buyers would be able to meet willing sellers and conduct their business in a safe, fair, violence-free environment. That business would be drugs and substances that were illegal in almost every jurisdiction in the world. He wanted to provide more than just a marketplace – he wanted to provide an environment of trust and exceptional customer service, based on the platform forged by popular legitimate e-commerce websites.

Three key emerging technologies could make this possible: Tor, a program that enabled anonymous web hosting and browsing; PGP encryption, which could scramble communications between users; and bitcoin, a borderless digital currency that existed only in cyberspace, which could be used to transfer funds with no identification of the parties required.

After considering and discarding other names, the budding drug czar settled on calling the website 'Silk Road' – a nod to the ancient Asian trade route that promoted cultural interaction between the East and the West by linking traders and merchants to buyers. The site's symbol would be a green camel, camel trains being the common method of transport in trans-Asian trade.

The difference between Silk Road and previous online black markets was a system of consumer protection. This involved an escrow system, whereby rather than trust the seller implicitly, the buyer would send the payment to the owner of the website, who would hold on to it in custody until the buyer confirmed that they had received the goods as described. The buyer would then release the funds, from which the website would skim a commission before passing the payment to the seller. A further layer of protection came by the feedback system: the buyer could rate the seller out of five and make comments regarding speed, communication, packaging and security ('stealth'), and quality of product.

This, of course, was nothing new in the world of online commerce. But in the world of black markets it was mind-blowingly revolutionary.

Silk Road's owner was no computer infrastructure whiz. He struggled to figure out how to set the site up, and nearing the end of 2010 despaired that he still didn't have a site, let alone a server. He asked questions on technical forums and tinkered with his idea until, eventually, he had the genesis of an anonymous online black market.

But first, the owner-operator of this new black market needed something to sell. He set up a lab in a cabin 'off the grid' where he produced several kilos of high-quality psilocybin mushrooms, also known as magic mushrooms, a popular psychedelic. Now he had a marketplace and he had a product. It was time to find the customers.

That wouldn't be hard. The internet was rife with websites where like-minded people got together to talk about getting high.

Silk Road entered the world with little fanfare sometime in early 2011. Its beginnings remain hazy; many of its digital footprints have been eradicated from the web, whether by those involved in Silk Road or by the owners of the websites where the messages sat – it's not always easy to tell.

The early evidence pointed to Silk Road testing the waters earlier on 4chan, an anonymous discussion group favoured by hackers and 'carders' (people who steal and use credit-card information for personal gain). Based on similar Japanese communities involved in manga and anime, 4chan is home to various subcultures and online activists, with users attracted by its anonymity and lack of censorship on posted content. It has been credited with being the genesis of hacktivist collective Anonymous.

'I first saw Silk Road . . . on 4chan in December 2010,' said Silk Road's first-ever moderator, 'Nomad Bloodbath'. 'At that time I just saw it as another scam.'

The earliest hard evidence to be found of the genesis of Silk Road was a posting on Shroomery. Established in 1997, Shroomery is a leading website for information about magic mushrooms. The owner of Silk Road had magic mushrooms to sell so on 28 January 2011, a new forum member calling themselves 'altoid' registered on the Shroomery forums and wrote:

I came across this website called Silk Road. It's a Tor hidden service that claims to allow you to buy and sell anything online anonymously. I'm thinking of buying off it, but wanted to see if anyone here had heard of it and could recommend it.

I found it through silkroad420.wordpress.com, which, if you have a tor browser, directs you to the real site at http://tydgc-cykixpbu6uz.onion.

Let me know what you think . . .

The gobbledygook site address, ending in .onion, was an indication that the site was one of those anonymously hosted by Tor. Sites hosted by Tor and other anonymity providers are colloquially known as the 'dark web'. Sometime before April 2011, Silk Road's address changed to ianxz6zefk72ulzz.onion. The Wordpress site included a cheeky reference to '420', slang for marijuana.

That was the only post ever made by altoid on the Shroomery forums, and the last time altoid logged on was 28 February 2011. The Wordpress site the post referred to was a short, basic guide on how to access Silk Road.

'This is not Silk Road, but you are close' was the heading that greeted visitors. It explained how to download the technologies that would enable you to find and use the drug marketplace. Soon afterwards, Wordpress closed the gateway and any attempts to access it returned an error message: 'silkroad420.wordpress.com is no longer available. This site has been archived or suspended for a violation of our Terms of Service.'

Altoid also registered and posted in the bitcoin discussion forums at bitcointalk.org. Bitcoin at the time was a fledgling crypto-currency, virtually worthless, and the forum's members were debating whether it could be used to enable online commerce anonymously. Specifically, they were considering whether it was viable to facilitate buying and selling heroin. In a lengthy thread called 'A Heroin Store', on 29 January 2011 altoid (who had only registered that day) helpfully chimed in:

> What an awesome thread! You guys have a ton of great ideas. Has anyone seen Silk Road yet? It's kind of like an anonymous amazon.com. I don't think they have heroin on there, but they are selling other stuff. They basically use bitcoin and tor to broker anonymous transactions. It's at http://tydgccykixpbu6uz. onion. Those not familiar with Tor can go to silkroad420.word-press.com for instructions on how to access the .onion site.
> Let me know what you guys think.

A suspicious reader might assume that altoid had more than a fan's involvement in the site he or she was so keen to spruik.

The only other early reference to Silk Road was from an apparent Silk Road seller calling himself 'maxvendor', who advertised his MDMA on topix.com, a website that allowed anonymous posting of news and gossip. 'Buy from the Silk Road!' the poster wrote on 12 February 2011 in a blatant advertisement for his ecstasy. 'Ships stealth/vac sealed regular airmail. Pretty much the only guarantee in the online vending world going, also no way to prove you paid – all transactions are decentralized and anonymous.' Maxvendor mentioned that payment would be made by bitcoin. Bitcoin is the preferred method of payment for goods and services on the dark web. Known as a 'cryptocurrency', it is a digital currency that uses cryptography for security. It exists only in cyberspace. Online multiplayer games such as Second Life use a virtual currency that has value and can be exchanged for real things outside of the game. Bitcoin is similar, but far more sophisticated.

It wasn't until 1 March 2011 that a thread brazenly and blatantly advertising Silk Road was started in the bitcoin forums by a user known as 'silkroad'; the thread was called 'Silk Road anonymous marketplace: feedback requested'. He stated: 'Silk Road is into its third week after launch and I am very pleased with the results. There are several sellers and buyers finding mutually agreeable prices, and as of today, 28 transactions have been made!' The poster asked for feedback on his site, which he said had been in development for four months.

'Thanks for this awesome idea, silkroad,' wrote FTL_Ian, host of web-streaming talkback radio site Free Talk Live, on 17 March 2011. 'I am so impressed, I promoted it on my national radio program tonight. Hope you don't mind the publicity.' On the program, he described Silk Road, the anonymity it provided and the escrow service, and cited the site as having 151 registered users, 38 listings and 28 transactions to date. The radio hosts enthused about the potential to remove violence from drug deals and other potential upsides of the site. 'This is an example of something really useful. This is a useful service. Allowing people to trade in whatever they want online completely anonymously . . . And you've got plausible deniability,' they reported.

'How cool!' silkroad enthused. 'How big is your audience?'

Silkroad's thread grew to be one of the longest the Bitcointalk forum had ever seen. Members raised questions and expressed concerns that silkroad responded to with explanations of the technologies, the escrow system and his vision for a viable market.

Bitcointalk had a healthy membership made up of the kind of people who live for computers, technology and the new and innovative uses they can be put to. Many were drawn to Silk Road from a technical perspective, even if they had no interest in drugs.

For many, checking out the site for themselves was their first experience of the 'dark web'. Host to all the sites that feature in contemporary horror movies or the cautionary tales of TV crime dramas, it is like the internet's evil twin, unknown by many and accessed by few.

And drugs are about the *least* illegal things to be found inside the dark web.

Technology continues to empower buyers and extend the reach of sellers.
— Australian Crime Commission, *Illicit Drug Data Report,*
2011–2012

Onionland

Almost as soon as Silk Road came into existence, obscure websites and blogs on the internet were providing instructions on how to find it. It seemed deceptively easy to locate the smorgasbord of illicit drugs waiting to wing their way across the world to your letterbox: download Tor, enter the URL and sign up for an account.

Googling 'Tor' brings up the Tor Project homepage. The site explains that Tor was originally developed in conjunction with the US Navy and its primary purpose was the protection of government communications; it continues to receive some of its funding from the US government. Tor has three main functions: allowing users to publish and read information with complete anonymity, circumventing censorship (i.e. getting around internet filters), and providing 'hidden services' – websites not visible or accessible to the outside internet, which can be found only within the network of the software provider.

24

Downloading Tor is as simple as a couple of clicks. And there it will be on your desktop – an innocuous little green onion (representing the layers of encryption and protection given by the program) providing entry into the dark web. It's like a gateway to another world, inhabited by felons and deviants engaging in activities that would never be allowed on the everyday internet. Double-clicking the onion feels wicked, as though the user is already doing something illegal.

The dark web is a home for people who have good reason not to want authorities tracing their movements on the web. But upon taking the plunge and clicking the icon, it doesn't really look like that. The onion simply opens up a new browser window containing a cheery congratulatory message on how you are now free to browse the web anonymously. It looks just like the Firefox browser millions use to surf the net. The difference, however, is that your computer's IP address is being 'onion routed' – software is routing internet traffic through a worldwide volunteer network of servers in order to conceal the computer's location or usage from anyone conducting network surveillance or traffic analysis. Original data is encrypted and re-encrypted multiple times until it reaches its destination. When that destination is a site on the regular internet, that site knows it has had a visitor but has no way of finding out who that visitor is or where in the world they were located.

It may look like a normal browser, but the other clever thing the browser opened by Tor can do is accept 'onion' URLs. An onion URL is a string of apparently random letters and numbers that ends in '.onion' instead of one of the usual domain identifiers, such as '.com' or '.org'. Any site that has an onion domain name is contained within the Tor network and is not part of the internet. The hidden network of sites is colloquially referred to as 'Onionland'.

As sites like Silk Road are not designed to be found by search engines, users either have to know the exact URL they want or use one of the available gateway sites. The most notorious of the latter is the Hidden Wiki, the starting place for hundreds of hidden websites.

The Hidden Wiki looks like any other wiki page, with links to external sites arranged under a variety of headings. Under 'Marketplaces' are two subheadings: 'Financial Services' and 'Commercial Services'. The financial services section contains links to sites that promise to sell stolen credit-card and Paypal details for a percentage of those accounts' balances; money-laundering services that claim they can wash any amount of dirty money and turn it into legitimate income for a hefty fee; shops that sell counterfeit cash; and services that promise to make your exchange of cash for bitcoin anonymous.

The commercial services section is significantly longer. There are online stores selling an array of goods and services, just like we're used to – but you won't find these shops advertising their wares over the regular internet. Drugs and guns are offered for sale, hit men advertise their services, and there are pornographic images to satisfy the most depraved of tastes.

The commercial services includes listings for fake IDs, dodgy university degrees and counterfeit coupons, services that research and write college papers, and a service that allows people to buy into fixed sporting events. Several stores offer stolen or counter-feit Apple products. One advertiser offers to steal goods to order, another offers bomb-making lessons and yet another says they can arrange for an enemy to be visited by a SWAT team. (This seemed a bit far-fetched, but 'swatting' is a real phenomenon in the United States, as security expert and blogger Brian Krebs discovered in March 2013. He had annoyed many hackers and shady websites over the years with his investigations, so someone placed a 911 call using instant message chats via a relay service designed for hearing-impaired and deaf callers. They said Russians had broken into Krebs' house, killing his wife. The result was something straight out of a movie – half a dozen squad cars with lights flashing and police leaning over their bonnets pointing guns at him when he opened his door. Krebs was able to convince the police it was a hoax, one he had warned them six months earlier was a favourite hacker retaliation.)

Hackers-for-hire compete against each other offering to deface the site of your most hated politician, hack your competitors' websites, or find out if your partner is cheating on you by providing access to his or her Facebook and email accounts. They also offer passwords to premium movie services or porn sites, allow you to change an inconvenient credit history or provide the private files of businesses you might want to cheat or destroy.

In the beginning, Silk Road featured in the commercial services section, but was not the only drugs marketplace. Other, smaller stores offered sales of a single product – marijuana, for example, or the prescription drug Xanax. One store was perhaps not as dark as the others: 'Medical marijuana market ONLY. No chems allowed.' Others, darker: they offered to sell cyanide, ricin and other poisons that had no discernible medical or recreational purpose.

Browsing the Hidden Wiki makes it obvious why many who visit the dark web want their activities to remain anonymous. Even before the Edward Snowden affair, where a former CIA employee leaked details of global surveillance operations by governments, people had become suspicious that authorities could track every site visited and every keystroke made, which could become rather inconvenient for those who wanted to purchase cocaine or heroin online. It was even more awkward for the people selling ecstasy or methamphetamine through the internet.

That's where Tor came in. As one of dozens of organisations offering anonymity software that can be downloaded for free, Tor provides 'hidden services' – the sites that are invisible to internet search engines. In the case of Tor, that is Onionland. Nobody – including those who work for the Tor Project – can determine who runs them or where they are located. Nor can they close the sites down. Where better to host your murky, illegal business than from premises that are invisible to everybody?

The dark web is not a single place, but a collective term for the many 'darknets', parallel internets that exist alongside the one we know and that facilitate anonymous browsing and publishing. Dark-web sites can be accessed only through special software programs that enable individuals and organisations to host private or illegal material while their identity and location remain secret. It is an environment that is beyond control or intervention by government and law enforcement.

The positive uses for Tor's functions of allowing users to publish and read information anonymously and circumventing censorship are obvious – they allow whistleblowers and human-rights workers to communicate with journalists, let dissidents in places such as China and Iran gain access to censored information or to circumvent laws against criticism of heads of state, and provide ordinary people with the means to surf the web without their information being harvested for marketers. But the third and smallest feature of Tor – providing hidden services – seems to have the least legitimate application. Hidden services are a way of creating meeting places where visitors can't discover where the host is and the host can't see where the visitors are coming from. Perfect for criminal marketplaces, but what other use might they have?

'We produce software that we give away for free to people [so that] anyone in the world who needs their privacy online can have it,' said Andrew Lewman, executive director of the Tor Group, in an interview. According to Lewman, the hidden services were developed by the US and Norwegian military as a research project to determine whether a completely anonymous platform could exist. Members of the Tor Project worked with experts from leading academic institutions such as Stanford and MIT to test security features and flaws and the ability of Tor to circumvent internet filters. Most of Tor's funding came from the US government and non-profit organisations and research programs, while around 5 per cent of its funding came from donations, some of which were anonymous. Several of the dark-web sites claimed to covertly direct a certain percentage of their profits towards Tor and some encouraged their customers to donate any spare bitcoins to the Tor Project.

Did it worry Lewman that some of his funding could be presumed to be coming from criminals? 'It concerns us, yes. We've turned down donations, sometimes sizeable, from organisations. You know when you get the hairs standing up against the back of your neck that there's just something wrong,' he said. 'And it's sometimes incredibly tough to turn down hundreds of thousands of dollars where someone says, you know, "I want to donate to you and thank you for what you do but don't ask where this money came from".'

He confirmed that Tor does accept anonymous donations, though, so it doesn't seem to be a stretch to assume that at least part of its funding is coming from criminals who have a vested interest in Tor's research. It is a little ironic that this is a project that is likely co-funded by the US government and organised crime.

'Tor's original design was to give users privacy and anonymity online and that's still the core of what we do,' Lewman said. 'The vast majority of Tor usage is by normal people who are just looking to not give out all their information; who they are, where they are and every website they visit. Of course jerks and criminals do use Tor but frankly they have far better options.'

WikiLeaks is one example of an organisation that took advantage of darknets to maintain the integrity of its submissions, recommending that those who required anonymity when whistle-blowing use Tor. Even if a server were to be confiscated, there would be little risk to users of the site, because there would be no IP trail and no typical user traffic trails that led out of the server. Conversely, traffic of visitors was also protected from their end, because they would not leave a trail of where they were going or what they were doing when they got there.

'Of course criminals will pick up on that too, but criminals are opportunistic,' Lewman said when quizzed. 'That's why they're criminals.'

It has become apparent that high-tech crime permeates tradi-
tional crimes with new crimes, for example, fraud, the theft
of electronic wealth using malicious software, cyber stalking,
extortion, espionage, hacking, child exploitation and the online
grooming of young people. The ability to use technology to
commit crime, attack critical infrastructure, engage in terrorist
activity and undermine the national security is a very real threat.

From a law enforcement perspective this means we need to
develop new methodologies to ensure perpetrators cannot hide
behind technological advances.

– Australian Federal Police statement on the dark web

The Internet's Evil Twin

Silk Road was by far the most famous site linked by the Hidden Wiki by mid-2011. Clicking on the link would bring a potential customer to a homepage that asked for login details, with a subtle link to register. All the site required was a username, password and a fake email address, and a buyer could get started.

A basic green-and-white themed web page filled the browser with pictures of some of the wares you might want to buy: 5 grams of hash, a gram of cocaine or MDMA, an enticing pile of pink pills, Xanax, something called 'shake'. A single vendor would have multiple listings for different quantities, ranging from a single pill or joint up to amounts that were clearly not intended for personal use. Underneath each picture was a price displayed in bitcoin or US dollars, depending on the setting chosen by the user.

Drugs were not the only goods for sale. The site also listed clothes, books, computer equipment and fake IDs. A link that said 'XXX' offered login details to premium clearweb (regular internet) porn sites. 'Books' proved to be a relatively harmless collection of self-published tomes offering assistance on picking up girls or setting up hydroponic gardens, as well as people offering downloads of 'banned books' for about half a bitcoin. The 'Money' listing didn't offer forged notes, but ways of obtaining bitcoin anonymously.

The 'Drugs' listing was broken up into sublistings: cannabis, psychedelics, stimulants, prescription and so on, all waiting to be popped into a shopping basket. They included hard-to-come-by designer drugs, such as a subcategory called the '2-C Family' – psychedelics in pill, capsule or powder form. Before the Road, the most popular, 2CB, was virtually impossible to obtain in Australia without a friend in a chemical laboratory.

Beyond Silk Road, the dark web is divided into porn, hacking communities, illegal commerce and crackpots. It is also a place where political activists can get together away from the prying eyes of their enemies. According to one source, Syrian rebels used Tor to communicate with their supporters worldwide and to help rebels jump borders into Turkey and Jordan, or get themselves hospital-ised in an Israeli hospital on the Syria–Israel border.

Not all sites can be found via a link in a wiki. As Lewman said, the idea of services being 'hidden' is that the people using them don't want them to be found. As .onion addresses do not use identifiable words, a person needs to know the URL in order to find a specific site. Thus, when activists or human-rights prac-titioners in hostile regimes want to communicate, they circulate addresses privately. 'They don't advertise anywhere, they don't link from anywhere and they actively try to protect their .onion site from discovery,' Lewman said. Those sites do not appear on the Hidden Wiki.

Delving into Onionland can become obsessive. Anyone can sign up to the black markets or spy on the forums. Some sites are completely incomprehensible to most mere mortals, like the hangouts of the hackers and phreakers (people who explore tele-communication systems).

Many of the sites on the dark web can be rationalised to at least some people, but once in the dark web, there is no escaping some of its nasty realities.

Child porn is one. Lots and lots of child porn. An entire section of the Hidden Wiki called 'Hard Candy' is dedicated to sites that provide images and videos of children being sexually abused. It is a place few would want to explore.

The 'assassination markets' purport to crowdfund the murders of high-profile people. They are based on an elaborate scheme described in Jim Bell's 1995 essay 'Assassination Politics', in which he imagined anonymous benefactors could order the killings of government officials and those who were seen to be violating citizens' rights. On the most prominent of these sites on the dark web, anyone can nominate someone for assassination, but they have to have good reason. 'Bad reasons include doctors for performing abortions and Justin Bieber for making annoying music,' the site says.

Those listed as potential victims are politicians from around the globe and executives whom some hold responsible for the global financial crisis. Attached to each name is a bitcoin address to which donations can be made to increase the pot. Every transaction is visible and anyone can independently verify that the money is actually there, waiting to be collected by the person who 'predicts' the date of death. 'Making the prediction come true is entirely optional,' the site says.

The dark web has spawned all types of myths, as well. Some people speak in hushed tones about real-life gladiator fights to the death, contract-killing services or live streaming of pay-per-view torture. Others will swear you can access details of live human experiments or obtain made-to-order snuff films. There is a black market in human organs, they'll tell you, and places you can buy genuine human slaves.

The hitman myth is particularly pervasive as there are dozens of services advertising contract killings. A typical blurb for services goes: 'I will "neutralize" the ex you hate, your bully, a policeman that you have been in trouble with, a lawyer, a small politician . . . I do not care what the cause is. I will solve the problem for you. Internationally, cheap and 100% anonymously.'

Another one promises: 'Will make dirt jobs for you, any kind of jobs. I will be glad to help you any dirt activity, my main interests is smuggling and teror [sic]'. 'Hitman Network' hoped satisfied customers would recommend its services to a friend once they were successfully rid of a nemesis: 'Tell others about this shop, and earn 1% from every purchase they will make.'

Some of them refuse to kill children (one won't kill women), though they vary with the age range of what constitutes a child. Others have higher prices for politicians, famous people and, comfortingly, journalists.

Trying to hire one of these, however, such as 'C'thulhu' ('You give us a picture; we'll give you an autopsy report!'), will lead to an amusing but creepy email exchange that is reminiscent of the scam emails that clog up our 'junk' inboxes every day. They may not need the entire hit price up-front, but they do need cash for travel, expenses and passports. The consensus on the dark web is that the hit-man-for-hire services are all scams, and most of the multi-product markets ban their listings for that reason.

The reality of the dark web is somewhat more pedestrian than the TV shows, movies and hysterical websites would have you believe. It is far less high tech than the regular internet. All those things that movie scripts are made of – fights to the death, snuff films, live streams, human experiments – seem to be mythical.

It's not possible to prove that something doesn't exist. But after years of looking into the murky bowels of the dark web, there is no evidence to support the existence of some of the more sensational allegations.

The greatest trick the devil ever pulled was convincing the world he did not exist. And like that . . . he is gone.

— Keyser Soze, *The Usual Suspects*

Bitcoin and the Man Who Wasn't There

It was apparent that commerce was thriving on the dark web in 2011. But how would people pay for the plethora of illegal goods and services that could be purchased online? It wasn't like you could meet in a dark alley and hand over a suitcase of cash when buying something from the other side of the world. Internet banking, credit card or Paypal weren't really options, with their pesky identification requirements.

Those who do business on the dark web typically don't want a paper trail of their transactions. This is where bitcoin comes in. In a nutshell, bitcoin is a borderless digital currency that started out as a valueless computer code. Within a few years, it had a market value closing in on US$3 billion. Bitcoin exchanges (much like stock exchanges) allow users to buy and trade bitcoin online, but those who want to remain anonymous will use cash over the counter at a local bank or exchange cash for bitcoin credit person-to-person. Pages of financial tomes have been dedicated to whether bitcoin should be categorised as a currency or a commodity, how it is created and traded, and its implications for fiat currencies, all of which are well beyond the scope of this book.

The important feature of bitcoin is that it is both completely transparent and, if users know what they are doing, completely anonymous. It is transparent in that anyone can view any transaction that has occurred in any account (or 'wallet') at any time they want. Every transaction is recorded in a database known as the 'blockchain'. Several websites, which anyone can visit and view, keep track of all transactions on the blockchain. Without further information, however, it is impossible to tell who owns the account you are looking at. So while, for example, you might be able to see that $20,000 worth of bitcoin was transferred from bitcoin address 1LK5HQqU6M9qyWSUhfPnV6xtKBCocUp6PY to bitcoin address 13g7xpD27XWDg5NX9dRLEdqumUNL6koh6H, unless the owners of those addresses have advertised the fact, there is no way of knowing who owns either of them. One person can create as many separate wallets or addresses as they like at the click of a button and transfer bitcoin from one to another almost immediately and without incurring any costs.

The cryptocurrency's life started on 1 November 2008, when a message appeared on a cryptography mailing list from someone calling himself 'Satoshi Nakamoto'. 'I've been working on a new electronic cash system that's fully peer-to-peer, with no trusted third party,' said his first posting. He linked to a white paper and invited discussion from other cryptographers.

Nakamoto took on advice and suggestions until bitcoin was properly unleashed in February 2009, when a modest post appeared on an obscure internet discussion forum, P2P Foundation, by

Satoshi Nakamoto (male, 38, Japan): 'I've developed a new open source P2P e-cash system called bitcoin . . . Give it a try.'

He went on to explain that technological advances had made encryption of information available to the average computer user – meaning users no longer had to place their trust in a system administrator who could access their password. This meant, he explained, that users could secure their own data 'in a way that was physically impossible for others to access'.

Nakamoto figured that the same principles that applied to electronic data could apply to electronic currency. He envisaged a currency that could be used by people completely securely, with no interference by banks or regulators.

'With e-currency based on cryptographic proof, without the need to trust a third party middleman, money can be secure and transactions effortless' was the lofty claim he made. In other words, this currency could be used to transfer money person-to-person instantly, without the need for oversight by a central authority, and in a way that provided protection from theft without anyone else knowing the user's details.

Later, Nakamoto would reveal that he had started the design and coding of the currency in 2007. But this first post gave some insight into his motivation and politics, and especially his thoughts about banks' roles in the global financial crisis of 2008:

The root problem with conventional currency is all the trust that's required to make it work. The central bank must be trusted not to debase the currency, but the history of fiat currencies is full of breaches of that trust. Banks must be trusted to hold our money and transfer it electronically, but they lend it out in waves of credit bubbles with barely a fraction in reserve. We have to trust them with our privacy, trust them not to let identity thieves drain our accounts. Their massive overhead costs make micropayments impossible.

Bitcoin was essentially something created out of nothing. Nakamoto's invention provided for a finite number of bitcoins that could be 'mined'. As more of them were mined, they became harder to come by and more valuable, requiring heavier and heavier machinery to find those that were left.

Rather than shovels and earthmovers, bitcoins were designed to be mined by computers performing complex mathematical equations, or what Nakamoto called 'proof-of-work'. In order to prevent people attempting to 'double spend' bitcoin, every transaction record had to be added to the blockchain, which became proof that a legitimate transaction had taken place and the bitcoin had changed from one wallet to another.

Mining involved computers adding those records to the blockchain. As more transactions took place, it became more difficult for a computer to perform the equation that confirmed the transaction. People who set their computers to compete with each other to be the first to solve the equation were known as 'miners', and the miner of the computer that solved the equation would be rewarded in bitcoin.

In the early days of bitcoin, anyone with a home computer could mine them. 'I made the proof-of-work difficulty ridiculously easy to start with,' wrote Nakamoto at the time, 'so for a little while in the beginning a typical PC will be able to generate coins in just a few hours. It'll get a lot harder when competition makes the automatic adjustment drive up the difficulty.'

When bitcoin were first unleashed, a person could literally set their home computer to mine them when they left for work in the morning and have a stash when they came home. At that time, the coins themselves had little to no value; each one was worth at best a fraction of a cent, and the added electricity costs to mine them outweighed their worth. During 2013 they reached a value of $1200 each.

But the chance of mining bitcoins with a home computer has long since passed. Nakamoto said that total circulation would be 21 million coins. In the first four years 10.5 million coins would be distributed to miners, and the number would be cut in half every four years after that. Thus, the number of bitcoins available to be mined would trickle to a stop by 2140. The computer equipment required to efficiently mine bitcoins now runs to tens or even hundreds of thousands of dollars of specialised machinery.

As one of the first people to engage with Nakamoto, forum poster and renowned cryptographer Hal Finney wrote, 'So the possibility of generating coins today with a few cents of computer time may be quite a good bet, with a payoff of something like 100 million to one! Even if the odds of bitcoin succeeding to this degree are slim, are they really 100 million to one against? Something to think about . . .' Finney later wrote that he had been the recipient of the first bitcoin transaction when Nakamoto sent him ten bitcoins. He left his PC running and mining until he turned it off because 'it made my computer run hot, and the fan noise bothered me'. He then went on to other things until:

The next I heard of bitcoin was late 2010, when I was surprised to find that it was not only still going, bitcoins actually had monetary value. I dusted off my old wallet, and was relieved to discover that my bitcoins were still there. As the price climbed up to real money, I transferred the coins into an offline wallet, where hopefully they'll be worth something to my heirs.

Another forum member who participated in discussions with Nakamoto during bitcoin's infancy, Sepp Hasslberger, said, 'So, the early adopter finds the worm in this system.'

'I never did get involved in actually owning or using any bitcoins,' he wrote later. In fact, he claimed to be a bitcoin critic. There did not seem to be any sense of regret or loss for his failure to follow up his own advice.

In the months following Nakamoto's initial posts and white paper, he created a new internet forum to discuss bitcoin at his domain bitcoin.org, which eventually broke away to become the wider unofficial forum Bitcointalk. He made a series of lengthy, thoughtful and technical posts on that forum, describing the project in detail. As experts recognised the genius in his invention, interest moved from a few early adopters in the IT sphere to more widely-read technology blogs.

The number of businesses and enterprises willing to accept bitcoin as an alternative form of currency was sluggish to begin with. But it found a niche in the black markets thanks to its ability to be acquired anonymously. A cash deposit could be made into a bitcoin trader's bank account over the counter of any bank. A reference number on the deposit slip would alert the trader to send the bitcoin to a specific bitcoin address, which had been supplied to the trader by anonymous email.

Although Nakamoto's initial posts had described his vision for an absence of regulation, his later posts remained technical and academic until WikiLeaks began to canvass the viability of accepting bitcoin. Nakamoto was adamant that he did not want his creation associated with the whistleblowing site. 'No, don't "bring it on",' he wrote. 'I make this appeal to WikiLeaks not to try to use Bitcoin. Bitcoin is a small beta community in its infancy. You would not stand to get more than pocket change, and the heat you would bring would likely destroy us at this stage.' He seemed more focused on the potential effects on his invention rather than any judgments about Julian Assange and his website.

Nakamoto's only other political statement was unearthed by cryptographers and was embedded in the source code of bitcoin itself, a little Easter egg for determined crypto-sleuths. Hidden in the code, he had provided a hint to his motivation by reproducing a headline from *The Times* from January 2009: 'Chancellor on brink of second bailout for banks'.

It would seem that someone who was wary about WikiLeaks bringing 'heat' to his invention would certainly have some issues with it being used as the cornerstone of dark-web markets. But he never made any statement about them. Nakamoto's appearances, postings and emails became increasingly sporadic, and then, in early 2011, he quietly disappeared, surfacing only for the briefest of moments in April 2011 to tell a bitcoin developer that he had 'moved on to other things'.

Naturally, some people wanted to stay in touch and tried to contact him. But they couldn't. Searches for a telephone number, an address, an alternative email to contact the man were fruitless. His name was not associated with any academic papers, publications or institutions in the profession in which he was so clearly an expert. It was becoming apparent that Satoshi Nakamoto (male, 38, Japan) had never existed.

And so began a hunt for the pseudonymous genius. The intrigue surrounding Nakamoto's true identity built into the type of frenzy reserved for characters such as British street artist Banksy. His English was faultless, suggesting it was his first language, with some even saying they recognised the marks of an Oxbridge graduate. Others pointed out that though the bulk of his communications were in British English, initially he had used American English. His website led to dead ends: the domain name had been registered through a privacy protection service. The other hints he had dropped from time to time contradicted each other and similarly led nowhere.

Journalist Andrew Smith, who spent months reviewing the 100,000 words known to be written by Nakamoto, came to the conclusion in a piece he wrote for *The Sunday Times* that Nakamoto had deliberately sown seeds of 'systematic obfuscation aimed at throwing us off the scent. One is tempted to further infer that Satoshi, having pointed us in the directions of the British Isles, Finland, Germany and Japan, is unlikely to come from any of these places . . .'

The 364 posts Nakamoto made on the bitcoin forums, while detailed and technical, revealed little about their author other than that he, she or they were a genius who had thought of nearly everything, responded quickly to flaws found by fellow cryptographers, and plugged every identified problem with, and potential attack upon, the currency.

As bitcoin gained value and mainstream publications began to take it seriously, the hunt for Nakamoto moved beyond the realms of internet sleuths and on to investigative journalists who saw the potential in the story.

One theory was that his name was drawn from technology multinationals **Sa**msung, **Toshi**ba, **Naka**michi and **Moto**rola. Some took this further, suggesting that top scientists from those companies had worked together to create bitcoin. It was a neat hypothesis, but no evidence that it was anything more than a coincidence has ever emerged.

Some surmised Nakamoto was an invention by those who have much to gain from the currency's success – perhaps the head of the Bitcoin Foundation (a lobby group dedicated to promoting bitcoin), or the world's largest cryptocurrency exchange, MtGox. Others believed it to be a pseudonym for a disruptive government or the CIA.

As attempts to locate Nakamoto failed, his cult status intensified. Mythology grew of the man who had apparently not made a single mistake – not in the code behind his invention, nor in covering his tracks, despite there being few people in the world who could possibly be him.

The mystery spawned an entire industry, with T-shirts emblazoned with 'Who is Satoshi Nakamoto?' and 'I am Satoshi Nakamoto' selling in worldwide stores dedicated to technology buffs.

If Nakamoto were a fictional character he would be the James Bond or Jason Bourne of cyberspace – a genius, an inventor, an outlaw with wealth beyond our imagination. He existed nowhere but in his online musings. He used his rare mathematical genius to create a virtual currency the value of which went from zero to a billion dollars in a couple of years and managed for years to evade every effort to track him down and unmask him.

He remained completely, utterly anonymous.

Now the question everyone was wondering was: just what were the 'other things' he had moved on to in April 2011?

[C]yber criminals will treat bitcoin as another payment option alongside more traditional and established virtual currencies . . .
– 'Bitcoin virtual currency: Unique features present distinct challenges for deterring illicit activity', FBI report, April 2012

Part Two
The Rise

So you can download drugs from a server run on onions? You guys are full of shit.

– Anonymous 4chan member

The New Silk Road

During the first half of 2011, as its owner tinkered with the interface and relied on the Bitcointalk forum and word of mouth for advertising, Silk Road was a fraction of the size it would eventually become. The earliest known screenshot of Silk Road showed 145 transactions to date, 60 current listings, mostly of drugs, and 655 registered users. Silkroad, the owner, was a vendor selling magic mushrooms and marijuana. The site hit 1000 registered users on or around 11 April 2011.

The members of the Bitcointalk forum had a new favourite topic as the desirability of this brazen black market for their fledgling currency was hotly debated. But even those who had no interest in drugs were fascinated by the potential provided by a commerce site that seemed to have a rational, business-savvy developer at its head. Members debated what should be sold online, other than drugs. 'Although I'd really not like to see any kidneys and slaves on silkroad, I don't see a point in disallowing fake ID's and passports,' posted 'Modoki'. 'Also, I think weapons should be sold (as long as they aren't weapons of mass destruction and stuff like napalm and agent orange). Things like pistols, knifes and such I'd like to see.'

Rumours of the website where illicit substances could be purchased spread to the online communities that would take a much greater interest in a black market for drugs – Reddit in particular. Like 4chan, Reddit is essentially a bulletin board where people can chat about anything and everything. Dubbing itself as 'the front page of the internet', it provides an online meeting place for every conceivable profession and hobby. Users can subscribe to 'sub-Reddits' dedicated to cute cat pictures or those discussing politics, cycling, Disney cartoons, lock-picking techniques or problems faced by the transgender community. Reddit has a large and active mainstream readership.

Bitcoin aficionados started getting worried about the Silk Road anonymous marketplace, fearing it would be the downfall of the cryptocurrency. Many didn't want it to be inextricably linked to the illegal trade in drugs. But it was apparent that the two were intertwined, with the success of one heavily dependent on the other. Silk Road needed bitcoin for anonymous trading; bitcoin's early rise in value seemed almost entirely attributable to the business being done on Silk Road.

Discussions became heated as fans and detractors debated the pros and cons of promoting the use of bitcoin on underground markets. The correlation between Silk Road and bitcoin was apparent, and it was very healthy for the value of bitcoin. On 15 May 2011, when Silk Road was shut down for maintenance, bitcoin immediately dropped by a couple of dollars. When Silk Road came back online on 18 May 2011, bitcoin bounced back with it.

Once back online, Silk Road's owner told the community in his usual cheery manner that 'We did a big update of the site over the weekend and are happy to say that it's back up and running!' New features included an integrated bitcoin tumbler (a kind of laundering service where funds were mixed in order to make it difficult to trace them to their original source) and dynamic pricing to smooth out exchange-rate fluctuations. The owner also promised an improved browsing experience and a more transparent ordering process. With its slick new look and ease of use, Silk Road's clientele grew steadily.

Many articulated why they liked the idea of the market. 'Reputation allows buyers to make informed decisions, escrow gives both buyer and seller added protection against fraud, arbitration gives both parties a non-violent recourse to disputes, and anonymity protects against any violent recourse outside the system,' posted 'BitterTea'. 'Notably, anonymity not only protects from violent recourse from other traders, but also from law enforcement.'

The website had variously been described as either the Amazon or the eBay of illegal drugs. It was more closely aligned with the latter in that the website itself sold no drugs (putting aside the mushrooms and marijuana listed by the owner during the site's infancy). Rather, it provided a marketplace where buyers and sellers could meet and do business.

If the drugs were not received or not what had been promised, the buyer and seller were expected to try to work out the issue between themselves before hitting the 'Resolve' button, which would put the transaction into resolution with Silk Road administration. Administration would arbitrate, taking into account the past transactions, reputations and statistics of the parties, to decide whether the funds should be released to the seller or returned to the buyer. The better a seller's feedback, the more customers they would get and the higher the prices they could charge. Sellers had an incentive to keep customers happy to ensure they would always receive that coveted five-out-of-five rating.

It wasn't only vendors who needed feedback and reputation for the ultimate Road experience. Sellers could also see information about buyers and might refuse to do business with those who had less than perfect statistics. Because of this, new sellers and new buyers often had to work together to build up their reputations.

Although anonymity was the cornerstone of Silk Road, the one point where it had to be given up was when the buyer provided an address for the delivery of goods. Nervous first-timers questioned why law enforcement wouldn't just open up an account and nab those who gave their address. They were placated by lengthy explanations as to why this would not be a feasible use of law enforcement resources.

For one thing, Silk Road charged $500 to set up a vendor account, an amount that was returned to the vendor after a certain number of successful transactions. Any efforts by law enforcement to use the system to harvest addresses would soon be spotted by the community and the vendor called out, their account cancelled.

Further, many buyers, especially those purchasing trafficable amounts, would use a 'drop' address rather than their home address. This might be a vacant house or apartment nearby, or a post office box opened under a false name. And even if a buyer did use their home address, there would still be the problem of proving that person had ordered the drugs online. Tor and bitcoin provided enough anonymity that no digital trail was left. Any person could send drugs to any other person, so the receiver had plausible deniability in the case of their parcel being intercepted.

So, in theory, honeypot (law enforcement sting) vendor accounts were certainly possible. But they would waste so much police time with so little reward that it would not be worth posing as a vendor selling small amounts. Law enforcement is rarely interested in busting small-time end users, so such vendor accounts could only possibly be worthwhile to sell bulk amounts that were of such a quantity that the police could be confident the buyer was buying the drugs in order to on-sell them. But bulk vendors needed a verified reputation before any high-quantity resellers would purchase from them.

By the end of May 2011, Silk Road had built up a healthy clientele through word of mouth among the communities of 4chan and Reddit. It had around 400 listings of all sorts of things, mostly drugs. It was a community built on trust and was generally considered to be secret and tight-knit.

That is, until a young journalist from a tabloid gossip site crashed the party.

Silk Road is going to become a phenomenon and at least one person will tell me about it, unknowing that I was its creator.
                                    – Dread Pirate Roberts journal entry, 2011

The Gawker Effect

'I'm just your normal, everyday half-Chinese half-Jew trying to make his way in our increasingly interconnected world,' said Adrian Chen when introducing himself as the new nightshift editor at Gawker in November 2009.

Gawker started life in 2002. The site recognised and embraced the emerging prevalence of technological distribution of news, and harnessed social media to find both stories and readers. It would employ tech-savvy young writers to trawl sites like Twitter, Tumblr, 4chan, Reddit and Craigslist, looking for entries by people that could be developed into news stories. Alongside sensational head-lines were interactive features such as 'Gawker Stalker', which pinpointed celebrity sightings on a live map so that fans could track down their favourite star if they were nearby.

Based in New York City, the site churned out thirty or forty stories a day, mostly salacious crime, celebrity news and happen-ings in the media. 'Today's gossip is tomorrow's news,' it proudly proclaimed. While most of the content was fluff, it occasionally teetered dangerously close to delivering real news – and even the odd scoop.

Chen worked hard for little pay, as is typical for those who are living their dream jobs – and for many a generation Y, writing blog posts for a gossip site is indeed a dream job. He started on nights and weekends, eventually moving from nightshift editor to regular staff reporter. He soon discovered there were stories to be found by scouring unregulated, anonymous online communities.

'It seemed like everyone was writing the same eight stories all the time,' he said in an interview. 'I found it was pretty easy to find different stories by just going below to where people were just talking and there was just people just shooting the shit.'

He wasn't afraid to expose some of the goings-on in those places and could lay claim to some genuine investigative features over the years. In particular, he was never afraid to openly challenge and taunt hackers and cybercriminals. In 2011 he wrote a scathing piece accusing a group of bullying an eleven-year-old girl; they hacked Gawker in retaliation. 'And that was the beginning of Lulzsec. That was the first time this group decided to get together and hack something,' Chen said.

Lulzsec went on to be responsible for some of the most notorious hacks in the world, including Fox News (they were upset that a rapper they liked was called 'vile' on air) and *The Sun* newspaper (they changed the front page to a story saying Rupert Murdoch had died of an overdose). They really didn't like Chen, calling him 'a brainless slug with no writing skills or friends' in a Twitter update.

In 2012, Chen exposed 'Violentacrez', a notorious and nasty internet troll and moderator of some of the most vile sub-Reddits, such as 'Creepshots' (candid photographs of bums or breasts of unsuspecting women taken during private moments) and 'Jailbait' (photographs of 'hot' or near-naked teen girls). Chen named and shamed Violentacrez in an article, causing the latter to lose his job and become reviled around the globe as mainstream media picked up the story and it was broadcast worldwide. Chen did this at considerable risk to himself – the Reddit community can be vengeful. All links to Gawker were banned from Reddit for some time, until the more clear-thinking members of the community pointed out that censorship of this kind didn't help anybody.

But in May 2011, when he first heard of Silk Road, Chen was still a 25-year-old doing nights and weekends and trying to carve a niche for himself. He had noticed that the virtual currency bitcoin was increasingly being featured in articles on specialist technology blogs but had not yet reached the mainstream. Sensing a story, he found his way to the Bitcointalk forum.

'I visited the forums and one thing that was always coming up was this Silk Road: there were these huge threads about whether it was good or bad for bitcoin. People were asking how to get on it, what is it?' Chen's first instinct was to assume it was a scam. 'I couldn't believe that's what they were actually talking about – that it was a drug market.'

It didn't take him long to figure out how to download Tor, although it was the first time he had heard of it. 'I installed it, went on to Silk Road and, you know, clicked around a little bit and saw that it looked like it was really real. But even then I was sceptical of it.'

Sceptical or not, he thought it was worth investigating and started messaging people on the bitcoin forum who claimed they had used the black market successfully. He found that many of them were open to talking about it and were excited about its potential. This gave him the confidence to contact the owner of the site. Silkroad was enthusiastic and forthcoming about the new venture, providing Chen with quotes for the article and lessons in his philosophy of agorism. But he also had a favour to ask.

'He said, "We want to get bigger, but can you hold off? We're not ready for the attention yet",' said Chen. 'And I just said, "No, I can't, I'm writing about this now. Sorry." And then I wrote about it.' After two days of research and a few hours of writing over a couple of lattes in a New York cafe, he filed his story and went right on to the next one.

On 1 June 2011, Gawker released an article called 'The underground website where you can buy any drug imaginable'.

At the time there were close to 400 listings of drugs on Silk Road, the website having steadily gained users by word of mouth. Chen described the site, its owner and the role of bitcoin and provided instructions for how to find Silk Road. He knew he had written a story about a niche internet subculture, but swears he didn't think it would make many waves: 'I thought it was interesting, but I didn't think it was going to be so huge, like one of the biggest stories I'd ever written. And it still is, I think.'

The story had an immediate impact on Silk Road, bitcoin, Gawker and those waging a war on drugs. Within three days, two US senators publicly called on US Attorney General Eric Holder and the DEA to shut down Silk Road.

'This audacious website should be shut down immediately,' Senator Joe Manchin of West Virginia said.

Fellow Democrat senator Charles Schumer wholeheartedly

agreed. 'Literally, it allows buyers and users to sell illegal drugs online, including heroin, cocaine, and meth, and users do sell by hiding their identities through a program that makes them virtually untraceable. It's a certifiable one-stop shop for illegal drugs that represents the most brazen attempt to peddle drugs online that we have ever seen. It's more brazen than anything else by light years,' he said. 'By cracking down on the website immediately, we can help stop these drugs from flooding our streets.'

True to their word, the senators wrote to the Attorney General and the DEA urging them to investigate bitcoin's relationship to online illicit substance purchases, co-signing the letter. 'As part of this critical mission, we urge you to take immediate action and shut down the Silk Road network.'

Silk Road's owner responded with a posting on the Silk Road forums, which by now had become a thriving meeting space for customers and vendors of the site to discuss all things drugs:

As many of you know, US Senators are aware of the site and aiming to take it down . . . The die have been cast and now we will see how they land. We will be diverting even more effort into countering their attacks and making the site as resilient as possible, which means we may not be as responsive to messages for a while.

I'm sure this news will scare some off, but should we win the fight, a new era will be born. Even if we lose, the genie is out of the bottle and they are fighting a losing war already.

'It's better to live one day as a lion than a hundred years as a lamb.'

The senators were not very successful in the efforts they made to shut down Silk Road in 2011. But terminating drug operations was a popular vote-winner, so as long as Silk Road was on the radar, politicians would have a vested interest in seeing it closed. Soon after the senators' letter, a multi-agency task force based in Baltimore commenced Operation Marco Polo. This operation would eventually encompass investigators from the FBI, DEA, Department of Homeland Security, Internal Revenue Service (IRS), US Postal Inspection, US Secret Service, and the Bureau of Alcohol, Tobacco, Firearms and Explosives.

But in the short term there was little that could be done about this new online black market. The combined technologies of Tor, bitcoin and easy-to-learn encryption were doing their job of hiding the tracks of users and administration alike. Within five days of the June 2011 Gawker article, bitcoin's price had doubled from around $9 to more than $18 per coin. Two days after that, it hit $30 as registrations on Silk Road boomed and demand for bitcoin grew. Within days, the post-Gawker rush resulted in membership jumping from around 1000 to north of 10,000 accounts.

Silk Road began to have stability issues as more and more people tried to log on to see what the fuss was about and, perhaps, to buy drugs. For a while, it seemed it was never accessible. 'Does it even exist?' demanded one Bitcointalk forum member. 'I've never been able to find it. I think it might be some joke they are playing on the politicians . . . it just sounds too far-fetched to be possible.'

Rumours started circulating that it had all been a hoax. The merely curious who had not been able to log on to have a look drifted away in the belief that it was just another media beat-up. Those who had been Silk Road members pre-Gawker were angry at

Chen, blaming him for what they assumed would be the market's inevitable demise. The article became the most discussed subject on the Silk Road message boards, which at the time were part of the main site.

'Some people were really mad,' said Stacey Long, a Melbourne-based early adopter. 'They wanted Adrian Chen's blood. Silk Road was supposed to be a secret.'

With the article bringing a flood of new users to the site, Silk Road went into damage control and on 9 June 2011 it shut down for an upgrade to cope with the influx – but it gave the faithful fair warning so they would not panic:

hey gang, here's the scoop . . .

The site went mainstream way faster than we were hoping and we weren't prepared for the traffic. Everyone on the site knows what a pain it is getting 502 errors [an error received when the servers involved in loading a web page are unable to communicate] all the time. So, we are working on setting up an even more secure server that can handle all the traffic as well. Once we get that set up, and make some more improvements here and there, we'll be opening back up, whether by invite, open registration, or whatever.

For everyone pissed at us, we just want to offer our sincere apologies. We really didn't expect all of the media to catch on so quickly, and we should have been prepared with a semi-closed system. We'll do our best to get out of the spotlight and hopefully the merits of bitcoin will become the focus.

Also, if there is anyone out there locked out of their accounts with bitcoins in them, pm [private message] us here with 'bitcoins in account' as the subject. Please don't pm for any other reason.

This is fun, love you guys/gals

When Silk Road reopened on 17 June 2011, much to the relief of its membership, new registrations had been disabled. The sudden inability of people to register led to a new market in already-created Silk Road user accounts being sold online at 4chan and Reddit and on the Bitcointalk forum. The Bitcointalk thread exploded with would-be 'Roaders' begging for 'invites' of membership that did not exist. Another major change was that Silk Road separated into two distinct sites. The discussion forums, which by now had thousands of threads and tens of thousands of posts, were moved from the marketplace and reopened on a different site, using a separate server.

Hey gang,

Really sorry for the dead time there. Hopefully most of you got the message on the bitcoin forum or at silkroadmarket.org.

The only major change is this forum. We have it running on a separate server with it's [sic] own url so if the main site ever goes down again, first check here for updates. Unfortunately this means we have separate logins for the main site and the forum.

As we mentioned before, everything was backed up and totally restored, but if for some reason a deposit didn't make it in to your account or something like that, just let us know and we'll track it down and credit you. Also, we're giving everyone a 4 day grace period on taking orders to the resolution center before they are auto-resolved, so sellers, you may see some orders past due for a few days.

Thanks everyone for hanging in there with us. This work is scary and exciting all at the same time, and I'm really very happy to be on this journey with all of you.

Cheers,

Silk Road staff

Although history would say it was Chen's Gawker article that alerted the public to Silk Road, in reality his piece didn't reach that many people in the mainstream. There were a few articles about it in the technology pages of newspapers, but it was soon forgotten. At the time, Silk Road was still relatively tiny. Gawker being what it was (and even worse, 4chan being the initial source), the story was treated with a healthy dose of scepticism. The vast majority of people who read about it would not have taken their curiosity any further. Silk Road's owner, however, was determined that the users of his site didn't become complacent.

Hi everyone,

Things are going really well here. There are many new buyers and sellers working well together, our servers are secure and humming along, and you may even start to feel comfortable.

DO NOT get comfortable! This is not wal-mart, or even amazon.com. It is the wild west and there are as many crooks as there are honest businessmen and women. Keep your guard up and be safe, even paranoid. If you buy from someone without reputation, get to know them really well through pm, and even then be suspicious. Unfortunately it only takes one bad apple to spoil the bunch, and there are bad apples out there. We've received some threatening messages and just want everyone to stay alert and careful.

Some people speculated that around this time ownership of Silk Road may have changed hands. The mushroom-loving nerd who had set up a little site to sell his fungi and herbs must have been as stunned as anyone to see its explosive growth, even as he courted it. You would have needed balls of steel not to be frightened by the public declarations of the senators. But the first Silk Road moderator later emphatically denied this rumour.

'There was no changing hands around the Gawker time frame,' Nomad Bloodbath said. 'He [Silk Road's owner] intentionally did the Gawker article to get every drug addict in the world to the market . . . to get all the drugs you had always wanted to try but never had the source.'

Registrations on the new separate discussion forum were swift, including those of Nomad Bloodbath, 'DigitalAlch' and 'Chronicpain', in the first couple of days. The three had been active on the original site and would become Silk Road's first global moderators – volunteers at the time who agreed to keep the forums tidy, move threads and posts into their appropriate places, and remove any information that could threaten the security or identity of Silk Road members. None of the three knew the true identity of the site's owner. He had chosen them as long-term members of the site who could be trusted.

Someone claiming to be Nomad Bloodbath said that he and the other moderators were offered the positions after they took it upon themselves to write up some self-styled 'FAQ' threads for the incoming members of the site. 'I guess [silkroad] got tired of the forum responsibility and one day when we were both in the forum out of the blue he sends me a PM saying that some moderators were gonna be needed and [asked] if I was interested,' Bloodbath said.

Bloodbath remained a well-respected moderator of the forums until October 2012. But it was Chronicpain, who later became the first administrator of the Silk Road Wiki created in November 2011, who would become the most significant person in later events.

On 26 June 2011, Silk Road announced it was reopening seller accounts, but with a major change: it was limiting the supply of new seller accounts and auctioning them off to the highest bidders. 'Our hope is that by doing this, only the most professional and committed sellers will have access to seller accounts. For the time being, we will be releasing one new seller account every 48 hours to the maximum bidder in that time frame,' the site's owner wrote.

In July 2011 Silk Road continued to innovate in the world of black-market commerce with the introduction of a hedging feature – providing the ability to offset potential losses or gains that could be incurred as a result of the time finances were tied up while buyers waited for their goods to be delivered. Bitcoin was prone to wild fluctuations and both sellers and buyers could lose out for transactions in escrow. Silk Road offered the option to sellers to hedge their escrow balances against fluctuations in the bitcoin/USD exchange rate, providing some 'much needed predictability and stability to the transaction process and allow sellers to price their items with confidence'. The hedging feature was a great success, giving promised stability throughout a time of high market volatility, and most sellers opted in.

In mid-July 2011, about half a dozen members allegedly had their Silk Road accounts drained. The immediate suspicion was that their funds had been stolen, either by hackers or Silk Road itself, but it was soon revealed that those affected had been using the same password for Silk Road as for their MtGox accounts. MtGox, a bitcoin exchange based in Tokyo, had been compromised on 9 June 2011 when large sums in bitcoin were transferred out, allegedly by a hacker who had been able to hack one of the exchange auditor's credentials. Silk Road's customers learned the lesson that their password should be unique to the site.

By August 2011, Silk Road's popularity had grown so much that the owner announced that the site needed more IT personnel, claiming his expertise and time were both 'maxed out'. Silk Road, once again making history, publicly put out to tender the role of a full-time experienced UNIX administrator, complete with a head-hunting incentive of $1000 to anyone who introduced the winning candidate. The job was a part-time, temporary position that could turn into a full-time, permanent position for the right person. The successful candidate could work from anywhere in the world and would have no access to sensitive information or the identity of his or her boss. Interested parties were instructed to answer a series of questions and apply to administration. Most of the questions were fairly standard for a job advertisement, with one notable exception: 'What is your drug of choice, if any?'

Silkroad later declared he was 'blown away' by the calibre of the applicants. No public announcement was ever made about the eventual appointment, but there was little doubt that the team behind what was fast becoming the largest and most notorious online black market in history was growing.

Another online drugs marketplace, Open Vendor Database (OVDB), had been launched at around the same time as Silk Road with high hopes of being the field leader. Its owners had a long history in online drug markets, and had previously been the 'council' of Binary Blue Stars (BBS), a private Tor-based forum for the sale of psychedelics.

'The council on BBS essentially came to the idea of a public drug site at the same time as and independently [of Silk Road],' said an OVDB moderator. 'We also had a massive history and honestly were kind of miffed that some noob was trying to steal the glory.'

But steal the glory Silk Road did. In December 2011, OVDB gave up trying to compete and shut down; it was later fully absorbed by Silk Road. It was a benevolent takeover of sorts.

By February 2012, Silk Road had become a team. The founder and public face of the website needed a separate identity.

Enter the Dread Pirate Roberts.

IT pro needed for venture-backed bitcoin startup

Hello, sorry if there is another thread for this kind of post, but I couldn't find one. I'm looking for the best and brightest IT pro in the bitcoin community to be the lead developer in a venture-backed bitcoin startup company. The ideal candidate would have at least several years of web application development experience, having built applications from the ground up. A solid under-standing of oop [object-oriented programming] and software architecture is a must. Experience in a start-up environment is a plus, or just being super hard working, self-motivated, and creative.

Compensation can be in the form of equity or a salary, or somewhere in-between.

If interested, please send your answers to the following questions to rossulbricht at gmail dot com

– Post by altoid on the Bitcointalk forum, 11 October 2011

State of the Road Address

From its humble beginnings, the Silk Road market was quickly populated with what has become a vibrant community full of interesting characters. From our superstar vendors and ever-helpful mods to all of the active folks on the forum, the people here are truly awesome. Silk Road would not be what it is or possibly even exist without everyone who has stepped up along the way to point out security flaws, contribute their ideas, and take this experiment on as their own and stand with us.

It didn't take long before word got out. Our little hidden market got the attention of the media and soon the politicians and law enforcement. But Silk Road was never meant to be private and exclusive. It is meant to grow into a force to be reckoned with that can challenge the powers that be and at last give people the option to choose freedom over tyranny. We fundamentally believe that people can thrive and prosper under these conditions and so far tens of thousands have done so in the Silk Road market.

A revolution has been born. So ideally, more participants means more prosperity. What we've found in practice is that if there is an opportunity to cheat, steal or lie for personal short-term gain, someone, somewhere will exploit it.

So, we've had two major challenges to face as Silk Road grows and evolves. One is making our systems tough enough and flexible enough to withstand and win a cyber-war with the most powerful organizations in the world, should they choose to start that war.

This is always and ever a top priority. The other is making the market a place where people can quickly and easily buy and sell just about anything without worrying about being attacked by gun-toting men in uniforms and thrown in a cage or worry about being ripped off by their trading partner.

I am proud to say we have been successful in achieving these goals up to this point. The site remains up and functioning (despite a few screw-ups on our part, like not having a full capacity backup server ready to go when a live server went down, and a poorly executed url switch, just to name a few). And, over 99% of all transactions conducted within the escrow system are completed to the satisfaction of both buyer and seller, or a mutually agreed upon resolution is found.

This success has in no way made us complacent, however.

New members are still being lured into trading outside of escrow by scammers and getting ripped off, and 'finalizing early', effectively cutting out the escrow process, is common practice. Still, I believe we can mitigate these risks and take our market to the next level in security, reliability, performance, and convenience for everyone involved.

First we must deal with trading out of escrow. Up to this point we have charged a flat 6.23% commission on all trades. This is much too high for transactions in the $300 and over range, making trading out of escrow for large transactions much more attractive than staying within the system. Now, instead of charging a flat commission, we will charge a higher amount for low priced items and a lower amount for high priced items, similar to how eBay does it.

We've worked hard to come up with a commission schedule that should work for everyone and will give scammers no excuse to make people send money outside of escrow.

. . .

With this change, there are no phoney excuses whatsoever for vendors to ask for out of escrow [OOE] payment. Any request should be interpreted as a scam attempt and reported to the Silk Road support team via the 'contact us' link on the main site. We are looking at several mechanisms for enforcing the ban on OOE transactions, from self-policing to bounties on offenders.

Together, we can beat the scammers and make the Silk Road market a place where you can buy with confidence and peace of mind. If we stay true to our principles of integrity, virtue, mutual respect and camaraderie that have guided us to this point, I believe our future is bright and this revolutionary experiment will be a success!

– Silk Road announcement, 9 January 2012

Enter Dread Pirate Roberts

There were black markets before Silk Road, and virtually identical online drug bazaars have popped up since. Yet none has achieved the notoriety or success of 'the Road', and this can almost certainly be attributed to the loquacious, enigmatic founder of the business.

If bitcoin's Satoshi Nakamoto was intriguing, Silk Road's founder blew him out of the water as the quintessential pseudonymous outlaw. He was prone to penning rousing epistles about life, liberty and his favourite philosophy, agorism. At first, he was simply known online by the name of his business, 'silkroad' – this was the username of the Bitcointalk forum member who announced he had started an anonymous online marketplace to sell drugs. As the site and its forums grew in popularity, the site's owner continued to call himself silkroad.

But as his legend grew, silkroad realised he needed an identity separate from that of the site. Or perhaps the site had become an enterprise run by a company of people and it needed a public face for the forum, which by this time was quite separate from the marketplace. In any event, rather than simply announcing a change of name, the founder made it into a game.

Who is Silk Road? Some call me SR, SR admin or just Silk Road. But isn't that confusing? I am Silk Road, the market, the person, the enterprise, everything. But Silk Road has matured and I need an identity separate from the site and the enterprise of which I am now only a part. I need a name. Actually, I already have a name picked out. It is a great name. You are going to love it. It is perfect on so many levels. But, I'm not going to reveal it until this weekend, when our customer appreciation sale is in full swing.

And, in the spirit of customer appreciation and love, we're going to play a little game. Sometime between noon Saturday and noon Sunday UTC I will announce my new name in this thread. The last person to post the top three items on their Silk Road wish list before I post my name will get those items express shipped to their front door for free!

The name he chose – Dread Pirate Roberts – was announced on 5 February 2012. 'I'll give it a couple of days to sink in before actually changing it on the sites, but there you have it,' he wrote. Switched-on forum members recognised the reference to the movie *The Princess Bride* (based on the 1973 fantasy novel by William Goldman) almost immediately.

In that movie, the hero, Westley, was captured by the Dread Pirate Roberts, a pirate with a reputation of ruthlessness who would kill all on board a ship if they refused to hand over their gold. Westley went on to become the first mate and eventually the pirate let him in on a little secret: the Dread Pirate Roberts was not so much one person's name as a job title, secretly passed on from man to man as each incumbent decided to retire. The fictional Roberts' infamous reputation meant ships would immediately surrender their wealth rather than allow their crew to be captured and killed. When the captain had gathered enough riches to retire, he would offload all his crew other than his first mate at a port. Engaging a new team, the captain would refer to the first mate as 'Dread Pirate Roberts' and once the crew were convinced, he would leave the ship and live out his days wanting for nothing.

It was perhaps the website owner's single most ingenious moment. By giving himself this name, he set up the premise that Silk Road was to move from owner to owner. The sins of one may not be the sins of another. Any person who might later be unmasked as the site's owner could have plausible deniability for crimes committed by a predecessor.

It immediately opened up questions. Was Silk Road's ownership about to change hands? Had it already? If it had, when had this occurred? Many speculated it had happened during the downtime after the Gawker article. Others thought it would be happening soon. Naturally, the enigmatic owner left all of these questions hanging. But he set in train the basis of conspiracy theories for the next couple of years.

Both the Silk Road forums and Reddit's Silk Road sub-Reddit held lengthy discussions debating whether there had been more than one owner of Silk Road and, if so, how many and in what time-frame. Many of the theories were plausible; some were fanciful.

Dread Pirate Roberts, affectionately known as DPR, became an active and visible member of Silk Road's large community, where he was hailed as a hero by those who believed it was their right to buy drugs without the interference of law enforcement bodies. More than that, his vision seemed to come from a place of peace, compassion and a genuine desire to provide a safer, better way for otherwise law-abiding citizens to procure and use recreational drugs. 'For the first time I saw the drug cartels and the dealers, and every person in the whole damn supply chain in a different light,' he wrote.

He subscribed to the belief that, despite what mass media and representatives of government would have us believe, the vast majority of drug users – even chronic drug users – were happy, non-violent people who were perfectly capable of holding down regular jobs. They weren't taking drugs because there was some-thing lacking in their lives: they imbibed because they enjoyed them – and because most recreational drugs did not cause the loss of control often associated with alcohol, and were far less likely to kill users than a product like tobacco.

Cartel atrocities notwithstanding, an online drug supply chain could assist in crime reduction. When end users ordered online, they could order direct from a large-scale dealer in Europe or North America, cutting out many of the middlemen usually involved before drugs arrived to the final customer in a face-to-face transaction.

What's more, anonymous online transactions completely eradi-cated any threat of violence from a drug deal. 'Some, especially the cartels, are basically a defacto violent power hungry state, and surely would love nothing more than to take control of a national government, but your average joe pot dealer, who wouldn't hurt a fly, that guy became my hero,' DPR said. (An academic study by two scholars that analysed Silk Road in retrospect some years later entitled 'Not an "eBay for drugs"', also cited the inherent inability to commit drug-related violence as a reason for the site's popularity. 'The anonymity that the cryptomarket provides reduces or eliminates the need – or even the ability – to resort to violence,' the study said.)

His utopian system would also contribute to harm reduction. Inconsistency in quality and content could lead to overdoses and unexpected reactions. The user in a face-to-face transaction rarely knew what purity their pill or powder contained, but with Silk Road's feedback system, the vendor's desire for repeat business and the lively discussion forums, the online purchaser could be comparatively confident about what they were ingesting.

The discussion forums were something else that DPR deliberately fostered, providing a support network for drug takers. He took his role of mentor, tutor and benevolent dictator seriously and nurtured and guided contributors to create the type of community he wanted. One of the most popular forums on the site was dedicated to drug safety. Users provided advice on the safest methods of taking and mixing drugs, as well as support and counseling for those who wished to quit using.

Drug safety and responsible use were 'incredibly important' to DPR and his team, he claimed in one interview. 'I care very much about the community of people that surround Silk Road,' he said. 'Many of the substances sold on Silk Road are quite powerful and if not used responsibly could lead to addiction, injury or even death. Not surprisingly, most people don't want these things for themselves.'

For the Dread Pirate Roberts, Silk Road was not merely a commercial enterprise: it was a revolution. DPR was determined to teach his followers his philosophy:

> Anything you do that is outside the control of the state is agorist, so in some sense we are all agorists whether we know it or not. Some people just take those actions because of the personal gain they can obtain, which is perfectly fine, but some do it as a conscientious objection and act of rebellion against the state as well.
>
> I'm out to turn unconscious agorists into conscious active ones. :)

By early 2012, Silk Road was firmly on the radar of authorities in the United States, Europe and Oceania. And everybody – law enforcement, journalists and followers alike – was curious about the charismatic founder.

Why, he was asked, was he able to remain anonymous despite manhunts by authorities, journalists and tenacious internet sleuths?

'Because my life, liberty and mission are more important to me than fame, convenience or comfort,' Roberts said.

Here's another thing that doesn't get said enough: I love you.
This is the most fun I've ever had and I feel closer to the people I
have met here than the vast majority of people I have to hide all
of this from in real life. Stay light, have fun, and please take this
on as more than a way to score drugs. Stand by me as we stand
up for ourselves.

         – Dread Pirate Roberts forum post, 11 January 2012

You've Got Mail

The occasional media article that emerged within the year or so of Silk Road's opening was often met with incredulity by readers. Many believed the whole drugs-in-the-mail thing to be a reporter's beat-up, a scam or a trap by law enforcement. It was absurd to think people were using something as banal as the postal service to send and receive the sorts of drugs that most of the general public had only a passing knowledge of.

One of the questions everyone asked was just how drugs could get through the mail. We've all seen news footage of dogs racing up conveyer belts of mail – why didn't they pick up the scent of heroin, cocaine, MDMA? How could a buyer be confident that the mail would get through? And what would happen if a parcel were intercepted – would the goods simply be confiscated, or would a SWAT team arrive at your door?

It is, of course, classified information as to how many and how often sniffer dogs are used for mail coming through customs.

There are many myths around the abilities or lack thereof of sniffer dogs. One such myth seems to have come straight out of the movie *Beverly Hills Cop*, in which drugs are packed in coffee beans because the smell of the coffee supposedly throws the dogs off the scent of the drugs. This, apparently, is complete bunk.

There are many technical explanations, but the one that best illustrates the point is that a dog's scent is similar to a human's sight. It can distinguish differences, no matter how much you try to mask them. That is, a dog can separate and differentiate scents the same way humans can with visuals. So hiding drugs in coffee is like painting three walls of a room red and one yellow, hoping the red walls will hide the yellow one from us. The dog can smell the drugs and the coffee. One does not mask the other from their sensitive noses.

In any event, drug dogs apparently are trained to sniff out only one or two types of drug each and can only work in half-hour increments, so the use of them can become prohibitively expensive. Few are trained to smell psychedelics, and that, coupled with the fact that such drugs are supplied on what looks like normal pieces of paper, makes LSD tabs some of the most popular items to import, especially for Australians. Those who prefer the drastically reduced prices of importing rather than buying locally take the risk and, anecdotally at least, it seems very few parcels are detected. The legal risk, however, is magnified: receiving drugs from overseas carries far harsher penalties than receiving the same amount of drugs from an Australian supplier.

On occasions that drugs have been detected for small-time buyers in Australia, there are reports of customs sending 'love letters' to the intended recipient. Stacey Long said she had received two – each for a small quantity of MDMA. The letters stated that customs had intercepted a communication they suspected contained a controlled substance and invited her to collect it if she believed there had been a mistake. She was blasé. 'I just ignored them,' she said, despite warnings on the letters that they should not be ignored. 'Never heard back.' She continued to have drugs mailed to her home and they continued to arrive. Apparently it is not uncommon for the authorities to let illegal drugs through if they believe they will be able to establish a pattern of deliveries to build a case showing intention, so that there is no defence of a one-off 'mistake'. Presumably Stacey's small, infrequent personal quantities were not enough to raise the alarm or effect an arrest.

Sometimes receiving drugs in the mail comes with unexpected consequences. Sam Tyler ordered a gram of MDMA from the UK and then, a week later, a gram of 2CB, an intense psychedelic. Both drugs come in the form of a white powder. When the first piece of mail turned up the following week, Sam assumed it was the MDMA he had been waiting a fortnight for and duly made up eight capsules of 125 milligrams each for him and his girlfriend.

'Kylie and I popped one each before heading out one night,' he said. 'When it hit us on the train, we knew something wasn't right. The carriage turned into a giant sea monster and we were swirling around in its stomach. Everything was wavy and sounds were distorted.'

It soon hit them that they hadn't taken ecstasy. The 2CB – which had a recommended dose of 20–25 milligrams – had arrived in record time and, mistaking it for the MDMA, they had taken a dose six times higher than they should have. They would be on an intense, and not particularly enjoyable, psychedelic ride for the next six hours or so. Fortunately 2CB is not toxic at such levels, but it could have been a tragic outcome had other drugs been involved.

Vendors on Silk Road competed to provide the best customer service. Packaging of goods was one of the important factors in determining the quality of a seller. Although it was strictly forbidden to discuss packaging on the forums – everyone knew that members of law enforcement were forever lurking – many people privately shared the often ingenious methods.

Most sellers, when providing small amounts of powders, would simply supply the goods in a vacuum-sealed pouch, flattened in a standard business envelope, complete with window and legitimate (or legitimate-looking) return address. Thus a gram of cocaine, ecstasy or heroin would arrive folded within a few sheets of blank A4 paper in an envelope from a real estate agent, bank or travel broker, undetectable to human touch or canine snout from the outside. Such envelopes were indistinguishable from the billions of other pieces of business mail circulating the globe every day.

In this case, should a person be unlucky enough to have their mail opened by customs or other authorities, the substance would be discovered. One vendor provided a little extra for the bureaucrat who intercepted the letter: dealer 'MarijuanaIsMyMuse' would provide a slip of paper inside the envelope saying, 'If you are the intended recipient, please use responsibly. If you are law enforcement, go fuck yourself.'

Other vendors were more creative with their packaging, especially those who supplied goods that could not be as discreetly secreted in a slim envelope. Those who were sending pills, plants or larger quantities of powders might hide them inside cheap plastic 'gifts', in cut-out pages of thick catalogues or behind false cardboard 'walls' of a padded envelope. One member received pills stuffed inside a hollow marker pen, and another was sent cocaine in hollowed-out batteries inside a toy. An article in *The Monthly* reported that a buyer found his foil package in the glue behind a shampoo sample inside a magazine.

Sometimes the stealth of a vendor was so ingenious that recipients would think they had been ripped off. If a buyer was not expecting a particular method of stealth, they could jump to the conclusion that they had been scammed; only by completely ripping apart the package would they find the goods cleverly secreted within. A sheet of acid might be disguised as a business card, or pills distributed inside the bubbles of a bubble-wrap package.

'I love vendors who use 007-style stealth,' said one member. 'Not only am I getting drugs in the mail, I get to have a little treasure hunt to find my goodies. So much fun!'

Occasionally the search for drugs inside a package was fruitless for the buyer. Some vendors were guilty of 'selective scamming', whereby they would send an empty package so that any tracking information would show that the parcel had been sent. The vendor would then use this as 'proof' they had mailed a package when the matter went to Silk Road's dispute resolution.

Then there were vendors who really screwed up. One over-worked seller, rushing to make the evening mail pick-up, forgot to include postage on all his packages. Ministers of a small church in southern USA were surprised to receive returned-to-sender mail that they had never sent out. Even more mystifying were the little packages of white powder inside, which they sensibly handed over to police. Addressees apparently received a frightening visit from law enforcement officers, but there were no reported arrests made.

Vendors had their own secret section of the forums. To access the Vendors' Roundtable, a seller had to have proven sales credentials over a certain amount of time and for a certain amount of money. In that forum, sellers could report suspicious buyers to each other and discuss suggestions for improvements or to otherwise make life easier for vendors. They would let each other know when they had 'bad LEO vibes', meaning they believed certain members were law enforcement officers nosing around, and warn each other about buyers who threatened to blackmail them with bad feedback. Just as some sellers would scam buyers by not sending out their drugs, some buyers would attempt to scam sellers by claiming their drugs never arrived and demanding a resend or refund. Certain user-names would be blacklisted and those buyers might never know why sellers wouldn't do business with them.

Buyers had an incentive not to scam sellers because some of the best sellers had the luxury of refusing to do business with anyone who did not have 'good stats'. When a buyer placed an order, vendors could see how much the buyer had spent in the past, how much they had had refunded and what percentage of their sales had been auto-finalised (i.e. where the buyer had not bothered to finalise the transaction and release the funds, it would auto-finalise after a long delay if the buyer had not disputed the sale). Auto-finalisation meant vendors could not access funds for at least thirty days.

Even if a seller agreed to deal with a buyer with no or bad stats, they might insist that they finalise early. Good buyer statistics put the member in a position of power. In fact, many buyers would finalise even when they did not receive their package if it was for a small amount so they would not ruin their buyer stats. Vendors who were also buyers would have different accounts for buying and selling, but occasionally would mess up by ordering from their vendor account. This, of course, meant somebody – the other seller – would have that vendor's address. But the general consensus was that an environment where dealers and users never had to meet face-to-face was beneficial to all.

Online drug marketplaces might claim to provide a safer environment for buyers and sellers, but they do not eradicate problems associated with the drug trade. In particular, the drugs have to come from somewhere. Despite Silk Road cutting out the middlemen involved in drug dealing and eliminating the violence that is always a potential in face-to-face transactions, millions of people are still harmed by the illicit drug trade. The purchase of the drugs contributes to the slaughter of thousands of people at the source, particularly in Central and South America, as drug barons fight to be the sole suppliers of the world's trade. Among other tragedies, the well-intentioned measures of the Afghanistan government, supported by NATO, to eradicate poppy fields led to farmers selling their children into sex slavery to 'compensate' traffickers or repay loans.

But such atrocities were something Silk Road users preferred not to think about. In early 2012, thousands of transactions were taking place over Silk Road every day. Much of the money within the site was simply recirculated as members bought bulk amounts from cheaper suppliers, then broke it up into smaller amounts to resell to local buyers at a marked-up price. These small-time sellers simply wanted to make enough money to cover their own drug purchases. Top vendors, however, were turning over tens – even hundreds – of thousands of dollars in bitcoin a month.

Unfortunately, bitcoin was worthless unless it could be converted into real money. Just as anonymity was lost for purchasers once they had to supply a delivery address, bitcoin's anonymity could be compromised when holders attempted to cash out large amounts. Silk Road's biggest dealers would have to learn money-laundering techniques in order to make a profit.

I am the only true money launderer on the Road so it's a lovely time right now.

– Self-styled money-laundering guru StExo

Money Laundering 101

As well as harnessing the e-commerce platform, one thing that set Silk Road apart from any of its competitors was its community. It had the liveliest online forums to be found on the dark web. Drug users from all over the world would engage each other in conversation and debate, share their musical tastes, ask questions, tell lies and generally interact in thousands of forum posts per day. Vendors would offer the more prolific members free samples of their wares in return for a public review. Members would lend each other fractions of bitcoin to complete an order.

One frequent conversation was small-time money laundering. It was one thing to buy bitcoin anonymously; it was quite another to sell thousands of dollars' worth of bitcoin at regular intervals without raising alarm bells. Members of the site discussed methods for cashing out bitcoin without being detected. It was a particularly hot topic in the Vendors' Roundtable.

One way was to make private transactions through Local-Bitcoins.com, which put buyers and sellers in touch with each other, but this could be expensive. 'I refuse to pay a bullshit ten percent fee especially on multiple grand cash outs,' grumbled one vendor.

The community of Silk Road were forever searching for other methods to cash out their bitcoin. Exchanging bitcoin for gold, which could be melted down and on-sold for cash, was suggested by some. Others bought gift cards for major retailers from private sellers at slightly more than face value, the difference being chalked up to a cost of doing business. Some set up online stores on legitimate art and craft websites, where they 'sold' worthless pieces of junk for outrageous prices. Or they would provide 'consulting services' or 'personal training' at highly inflated hourly rates. If queried, they could claim high-profile, wealthy clients and obligations of anonymity and privacy.

Then there was a method of explaining not only large hoards of bitcoin but also a high power bill caused by growing copious amounts of marijuana. By purchasing decrepit bitcoin-mining hardware, if ever questioned about the amount of bitcoin being cashed out on an exchange, the cannabis seller could claim they had been mining bitcoins since their genesis. The mining hardware could also be responsible for the high power bills for the property over those years before the machine broke down.

Using bitcoin for online gambling was another strategy. The user would place a bet on the highest probability or lowest odds bet (like betting on both red and black on the roulette table at the casino) and have the winnings delivered to a number of different bitcoin wallet addresses. The small losses would simply be the cost of laundering.

More sophisticated methods involved starting a legitimate-looking bitcoin-based business that purchased a high volume of low-cost goods and then 'sold' them at a massive mark-up to a number of shill accounts owned by the user themselves. Members who recommended this method suggested that proper books be kept and taxes paid if the income was substantial.

A variation on the theme was to set up a small company that mined bitcoins, and over-report the earnings. This could be a simple matter for those earning an average wage from selling, but needed to be a more sophisticated system for the high-volume sellers earning millions of dollars. They would need to actually purchase mining equipment for tens of thousands of dollars and attribute their bitcoin earnings to the machine. The machine would never be used – it would be sold elsewhere on the black market for cash.

Many speculated how Dread Pirate Roberts was laundering his earnings from commissions. In the early days, the values of deals being made were visible to all, providing some insight into the massive turnover being enjoyed by the site. Roberts' commissions would be substantial, as would be the interest of authorities in tracking him down. Most theorised he was probably holding on to his commissions in a number of bitcoin wallets dotted around cyberspace. Perhaps he was living in a country with more lax money-laundering laws.

One highly paranoid person, 'A', claimed to have uncovered the money-laundering trail of Silk Road and some of its largest vendors. He said he had engaged with a hidden service that offered money-laundering services to DPR as well as to a few senior staff and vendors of Silk Road. He said he had traced the flow of bitcoin in quantities and patterns that left him in no doubt he was following the proceeds of sales from Silk Road.

Further, he claimed to have posed as a customer and actually met the man responsible for the laundering of Dread Pirate Roberts' money, as well as that of two of the Road's largest vendors, in a hotel in New York. The money-laundering process was, he claimed, undertaken by a group of former private bankers and accountants, using legitimate bitcoin exchanges and part-ownership of a tiny European bank. The consortium, he believed, was purchasing a mid-sized property portfolio, comprising multiple suburban residential homes and a commercial building out of which a legitimate IT company was operating, through loans made to a Delaware company from a small boutique bank in Europe, arranged by a Toronto-based corporate finance group.

There seemed to be little verifiable in A's claims and no way of determining whether they were true, or even whether A believed them to be true or was simply trolling.

Then there was StExo. StExo was an increasingly prolific presence on the Silk Road forums who claimed to be a security expert and large-scale money launderer. He openly courted the media, contacting a number of journalists who had written about Silk Road. He bragged that he was Silk Road's number-one money launderer and hinted that he laundered the money of the Pirate himself. 'I am the only true money launderer on the Road so it's a lovely time right now,' he said.

He was prone to grandiose statements and juicy titbits about the site, its top vendors and its founder. 'I've been extremely busy recently due to a major shift in business,' was one typical statement he made after he hadn't been around for a couple of days, 'which will probably be noticed within the next five days since, as per my usual style on Silk Road, it is a pretty "ballsy" move, something I now kind of take in my stride since I've realised the potential pay off for being bold and brazen.' Forum members were split on whether StExo was legitimately a major player or full of hot air.

He implied that he had a close personal relationship with Dread Pirate Roberts. 'Of course, one thing I absolutely cannot discuss is DPR's personal circumstances,' he said. 'Some theories have been flying around SR recently speculating of why I have suddenly returned in such force and one of them is because DPR obviously has a lot of bitcoins and there are very few people capable of undertaking such an operation, that's fair game to probe but don't expect any direct answers.' He dismissed the revelations of A as ridiculous.

StExo wrote reams of self-congratulatory posturing. Patrick O'Neill of Weirder Web wrote up StExo's claims as a story about a forty-something money launderer living the high life in London. O'Neill may have had his suspicions, though. He wrote a disclaimer of sorts:

In reading about StExo, it's important to note that it's impossible to verify the numbers he's supplied and many of the stories he's told. It's equally important to understand that they are still of serious worth. There is no doubt that his dealings and the numbers behind them are significant but, approaching the specifics of it all, this is his story as he tells it. It's a story worth telling.

In reporting this story, I have spoken to and seen proof of several clients of StExo's, including those among Silk Road's most popular vendors. While that still does not verify the numbers, it strengthens the foundations of the story.

StExo claimed he was in charge of a group that sold MDMA whole-sale in the UK and originally visited Silk Road to find more dealers to work for him. He claimed to have been there, lurking, from the beginning, but after the Gawker article, he said he:

> decided to start purchasing things from Silk Road to test vendors out, see their packaging, get to know them etc as vendors are much more comfortable talking to or working with their customers than somebody who has never purchased before – they like to see your words of money are backed by money. Of course I had to get one of my guys to setup a mailbox under false passports and driving licenses and then it'd be a different guy every week picking up the shipments. After it is picked up we have our methods of getting it to me without them ever seeing me or knowing my address for safety reasons as even amongst my own crew I must be careful simply because of who I am.

StExo's tales read a bit like a lame crime novel. He said he bought other vendors laundering consultations, 'playing it all quite dumb so I could see the depth of their knowledge which to be frank, wasn't deep at all'. He claimed most major Silk Road vendors had been in touch with him, he laundered most of the top-ranked sellers' money and they were all really happy with him. But, of course, he couldn't provide any details 'for opsec [operational security] reasons'.

It all sounded like the deluded fantasies of a wannabe gangster.

Upon checking the forums' archives to read StExo's old posts, it was revealed he had deleted all of them – hundreds – a couple of months earlier. This would have been done manually, post by post; it is a job only someone dedicated to hiding something would do. However, when a user deleted his or her posts, it didn't affect the posts of other members who had quoted him. Trawling through months of replies to StExo turned up snippets that built a picture of a clueless twenty-year-old trying to make a name for himself in the criminal world.

It looked like StExo was full of shit. But he remained prolific on the forums. His reputation as a money launderer and security expert grew and he became one of the most trusted members of the site.

He may not have been the person he tried to project. But that didn't mean he wouldn't become a force to be reckoned with on Silk Road.

Meet Tony76

Silk Road's top-ranked sellers chopped and changed over time. But some were there from the beginning, racking up thousands, hundreds of thousands, perhaps even millions in sales by keeping customers happy and providing top-quality product and reliable service. In January 2012, a new Canadian vendor arrived on the scene. Tony76 blundered on to the forums offering free samples of heroin and MDMA, oblivious to the rules that stated in no uncertain terms that anyone who wanted to sell their wares on Silk Road had to purchase a vendor account.

He swept in with extravagant statements about the quality of his Afghanistan-origin heroin (known simply as 'H' on the streets). 'I know everyone claims to have the best shit, but I actually guarantee my H is the best you will ever find. I am that confident,' he said. 'That isn't just a sales pitch because I am not going to say that about my MDMA.' He assured potential customers that his MDMA was 'really great' but he couldn't say whether it was the best MDMA on Silk Road simply because he had yet to sample anyone else's.

Tony laboured at the beginning. He was paranoid about his physical safety, worrying about lurking cameras at the post office or bank. He had no idea how to purchase bitcoin and struggled with the technology. He couldn't open a vendor's account because of the restrictions placed on new accounts at the time.

But after this somewhat childish and try-hard entrance, which belied his claim he had been 'doing this for 20 years', it didn't take long for Tony to become educated in the ways of the Road. He engaged with the senior members of the site and learned about the technologies that made online black markets work. As soon as vendor registrations reopened, he purchased a vendor account and listed heroin, ketamine and MDMA of the highest quality. He was eager to please the stakeholders in his business – Silk Road's management, members and customers. He sent out samples to trusted members and solicited their feedback, dealt with complaints swiftly and acknowledged those who publicly praised him with little 'extras' in their next orders. He marketed himself and his goods on the forums, engaging members, offering incentives and being friendly and personable, if a little rough around the edges.

When some buyers tried to extort him by threatening to give bad feedback if he did not supply free drugs, he dealt with them openly and with the plaintive cries of an honest businessman who was being hard done by. And when he heard of his loyal customers getting scammed by other sellers, he offered them freebies. 'Chiefrogan: Send me your address and i'll send you a free 0.5 g of H . . . You were one of my first customers and i hate to see you hurting and getting fucked over like that.'

It was a fantastic business plan. From the bumbling sole trader grew a slick, professional business force, and within a couple of months Tony76 became the number-one heroin and ecstasy seller on the Road. As the site continued to grow, new buyers were quickly turned on to the most professional vendor it had to offer. When a member performed a search for their drug of choice, the site would list them in order of popularity, and soon Tony's wares appeared at the top of the page. The accolades poured in from all over Canada and the US, Tony76 having made the decision to contain his business to North America despite repeated requests from those outside the jurisdiction to sell to their countries.

He was actively involved and made sensible suggestions in the Vendors' Roundtable. He championed the Roundtable section being made private from all but verified vendors. When he got his wish, he said to Dread Pirate Roberts: 'While you are here . . . Can you remove "stats" from the forum? I can click anyone's name, and click "view stats" and see exactly what hours of the day they are online . . . Which is a huge security risk in terms of time correlation attacks.'

Tony was concerned that law enforcement would be able to determine a vendor's location by the hours the vendor kept. Dread Pirate Roberts implemented the change.

Silk Road's 'Rumor Mill' forum was where drug users rated and reviewed the sellers. 'Tony76 Official Thread – Reviews/Updates/ Products' soon became one of the busiest places in the forum. And there were few negative reviews: Tony had a legion of fans raving about his products and service. He didn't even seem to use the tactic many new sellers used of 'purchasing' from himself in order to rack up sales and accolades. According to the feedback, you could trust the descriptions of his product. He guaranteed shipping. His packaging was first rate. His sales grew and within a few months, Tony76 was raking in tens of thousands of dollars a day by doing exactly what Silk Road was set up to do. His feedback held steady at 100 per cent satisfaction. Members recommended him to their friends: 'Tony76 is DA MAN'. He was the ultimate Silk Road success story, one of many.

He remained modest, too. 'Wow thank you guys for the amazing feedback on my H!' he wrote. 'I plan on sticking around here for a long time to come! Cheers!'

He held a sale with unbelievable prices at the beginning of February 2012 and the reviews continued to be brilliant, despite him making customers finalise early so as not to have bitcoin tied up in escrow as he was 'practically giving it away for free'. Those who didn't want to finalise could buy in escrow at his usual prices, but such was Tony's reputation that few people felt the need for third-party protection. The customers who bought during the sale were very happy with the price and the product that soon arrived in their letterboxes.

Later in February, Tony added cocaine to his wares and his fan base grew. He could do no wrong. He was a vendor that others could emulate if they, too, wanted to be a Silk Road success story. Dread Pirate Roberts was no doubt proud to have him on board.

Hey guys,

I read more than I post in the forum, and my posts are rarely of a personal nature. For some reason the mood struck me just now to put the revolution down for a minute and just express a few things. There is a curtain of anonymity and secrecy that covers everything that goes on behind the scenes here. It is often fast paced and stressful behind this curtain and I rarely lift my head long enough to take in just how amazing all of this is. But when I do I am filled with inspiration and hope for the future. Here's a little story about what inspires me:

For years I was frustrated and defeated by what seemed to be insurmountable barriers between the world today and the world I wanted. I searched long and hard for the truth about what is right and wrong and good for humanity. I argued with, learned from, and read the works of brilliant people in search of the truth.

It's a damn hard thing to do too with all of the misinformation and distractions in the sea of opinion we live in. But eventually I found something I could agree with wholeheartedly. Something that made sense, was simple, elegant and consistent in all cases.

I'm talking about the Austrian Economic theory, voluntarism, anarcho-capitalism, agorism etc. espoused by the likes of [Ludwig von] Mises and [Murray] Rothbard before their deaths, and [Joseph] Salerno and [Lew] Rockwell today.

From their works, I understood the mechanics of liberty, and the effects of tyranny. But such vision was a curse. Everywhere I looked I saw the State, and the horrible withering effects it had on the human spirit. It was horribly depressing. Like waking from a restless dream to find yourself in a cage with no way out.

But I also saw free spirits trying to break free of their chains, doing everything they could to serve their fellow man and provide for themselves and their loved ones. I saw the magical and powerful wealth creating effect of the market, the way it fostered cooperation, civility and tolerance. How it made trading partners out of strangers or even enemies. How it coordinates the actions of every person on the planet in ways too complex for any one mind to fathom to produce an overflowing abundance of wealth, where nothing is wasted and where power and responsibility are directed to those most deserving and able. I saw a better way, but knew of no way to get there.

I read everything I could to deepen my understanding of economics and liberty, but it was all intellectual, there was no call to action except to tell the people around me what I had learned and hopefully get them to see the light. That was until I read *Alongside Night* and the works of Samuel Edward Konkin III. At last the missing puzzle piece! All of a sudden it was so clear: every action you take outside the scope of government control strengthens the market and weakens the state. I saw how the state lives parasitically off the productive people of the world, and how quickly it would crumble if it didn't have it's [sic] tax revenues.

No soldiers if you can't pay them. No drug war without billions of dollars being siphoned off the very people you are oppressing.

For the first time I saw the drug cartels and the dealers, and every person in the whole damn supply chain in a different light.

Some, especially the cartels, are basically a defacto violent power hungry state, and surely would love nothing more than to take control of a national government, but your average joe pot dealer, who wouldn't hurt a fly, that guy became my hero. By making his living outside the purview of the state, he was depriving it of his precious life force, the product of his efforts. He was free. People like him, little by little, weakened the state and strengthened the market.

It wasn't long, maybe a year or two after this realization that the pieces started coming together for the Silk Road, and what a ride it has been. No longer do I feel ANY frustration. In fact I am at peace in the knowledge that every day I have more I can do to breathe life into a truly revolutionary and free market than I have hours in the day. I walk tall, proud and free, knowing that the actions I take eat away at the infrastructure that keeps oppression alive.

We are like a little seed in a big jungle that has just broken the surface of the forest floor. It's a big scary jungle with lots of dangerous creatures, each honed by evolution to survive in the hostile environment known as human society. All manner of corporation, government agency, small family businesses, anything that can gain a foothold and survive. But the environment is rapidly changing and the jungle has never seen a species quite like the Silk Road. You can see it, but you can't touch it. It is elusive, yet powerful, and we are evolving at a rapid clip, experimenting, trying to find sturdy ground we can put roots down in.

Will we and others like us someday grow to be tall hardwoods?

Will we reshape the landscape of society as we know it? What if one day we had enough power to maintain a physical presence on the globe, where we shunned the parasites and upheld the rule of law, where the right to privacy and property was unquestioned and enshrined in the very structure of society.

Where police are our servants and protectors beholden to their customers, the people. Where our leaders earn their power and responsibility in the harsh and unforgiving furnace of the free market and not from behind a gun, where the opportunities to create and enjoy wealth are as boundless as one's imagination.

Some day, we could be a shining beacon of hope for the oppressed people of the world just as so many oppressed and violated souls have found refuge here already. Will it happen overnight? No. Will it happen in a lifetime? I don't know. Is it worth fighting for until my last breath? Of course. Once you've seen what's possible, how can you do otherwise? How can you plug yourself into the tax eating, life sucking, violent, sadistic, war mongering, oppressive machine ever again? How can you kneel when you've felt the power of your own legs? Felt them stretch and flex as you learn to walk and think as a free person? I would rather live my life in rags now than in golden chains. And now we can have both! Now it is profitable to throw off one's chains, with amazing crypto technology reducing the risk of doing so dramatically. How many niches have yet to be filled in the world of anonymous online markets? The opportunity to prosper and take part in a revolution of epic proportions is at our fingertips!

I have no one to share my thoughts with in physical space. Security does not permit it, so thanks for listening. I hope my words can be an inspiration just as I am given so much by everyone here.

– Dread Pirate Roberts forum post 'Chat', 20 March 2012

The Growth of a Legend

Over the ensuing eighteen months, the identity of the Dread Pirate Roberts became the subject of debate, news articles and the work of internet sleuths. But nobody could link the name of a real person to him. The only names that were raised in speculation of Roberts' identity at that time were other pseudonyms.

One such name was 'pirateat40', a Bitcointalk user who ran a suspected Ponzi scheme through the forum during 2011 and 2012. Carrying out a business under the name Bitcoin Savings and Trust (BST), pirateat40 promised returns of 7 per cent per week. As with most sham schemes, BST provided the returns to those who wanted them, and 'reinvested' for those who wanted the cumulative interest effect. It managed to run until August 2012, collecting around 700,000 bitcoin, until Bitcointalk became filled with complaints and suspicions.

As people examined the blockchain in the aftermath, the internet sleuths of Bitcointalk uncovered a very large wallet that they soon determined belonged to Silk Road. From this, some concluded BST was in fact a clever money-laundering scheme that accepted investors' bitcoin and returned to them Silk Road's funds, effectively 'washing' the dirty money.

Pirateat40 disappeared when it became clear that he was no longer making returns, and investors realised that the chances of recovering their money – let alone any profits – were slim to none.

The suspicions that BST could have a link to Silk Road continued until July 2013, when a thirty-year-old Texan, Trendon T. Shavers, was charged by the US Securities and Exchange Commission (SEC) on fraud charges related to BST. The SEC complaint alleged that Shavers was pirateat40. Any thoughts that the two pirates shared anything other than a sea-based fantasy were put to rest.

The other name that was bandied around as being the alter ego of the Dread Pirate Roberts was Satoshi Nakamoto. This theory had a lot going for it; for one thing, the value of bitcoin during the early days had depended heavily on its use in the online black markets. Nakamoto had disappeared around the time of Silk Road's birth and resurfaced for the last time in April 2011, when he said he had 'moved on to other things'.

But the evidence for Nakamoto and Dread Pirate Roberts being the same person was as flimsy as that linking DPR and pirateat40. Although both Nakamoto and DPR were prone to writing lengthy missives in their respective forums, Nakamoto's were technical and scientific in nature while Roberts espoused his agorist philosophy, set reading challenges for member discussion and even hosted a movie night, with site members around the world simultaneously watching and discussing *V for Vendetta*. Nakamoto used UK English; Roberts' writing was in US English.

In October 2011, *The New Yorker* ran a well-researched piece that identified Nakamoto as Michael Clear, a student of Trinity College, Dublin. Shortly after, *Fast Company* magazine countered with equally compelling – and equally circumstantial – evidence that Nakamoto was a pseudonym for not one but three Munich-based men who had worked together to create bitcoin. Both explanations were plausible. Both were apparently wrong.

The accused – Clear and the three Germans – all emphatically denied it. But as Clear told *The New Yorker*, 'Even if I was I wouldn't tell you.' Another accused, Neal King, told *Fast Company*: 'I'm cashing in on Warhol's prediction of fifteen minutes of fame – albeit for something I didn't do.'

Like that of Nakamoto, Dread Pirate Roberts' cult status grew. Articles painting him as a hero and visionary were no longer confined to a few fringe online publications. *Forbes* started to report regularly on Silk Road and its owner in positive terms. The magazine published a collection of Roberts' quotes, describing him as a 'principled libertarian and cypherpunk in the same vein as WikiLeaks founder Julian Assange and bitcoin creator Satoshi Nakamoto'.

Although many would be appalled at the notion of a drug dealer as a hero, those who were against prohibition believed Silk Road offered a better, safer way for users to buy the drugs they would acquire anyway. As one member put it, 'I came for the drugs and stayed for the revolution.'

That revolution played out largely in an entire section of the Silk Road forums called 'Philosophy, Economics and Law', which hosted many passionate debates about prohibition, legalisation and decriminalisation. Not everyone, including Roberts himself, was interested in seeing drugs regulated by the state. They believed governments were every bit as corrupt as the cartels they would replace.

DPR claimed that Silk Road was evidence that the war on drugs had been lost. 'With Silk Road, you can now get virtually any drug you want delivered directly to you, with little chance of them even knowing about it,' wrote Roberts. 'In a very real sense, we've won the war on drugs. I'm not saying it's time for a victory lap, but I can at least see the light at the end of the tunnel.'

The Philosophy, Economics and Law section was home to 'DPR's Book Club', which was launched in August 2012 with the following introduction:

> Welcome to DPR's book club! Knowledge is power, and reading is one of the best ways to expand your knowledge. Each week, we will select a reading designed to expand our understanding of the issues that face the Silk Road community and have a group discussion on the material. My hope is that a high level of discourse will be fostered, and as a community, we can become strong in our beliefs, with a coherent message and voice as the world begins to take notice of us.
>
> We will focus on agorism, counter-economics, anarchocapitalism, Austrian economics, political philosophy, freedom issues and related topics. My hope is that through this, we will discover what we stand for and foster a culture of peace, prosperity, justice and freedom. There is so much double-speak and misinformation in the world today that we must take our education into our own hands, and defend our minds with reason and critical thinking.

The forum became a place not only for the book club (and, later, the movie nights), but for philosophical debates and discussions of all types. Trolls and illiterates steered clear and many of the threads were more akin to the debate sections of a university alumni website than to the discussion arm of a black market for narcotics.

In true cult style, Dread Pirate Roberts' devotees seemed to forget he was running a highly profitable business and thought of themselves as part of a movement. The faithful would practically beg to give him more money, despite the huge sums he was earning in commission. They offered their services in IT or to work as moderators of the forums for free. When the site was unavailable due to malicious attacks or infrastructure failure, members offered to take up a collection to help instead of demanding it be fixed with the profits they had already provided. Dread Pirate Roberts rarely, if ever, accepted such offers, though the moderators of the forum were unpaid until early 2013 and some people donated money to the cause anyway.

When journalists contacted Dread Pirate Roberts from time to time, he was very guarded but always polite, and he always provided the briefest of quotes for articles. Although he never failed to respond to a private message, most of the time the responses were short, revealing little of the man behind the keyboard. He never bothered to use PGP, even in response to encrypted messages.

When it was put to him that he had many of the attributes of a sect leader, Roberts denied he was the object of cult-like devotion with a curt admonishment: 'don't go getting sensationalist on me now'.

Shouldn't you get in touch with me when it's time to write? I'm not going anywhere.
— Dread Pirate Roberts' response to the author when asked if he would consider contributing to a book, August 2012

Sam's Vegas Adventure

It was pretty clear that on a per capita basis, Australia had one of the highest usage rates of Silk Road – if not the highest – of any country in the world. Australians were over-represented on the discussion forums, where they would start their own threads to confer on which overseas vendors had the highest success rates of beating Australian Customs, or which Australian vendors had the best drugs. The large number of Australian members could be attributed at least in part to the incredibly high prices Australians paid for their party drugs. We have always paid a premium for illicit drugs thanks to our geographical isolation and relatively small population. Silk Road offered an alternative.

As the use of the site by Australians to purchase their drugs cheaply from overseas grew, so too did a sideline in vendors using Silk Road to resell those exact same drugs at four times the price to their fellow Australians. The number of vendors shipping exclusively within our borders grew. For the buyers it meant receiving quality-tested drugs overnight at similar prices to those they were used to paying on the street. There was also the comfort of parcels not passing through customs, which meant both a better probability of arriving and much lower penalties if a package happened to be intercepted.

For the Australian vendors, it was a quick and easy way of getting a 300 per cent or more return on investment. Five grams of very high-quality MDMA, for example, could be purchased from Europe for about $340 and used to create forty effective capsules that could be resold for around $35 each to Australian Silk Road users – still a better deal than the up to $50 they might be expected to pay at a nightclub for unknown goods.

Once he was introduced to Silk Road, Sam Tyler never looked back. Initially only purchasing from Australian dealers, he eventually realised that he could obtain the same drugs far more economically by buying direct from overseas. He experimented with drugs from Germany, the Netherlands, the US and the UK and eventually settled on a couple of vendors he could trust.

An avid traveller, Sam soon discovered that another pleasant effect of Silk Road for recreational drug users was the fact that suddenly dealers were available in any town, anywhere in the world. He became most appreciative of this when he travelled to Las Vegas in 2012. Usually when holidaying he simply took a hiatus from drugs, unless he happened to meet a friendly local with a penchant for the same substances. This year things were going to be different.

After three days of research into American vendors who had a good reputation for servicing the area, scouring the forums for other people who had ordered to hotels, asking questions and prevaricating over whether it was a wise move, Sam settled on a seller. Worried that the package would arrive too early or too late, he messaged back and forth until he was satisfied that the seller, 'Morpheous', was aware of the importance of the mission before finally placing an order.

Sam loved the tackiness of Vegas, the excess, the colours and sounds and vibe of the place. And how much would each of those things be enhanced by the 2 grams of molly (the name given by dance enthusiasts to MDMA) that was due to arrive at his hotel on his second day there, a couple of days before the Electric Daisy Carnival dance party.

His MDMA didn't arrive on the second day. About an hour after he'd settled into his room, just as he was considering his options for the afternoon, the phone rang.

'Is this Mr Sam Tyler?'

Sam agreed it was.

'We have a package here for a Mr S. Tyler. Could you come to hotel security, please?'

Hotel security did not sound like the proper place for what was ostensibly a package of papers – reception sounded like the proper place to hold mail. Sam wasn't exactly a super-criminal. He'd sent himself a greeting card from New York City, where he had spent a few days before arriving at Las Vegas, so that he would have more than one piece of mail arrive while he was there. But he deduced it couldn't be that because the security officer would have mentioned a card, not a package.

Sam's voice was a high-pitched squeak: 'Sure, I'll be right down.' He had heard about controlled deliveries. That was where a consignment of illegal goods was detected by customs or postal workers, who would contact law enforcement. Police would then allow the delivery to happen under their surveillance and swoop once the target had taken possession. Could this be a controlled delivery? Sam had also heard about American jails. Consequences for drug offences were more severe in the US than they were in Australia. Suddenly, ordering to his hotel room didn't seem such a good idea after all.

But then, what were the chances really of all those resources going into busting a tourist for what was clearly a small amount of ecstasy for personal use? Calming down a little, Sam took a couple of deep breaths and took the lift down to the security office.

Trying to act natural when you feel guilty as hell is, Sam discovered, really difficult. The security guard requested ID, then told Sam to wait as he made a call. A cold shiver snaked down Sam's spine as the security guard told whoever was on the other end of the phone that Mr Tyler was here to collect some documents. The security guard listened down the telephone, all the while keeping his eyes on Sam. Eventually he raised his eyebrows and asked Sam if he was sure it was documents he was expecting.

'Yes,' Sam's voice was scratchy. 'I'm expecting some papers for signing.'

He hung up the phone and another security officer entered the room. This guy asked Sam's name and also demanded ID. He asked if he was expecting a package. Sam repeated that he was expecting documents. The guard showed him the large priority-mail envelope and asked if that was him on the address label.

Sam agreed it was. How many different ways could they ask the same question? As his stomach churned and his face reddened, he wondered how the controlled delivery would work. Would they arrest him the moment he admitted the parcel was his? Or would they wait until he opened it in the privacy of his room, swooping on him red-handed with the product? Could he plead innocence, insisting that somebody must have sent the powder as a joke or a setup?

The security guard said they weren't sure Sam was the correct recipient because the parcel was addressed to his first initial and surname, and didn't 'match' his full first name and surname, as per his room reservation. Being such a common name, they couldn't be too careful and risk handing it over.

Sam assured them that as it was addressed to a person with the same surname, to this hotel, and that he was expecting documents for signing, he was pretty sure it could be released to him.

At last the security guard handed it over. What should have been a two-minute pickup from security had turned into a five-minute process that felt like a thirty-minute ordeal. Sam grabbed the 'documents' (as well as the greeting card that had coincidentally arrived at the same time) and ran.

Back in his room, he gave in to the extravagance of the minibar and poured himself an outrageously priced scotch before examining the A4-sized USPS cardboard envelope. Tearing open one end, he discovered another envelope within, folded into four.

Inside this envelope was what he had gone through all that trouble for – a vacuum-sealed baggie containing what Sam's trained eye had come to recognise as 2 grams of MDMA.

This was going to be a good holiday after all. Smiling, Sam flicked open his laptop, logged on to Silk Road and released the funds from escrow to the account of Morpheous.

Voyeurs, Guns and Money

'**T**hose claiming to be selling slaves and radioactive material on Silk Road worry me slightly, even though they may be trolls. The slavery post seems like nonsense to me, but the radioactive materials one is chilling,' wrote user 'CharlieContent' on the Bitcointalk forum on 19 April 2011. 'Silk Road, do you feel anything is crossing the line? Is there anything that you would step in and stop from being sold on the site?'

The user silkroad never responded to that question directly, but from the beginning, Silk Road had declared it would not allow the sale of any items 'the purpose of which is to harm or defraud others'. It was part of the owner's agorist philosophy that the only laws the site should break were those its owner considered 'victimless'. In April 2011, the Road's 'New Listing guidelines' stated:

Restrictions

Please do not list forged documents including fake ids, passports, and counterfeit currency.

Please do not list anything who's [sic] purpose is to harm or defraud, such as stolen credit cards, assassinations, and weapons of mass destruction (chemical/bio weaponry, nukes, and anything used to make them).

This was a different approach to most other black markets in Onionland. As a rule, the commercial sites believed in absolute freedom of trade and would accept listings for the most morally bereft goods and services.

Eventually the new listing guidelines morphed into a more complete 'Silk Road's Sellers' Guide'. The examples of goods and services that the site prohibited became: child pornography, stolen credit cards and goods, assassinations, personal information, and 'weapons of mass destruction (chemical/bio weaponry, nukes, and anything used to make them)'.

Dread Pirate Roberts called it 'taking the high moral ground (pun intended)'. This decision led to many debates over the years about what should and should not be available on the market. Notably, forged IDs and counterfeit currency had dropped off the list of prohibited items.

Some members of the site would argue that a truly free marketplace would not impose any limits. If Roberts were a true libertarian, they contended, he would not ban items simply because he did not agree with them. The site's owner rarely engaged in such debates, but if they raged long enough he would respond with a curt 'This is my site. I decide what you can and can't sell here.'

Few disagreed with his position when it came to child abuse materials. 'I am completely opposed to child porn and hitmen and would never sell on any marketplace that allowed that,' said vendor 'AussieDomesticDrugs'. It was a stance that united vendors and buyers alike and even the most militant libertarians shied away from any debate about allowing such services and sites to be advertised. Being associated with an enterprise that provided illicit substances was one thing; nobody wanted to sell or shop in a market that supported those who would profit from harming children.

For owners of black markets, child pornography was not just morally reprehensible, it was bad for business – and not just in terms of losing vendors and customers. Allowing the sale of child pornography was the sort of thing that raised emotions so high that any site that did so risked the wrath of activist hackers. The Hidden Wiki discovered this the hard way.

In October 2011, members of the vigilante hacktivist collective Anonymous launched 'Operation Darknet'. When the Hidden Wiki refused to remove links to offending pornographic images and videos, Anonymous launched a distributed denial of service (DDoS) attack, making the entire site inaccessible. It prompted the Hidden Wiki to post a message imploring Anonymous to stop the attacks: 'To Anonymous: This site is simply a Wiki. Anti-pedo? Attack the pedo sites. You didn't attack Wikipedia for hosting information about your enemies. Wake up.'

Instead, Anonymous stepped up the attack, crashing the server of Freedom Hosting, the service that hosted nearly all of the child porn linked by the Hidden Wiki. The group also used a clever bit of social engineering (psychological manipulation rather than technical intervention) to fool visitors to Lolita City, the most popular site in the Wiki's 'Hard Candy' under-age porn directory, into clicking on a button that harvested their usernames and IP addresses. Anonymous posted these publicly, alerted the media and supplied the details to law enforcement. 'We vowed to fight for the defenseless, there is none more defenseless than innocent children being exploited,' they said.

Sadly, their efforts were mainly in vain. Law enforcement was unable to use the IP addresses, illegally obtained, to track down users of child pornography. Lolita City returned, its members hidden, its administrators triumphant. 'It is our GOD given right that we can choose to have our sexual preferences for youth,' the site reported. 'It is the same for any other porn community. It is not what we choose to become, it is who we are. You Anonymous aka #OpDarknet do not have the right to censor us.'

Anonymous vowed to continue the fight against child abuse sites: 'We will continue to not only crash Freedom Hosting's server, but any other server we find to contain, promote, or support child pornography.'

Although the debate of child porn would rear its ugly head from time to time, particularly in the philosophy forum, Silk Road's community were united and adamant. That sort of material had no place in their market.

Many visitors to the site were surprised at the ban on stolen credit cards, hacked Paypal and bank accounts, and personal information that could allow the owner's identity to be stolen. These were, after all, staple sales items on the dark web. But the majority applauded the vision of Dread Pirate Roberts to create a utopian online society where the rule was 'personal freedom, but do no harm unto others'. Let those who wanted to commit crimes against others visit one of the many other black markets, where the owners didn't care who you hurt or what you bought as long as they got their cut.

Silk Road's philosophy of not listing anything of which 'the purpose is to harm or defraud another' did not extend to fake IDs. Identity items were a high-demand black market product. They ranged from $5 licence copies that might fool a sleepy liquor store attendant but not much else, to passports that were 'genuinely generated from within the IPS system of the UK government and guaranteed good for travel' for $4000.

One Silk Road seller offered Australian driver's licences, alone or in conjunction with a forged credit card and Medicare card to make up 100 points of ID (i.e. the necessary pieces required to open a post office box or bank account in a fake name, or the beginnings of acquiring genuine pieces of identification in order to assume an entire new identity). 'AUSID' was selling NSW licences for around $800 apiece. The quality of the fake licences was high, almost indistinguishable from the real thing other than some slight differences in the holograms that would never be noticed by the casual observer. But AUSID failed to attract many customers, finding the Silk Road community hostile and suspicious, and unwilling to provide the necessary photograph to an anonymous vendor. Frustrated, he left the site, claiming his team had enough work 'in real life' selling their wares.

Some time later the community discovered that AUSID may have been busted. A Western Sydney house that had been specifi-cally set up as a factory mass-producing fake credit cards and identities was exposed in 2013. The factory housed embossing machines, laptops, scanners and plastic holograms. The goods being manufactured and the description of one of the men arrested accorded with much of the information that had been provided by AUSID in his online communications.

The large-scale criminal operation was an indication that Silk Road's vendor database was not necessarily just made up of the 'little guy'.

While most members were united in agreement on the list of banned items, the one point of debate was the sale of weapons that were not of the mass destruction variety.

'While I support the right of someone being able to have a single-shot gun for self-defence, I am not comfortable with the idea of automatic and semi-automatic weapons being made available to anyone with the money to buy it,' AussieDomesticDrugs said. 'Just because we support the rights of people to put what they like in their own bodies, doesn't mean that we are evil people, in spite of what the government would often have the general public believe.'

Dread Pirate Roberts had no philosophical objection to selling guns. On 1 March 2011 he wrote:

My hope is that eventually, more than just drugs will be listed there. Drugs are an obvious direction to go in, however, because there isn't a good market for them currently. I have a category for weapons as well because many people are restricted from purchasing these, but no one has listed in that category yet. It would be great to hear if anyone has ideas for other kinds of products that would fit well at Silk Road.

Later that year, within a couple of weeks of the Gawker article bringing the site to the attention of the world, guns, knives and knuckledusters were listed for sale. Sellers were mostly from the USA and selling only to the USA, though at least one claimed to ship internationally 'hidden in appliances'.

Not everyone agreed with Roberts' stance on weapons. Surely guns were quintessentially items the purpose of which was to harm others? On 1 August 2011, someone started a poll on the forums, asking, 'Would you like to see the sale of guns removed from the Silk Road?' Responses from the members were split nearly 50/50 but leaned very slightly to allowing the weapons section to stay.

By this time, the community had become strong and tight and debates on all manner of subjects raged over days and weeks among the members. Dread Pirate Roberts enjoyed the lively interaction of his customers. 'Just make sure you keep it civil,' he warned. The suggestions and opinions of the community would occasionally lead to changes and improvements to the marketplace or the discussion site, but rarely would the site's leader allow a debate to change his position on anything.

But those who felt strongly against the sale of guns campaigned hard. 'No guns on Silk Road' became the automatic signature at the bottom of many members' posts.

Initially the reasons given for not wanting the sale of weapons came from those who were morally opposed to the private ownership of firearms, and the counter-arguments from those who supported the USA's second-amendment right to bear arms and protect self and family.

But the debate was many-faceted and the most compelling argument to emerge came from those who were not necessarily against gun ownership but were afraid that the sale of weapons would bring more heat to Silk Road. Drugs, they argued, were one thing. Semi-automatic rifles were something completely different: a guarantee of a fast track to attracting unwanted attention from law enforcement agencies and politicians. Although drugs might be controversial, a growing number of people were questioning the effectiveness of absolute-prohibition drug policies and favoured the legalisation of 'soft' drugs, such as marijuana and ecstasy. Some of those people might tolerate a marketplace dedicated to providing drug users with drugs, but selling illegal guns would likely alienate those liberals who might otherwise leave Silk Road's customers alone. Illegal firearm sales accounted for only a minuscule part of Silk Road's business, but could attract disproportionate attention to the site.

'I am in favor for the ex-cons, the radicals, the communists, anarchist, the oppressed, and those who suffer abuse from the dominant Anglo culture in America to possess all the guns and ammo they can get (including C4 with proper training),' one forum member claimed. 'This is with the implicit intent to bring about change in this failed system called America. I am as libertarian as the next guy about most things but the sale of guns will be the downfall of [Silk Road].'

'We have something very good going for us here and I would hate to see it fucked up over some idealist beliefs that the right to buy guns online is important enough to risk it all,' said another.

Another online dark web marketplace, Black Market Reloaded (BMR), sold guns and other weapons. BMR did not subscribe to the Silk Road's philosophy of limiting the type of goods sold – other than child pornography – and many Road members suggested that those looking for guns do their shopping at BMR. While Silk Road grabbed all the media attention, BMR quietly but steadily grew in its shadow, attracting the customers who preferred an open market over an ideology.

Another argument against guns on Silk Road was that the people who would buy overpriced guns illegally from an anonymous website were probably the types least likely to use them responsibly. In countries where guns were available through legal channels, what reason would someone have for paying a much higher price to obtain one anonymously, if not to use the weapon for illegal purposes or because the purchaser was already precluded with good reason from legally owning a firearm?

Others argued that the philosophy behind Silk Road was that of a free market and it could not truly be free if it did not allow the sale of weapons. 'I just found the freest place ever and now someone seems to be trying to REGULATE it and it irks me,' said one member.

Tony76 was one who opposed the sale of weapons. The Canadian heroin dealer's rationale was purely from a business perspective: he was frightened that gun sales would be a catalyst for extra funding for, and scrutiny by, law enforcement. 'I don't want to see guns here either. I am not going to give my view on if guns should be sold or not, but let's pick our battles, guys . . . This is the perfect opportunity for media to blow this place way out of proportion,' he said. 'Maybe we can specialize in a drug marketplace, and let another market take care of the weaponry stuff? So not take a stance on whether we are for or against guns, but just that it is sort of off topic for this marketplace.'

Many members expressed surprise that the peace-loving Dread Pirate Roberts was comfortable with the sale of implements of death on his website. And it seemed at odds with what he had stated publicly on previous occasions. 'Back when we broke the story in June, Silk Road's anonymous administrator said he wouldn't allow weapons to be sold on the site,' wrote Adrian Chen in another Gawker article in January 2012. When Chen asked the site's owner to comment on the weapons debate, he was asked to wait a few months until they were prepared for another 'influx of attention'.

Silk Road's administration was not just remaining silent with media – it also stayed away from the debate raging on the site's forums. But Dread Pirate Roberts wasn't ignoring the controversy. Not wanting to back down on his philosophical stance on the sale of firearms, but cognisant of the negative effects on his business, he made an announcement on 26 February 2012:

We are happy to announce a brand new site called The Armory. It focuses exclusively on the sale of small-arms weaponry for the purpose of self defense.

The issue of whether weapons should be sold on Silk Road has been brought up and debated too many times to count. I have heard good arguments on both sides of the debate and had to really think hard before choosing to take this direction.

Here is a brief summary of my thoughts on the matter and why I chose to spin-off a new site rather than ban weapon sales completely, or allow them to continue here:

First off, we at Silk Road have no moral objection to the sale of small-arm weaponry. We believe that an individual's ability to defend themselves is a cornerstone of a civil society. Without this, those with weapons with eventually walk all over defenseless individuals. It could be criminals who prey on others, knowing they are helpless. It could be police brutalizing people with no fear of immediate reprisal. And as was seen too many times in the last century, it could be an organized government body committing genocide on an entire unarmed populace.

Without the ability to defend them, the rest of your human rights will be eroded and stripped away as well.

That being said, there is no reason we have to force everyone into a one-size-fits-all market where one group has to compromise their beliefs for the benefit of another. That's the kind of narrow thinking currently used by governments around the world. It's why we are in this mess in the first place. The majority in many countries feel that drugs and guns should be illegal or heavily regulated, so the minority suffers.

Here at Silk Road, we recognize the smallest minority of all, YOU! Every person is unique, and their human rights are more important than any lofty goal, any mission, or any program. An individual's rights ARE the goal, ARE the mission, ARE the program. If the majority wants to ban the sale of guns on Silk Road, there is no way we are going to turn our backs on the minority who needs weaponry for self defense.

So, without further ado, I give you our answer to this whole conundrum:

The Armory: ayjkg6ombrsahbx2.onion

The Armory is run on the same codebase that runs Silk Road, with all of the same features you know and love. However, it is run completely independently with it's [sic] own servers, bitcoin wallets, databases, etc. If it becomes popular, we'll even look into putting it under separate management.

A note to vendors: If you have items in the Silk Road weapons category, please relist them at The Armory asap. We will be shutting down weapons sales on Silk Road on Sunday March 4th.

The announcement of the Armory was met with mixed reactions. Those who wanted the unrestricted sale of weapons were glad to have a new market available to them. Some who were opposed to guns on Silk Road were appeased by the compromise. But to many, the opening of a sister site illegally selling weapons that was obviously affiliated with Silk Road, bearing an identical interface and the same owner, was a sham that was never going to fool the authorities.

'The armory is a completely other thing that i think needs to go,' said Tony76 in the Roundtable a few weeks after the new site's inception. 'Not only are we going to get DEA/FBI/CIA watching this site . . . now we're going to taunt homeland security / terrorism departments?'

But once the weaponry section was hived off and pictures of guns no longer greeted visitors to the marketplace, the debate petered out as the community went back to discussing their favourite subject: drugs. A discreet link to the Armory on Silk Road's homepage led those who were interested to the new site.

Despite operating on the same business model as Silk Road, and receiving the free publicity offered by the news outlets that duly reported on the new venture, the Armory was a colossal failure. Few firearm sellers were motivated to pay the vendor fee for an account on such a quiet marketplace. Complaints poured in from potential customers of scam listings and rip-offs.

While BMR had a healthy volume of weaponry sales, there was never a single verified instance of a firearm being sold on the Armory. Less than six months after it opened, Dread Pirate Roberts made another announcement:

As most of you have figured out, we are closing the armory. Your first question is probably 'why?'. Well, it just wasn't getting used enough. Spinning it off originally was done somewhat abruptly and while we supported it, it was a kind of [a] 'sink or swim' experiment. The volume hasn't even been enough to cover server costs and is actually waning at this point. I had high hopes for it, but if we are going to serve an anonymous weapons market, I think it will require more careful thought and planning.

The next question is probably 'can we now sell guns on Silk Road?'. The answer there is most definitely NO. If we do support weapons sales once more, it will be on a separate site.

As the banner on the site says, finish up your business there and withdraw your coins before the end of the countdown. If you recently bought a seller account and haven't made enough sales to at least break even on it, contact us on the armory and we'll get you a refund.

So in the end, Silk Road stopped selling firearms not because of any lofty ideals, not because of unwanted heat from media or law enforcement, but simply because the business venture was unprofitable.

Customer Appreciation Sale this Weekend!

Let's face it, the Silk Road vendors and staff are here for the customers. Without you, we'd be out of business: Each and every person that takes the plunge and makes a purchase is standing up for themselves and setting an example for their fellow man. The commerce that happens here is out of the reach of the oppressors and control freaks of this world. The bigger our world gets, the smaller theirs gets, and YOU are making that possible.

To show our love and gratitude for you, we are discounting every item on the site by up to 10%.

– Dread Pirate Roberts announcing Silk Road's first 'sale',

31 January 2012

The Great 420 Sale and Giveaway

One April evening in 2012, half a dozen people were gathered in Stacey's funky inner-city apartment, sipping beer and wine, each tapping away at a laptop. You would have thought you'd stumbled on a geekfest of World of Warcraft players, except the people here didn't look like the stereotypical socially challenged gamers. They were all Silk Road customers hoping to nab a bargain.

Keeping up the cheeky, thumbing-the-nose-at-the-man theme, Dread Pirate Roberts had announced a sale – the inaugural Silk Road Great 420 Sale and Giveaway. It was on 20 April, in US style written as 4/20, and '420' is slang for marijuana. Silk Road had held small 'sales' before, but never a prize draw, and never on this scale. Every illegal drug purchase during the sale would put the buyer into the draw for a giveaway every 420 seconds until 420 prizes had gone.

Dread Pirate Roberts had announced his intention to have a sale in the Vendors' Roundtable forum on 26 March, to some hilarity. 'An important message went out to active vendors today from the Vendor Support team. Take a look when you get a chance,' he wrote.

Dread Pirate Roberts announced that Silk Road would not take commissions on any of the sales made during the sale and he expected the sellers to pass on the savings to their customers. Vendors came on board, supporting the event by offering discounts on their wares for the duration. The competition was to culminate in a draw for a grand prize of a trip for two, including airfares, accommodation and $2000 spending money.

'Are you really sending someone on holiday, or is it a joke????' asked vendor 'Googleyed1' incredulously. Googleyed1 was assured it was no joke.

Dread Pirate Roberts announced the sale to buyers a few days before it was due to start:

Grab your sleeping bag, stock up on supplies and get ready to camp out on your computer for 49 hours, because on April 20, 2012 at 4:20 PM, the greatest sale in the history of the Silk Road kicks into gear, and you're not going to want to miss a minute of it.

This 4/20, every 420 seconds, some lucky buyer will win one of our 420 great prizes! From $50 gift certificates to a brand new iPhone 4s, some lucky person will be chosen every 420 seconds to win a prize.

Of course, we aren't stopping there. We are also offering a grand prize trip of a lifetime. A trip for two with all the trimmings to paradise, all expenses included. 12 days of the nicest weather, the clearest blue waters, and the finest accommodations you can imagine are all included. You won't even need to pack for this one, as we're including $2000 spending money for your travel wardrobe and incidental (cough *weed* cough) expenses. From the time the limousine picks you up at your front door, until you're swimming with the dolphins or taking in a helicopter tour, you just aren't gonna believe your luck!

Every time you complete a sale you can win one of our 420 second prizes, and for every btc you spend during the sale, we'll put in one entry for you for our Take a Trip to Paradise Grand Prize. Seriously, why would you be anywhere else but on your computer from 4:20 PM (UTC) on Friday, April 20, until 5:20 PM (UTC) on Sunday, April 22, 2012. One great prize every 420 seconds, and the mother of all Grand Prizes could be yours with a single purchase.

But wait, you also get these six Ginsu knives – wait, wrong script. Wait, there's more – Every item on the site will be discounted up to 10%! IN ADDITION to this, our vendors have put together some deep discounts on your favorite 420 goodies. More info and links here: silkroadvb5piz3r.onion/silkroad/four_twenty

PS – if you are a vendor who isn't on the sale list and would like to be, just send a description of your sale over to Vendor Support and we'll add you asap.

The most enthusiastic of the vendors was Tony76. 'At first I wasn't going to participate in this 4/20 sale,' he said, 'but seeing all these other amazing deals from vendors got me excited (and maybe brought out my competitive side a bit. I don't like being one-upped).'

Tony listed MDMA, heroin, cocaine, LSD and ketamine at outrageously low prices and the crowd went wild. Nobody had better product, better customer service, better feedback than Tony. A gram of MDMA for $40, pure Afghan heroin for $190 – Tony was going to be very busy in the days after the sale.

And then his next announcement created even greater excitement: 'Also for the first time, I'm going to be allowing international buyers, as I did a trial run with some of my loyal customs [sic] and my success rate was very high.'

Finally Tony76, one of Silk Road's most popular vendors, was opening up to customers beyond North America. The gushing thanks came rolling in during the days leading up to the sale: 'I for one am very excited for tony to finally open up his wares to us outside of yankeeville,' wrote 'Greatgreatgrandpa'. 'Will have bells and whistles on mate!'

'Low [sic] and behold, tony exceeds my expectations time and time again. #1 vendor for a reason,' said 'Icculus97'.

'Deadra7' enthused, 'World buyers – I hope your orders come in fast and heavy – tony is truly an awesome vendor – especially when your [sic] loyal.'

So excited was he that Tony76 launched his own sale a day earlier than the Great 420 Sale and Giveaway. 'To stay No. 1 I have to be ahead of the competition,' he said.

As with his previous customer appreciation sale in February, Tony76 told his buyers they would have to release their funds from escrow immediately. Trusted vendors had always been allowed to bypass Silk Road's escrow system and request that users finalise early. New members of the site were often asked to do so until they had proved themselves to be trusted buyers, and sellers would sometimes ask for early finalisation when bitcoin was fluctuating wildly.

'I can't afford to have so much money tied up in escrow and have it affect my ability to reload on product,' Tony said. 'If you are uncomfortable finalizing early, I completely understand but it is not optional for this order and I advise you to not order.'

By now Tony's success had made him a target for scammers and rival vendors. A few days before the great sale, he posted in the forums that he was being targeted by a vindictive competitor who had threatened to set up bogus buyer accounts to order thousands of dollars of drugs in 'multiple orders, in multiple names, from multiple states'. Tony would have no way of knowing which were the bogus accounts and would lose the money not released from escrow. His supporters told him he should have *all* customers finalise early until he was rid of the malicious potential scammer.

Nobody found the request for early finalisation from the site's highest-grossing and most trusted vendor to be strange. He'd had countless transactions that went smoothly, and anyway, to not finalise might mean missing out on a bargain. Orders flooded in from users well accustomed to receiving high-quality goods from Tony76 and from new users excited to have the chance to buy from such an esteemed identity.

During the party at Stacey's apartment for the 420 sale, the little crowd discussed Tony76 and his sudden decision to allow international buyers to purchase his wares. Each of the attendees was making small individual purchases, because every seven minutes a lucky user somewhere in the world was receiving a private message telling them they'd won a prize. Each purchase gave a buyer one entry into the draw.

'I'm definitely tempted by that MDMA,' said Sam. The gram that Tony was selling for $40 would cost him at least $200 in Melbourne; more if it were broken into individual capsules. A gram would make eight decent ecstasy capsules, enough to see Sam through three weekends of partying.

As Sam was contemplating a switch from his usual vendors, a cry rang out from a young man in his late twenties. 'Woohoo! Seventy-five-dollar voucher!' Everyone crowded around him to see what the winning message looked like. Nobody begrudged him his good fortune; everyone was just happy to be grabbing bargains. Sam decided to stick with his favourite vendors from Germany and the Netherlands.

The party lasted well into the next day, with people popping in and out until their bitcoin balances were exhausted. There were no more winners among Stacey's friends, but there would certainly be some heavy partying in the weeks to come.

Halfway through the sale, some buyers complained that their regular vendors' prices hadn't changed to reflect the discount they should have been offering thanks to their sales being commission-free.

'Sorry to those who were expecting deeper discounts,' Dread Pirate Roberts wrote reproachfully of the spoilsports. 'Some of the vendors did not opt in to the "up to 10% off" part of the sale, so instead of their items being discounted, they stayed the same and the discount is passed to them instead. Still, there are some amazing deals on the market right now, so keep looking if your original plan isn't panning out.'

Two days later the sale was over. Dread Pirate Roberts was pleased with the excitement it had generated:

OK, the sale is officially over! What a ride! To those who won a prize, but the message was blank, you can expect your prize within 24 hours. Also in the next 24 hours, we will be picking the winner of the grand prize trip of a lifetime to paradise all expenses paid you'll choke on your sandwich when you win and still somehow scream so loud the neighbors come over.

For security reasons, the winner won't be announced, but we'll leave it up to them if they want to brag about it. And we'll tell you when someone's been picked so you can let out a moan and move on with your day if you weren't the one.

The winner of the grand prize was a member by the name of 'kiwibacon'. He seemed pretty excited about it:

omg thanks alot sr!!!
cant beleive [sic] i actually won something!!!!!!!
WTF!!!!!!!! when i saw msg i was like must be a scam ill never win anything!!!!!!!!!!!!!!!!!!!!!!!!!!!!!!
thanks guys!!!!!!!!! zomg

Probably wisely, kiwibacon did not post in the forums where he or she took the holiday prize, nor did the Silk Road administration reveal any details of how it was arranged. But the sale was a roaring success and yet another online black market first.

A week later, a rumble began on Silk Road. Nobody expected international orders that had been placed during the sale to have arrived yet, but people had started to report and rate their domestic deliveries. And shoppers began to ask Tony76 when their domestic deliveries would arrive. His service was usually so good – his customers hoped his standards weren't slipping.

On 25 April, Tony76 wrote:

> In 12 hours i will be taking my listings down for 24–48 hours to catch up with the sale orders. If you have an order you want to get in you have 12 hours. I will leave sale prices up for the 12 hours. When i put my listings back up in 24–48 hours prices will be back to normal with NEW PRODUCTS AS WELL.
>
> Thanks to an angel investor, i will be bringing a much in demand product to SR as well.
>
> Please keep messages to a minimum as i have been having a hard time keeping up with all the pointless messages.

Some people weren't too happy, but Tony's fans reassured both them and him it was okay.

That was the last anyone would ever hear from Tony76.

Two weeks later the rumbles became a roar as buyers demanded to know where their goods were. They compared notes and realised Tony wasn't responding to messages, even as he logged on. It slowly became clear that the most trusted vendor on Silk Road had absconded with what buyers estimated was over $100,000 for a single weekend's work; one moderator of the forums placed it at a cool quarter of a million dollars.

Some of the faithful remained hopeful for weeks, even months later. Others offered explanations other than his actions being a massive scam. Some believed Tony76 had been killed by Mexican drug lords. Others assumed he had been busted. Many refused to believe that someone in their community would do such a thing. Then came the conspiracy theories: he was already selling under another name; Silk Road's owners were in on it; it was all part of a worldwide sting and nobody was safe; Tony76 was actually a Canadian bikie gang.

A lot of customers demanded Silk Road do something to recover their bitcoin. But Silk Road's administration was unsympathetic. Dread Pirate Roberts had developed a system to protect buyer and seller – that system depended on the escrow service being used. Buyers had been warned that if they traded outside of escrow, they were unprotected.

The members of Silk Road had learned a hell of a lesson, some to the tune of tens of thousands of dollars.

Attempts to reach out to Tony76 through Twitter and blogs were met with silence.

Perhaps he took the money, bought a house and gave up the drug business for good. Or maybe he became a more significant figure in Silk Road's story – perhaps Dread Pirate Roberts' greatest nemesis.

Greetings everyone! It has been some time since I have made an official announcement, and I am very pleased to be making this one today: The look and feel of our beloved market will be transformed in just a few days time!

We have been working tirelessly to deploy many 'behind the scenes' upgrades over the past few months that have vastly improved our security, flexibility and availability. These advances aren't sexy, and don't get much fanfare, but hopefully you've noticed the site running smoothly even as our community grows.

This kind of work rarely gets acknowledged, so I would just like to applaud everyone on the Silk Road team that has put in the effort to make this possible.

But now, in just a few days, I will have the honor of rolling out a sleek new look that will be impossible to miss and I am sure you all will love. I feel it matches the integrity and profession-alism of our community and the robust technology that empowers it. Newcomers will now have the confidence they need to take that leap of faith and make their first purchase.

My hope is that this day will be looked back on as one where we really came into our own and started a new chapter in our quest to stand up for our freedom and declare ownership of ourselves and our bodies.

Much love to you all,
Dread Pirate Roberts

— Dread Pirate Roberts forum post, July 2012

The Scientist

Silk Road attracted the attention of not just drug users and law enforcement, but academics and researchers who were interested in what the site meant for current drug policy. Dr Monica Barratt was a research fellow at Australia's National Drug Research Institute (NDRI) whose focus was on harm reduction. She took an evidence-based approach to drug policy and wrote her PhD thesis on drugs and the internet. Barratt had been a moderator on the Bluelight forums on the clearweb for some time before discovering and studying Silk Road. The Bluelight forums were a place where people could safely discuss drug use without the judgment of others.

Barratt was balanced, well respected and clearly intelligent. She had also published a couple of academic papers on Silk Road. Funky, smart, articulate and passionate about drug reform, she had a refreshing outlook on alternatives to prohibition based squarely on data acquired through research and that was devoid of moral judgment. She was interested in the impact of technology on the drug debate.

In an interview in a cafe below the State Library of Victoria discussing all things Silk Road, I asked if she was surprised at the intelligence and courtesy on display in the posts on the forums and if she had any statistics on the number of Australians using the site.

The 2012 United Nations World Drug Report stated that around 230 million people, or 5 per cent of the world's adult population aged fifteen to sixty-four, were estimated to have used an illicit drug at least once in 2010. Of those, about 27 million people worldwide were 'problem' drug users, being people with dependence or who had contracted diseases such as hepatitis C or HIV through drug use. Approximately 200,000 people worldwide died per year from heroin, cocaine and other drugs. That same report claimed that Australians and New Zealanders were the world's biggest recreational drug users, with a use that was higher than the global average for all drugs other than heroin. The presence of a high per capita use of Silk Road by Australians, therefore, echoed the empirical data gathered elsewhere.

'There's really only a particular type of person that's going to use the site,' Barratt said. 'It's someone who is able to get over the technical barriers, which aren't dramatic, but a good proportion of the population wouldn't do it, so you've already narrowed down the potential users of the site. But it's pretty clear from looking at the forums that Australians are very interested in the site and I think it's pretty clear that they're successfully using it.'

The growing Silk Road community was, in her experience of being involved in non-marketplace forums for years, reflective of similar discussion sites where drug users converged. 'With the study I was doing for my PhD over the last five years, in the end it was much more about sharing information and community online, so drug users were able to find other people like them,' she said.

With the price differential between Silk Road and the street, she wasn't surprised at the uptake by Australians. She believed prohibition was futile, although she did not outright advocate full legalisation: 'In Australia there's a lot of barriers to drugs getting in so, as a result, drugs are overpriced. In the end, I just think in this globalised world we're living in and especially in an internet-saturated society, maybe we just have to have a rethink of how we manage flows of drugs and information into the country, because you don't have the same ability to erect barriers around our island that we once did. So I guess I've been thinking about this and thought Silk Road should actually prompt us to reconsider prohibition in its totality, especially given the evidence around supply reduction methods currently in use being really weak. We spend a lot of money and they may work partially but there's not a hell of a lot of evidence they work well. In some instances they make things a lot worse.'

At the time of the interview, the NDRI had applied to do a pilot study on Silk Road, but it was early days. From an academic perspective, Barratt was excited at the potential offered by a study of Silk Road and its users. Over a couple of glasses of shiraz she, too, speculated about the real identity of Dread Pirate Roberts and why he was so revered.

'Having a mission statement – really spelling out the philosophy behind the venture – allows people to see it as a movement, a political action, rather than just a place to buy drugs,' Barratt said.

'However, the cynic in me wonders whether in fact this is simply a clever marketing ploy which really just masks the 100 per cent profit motive. It's hard to know what is truly happening behind the scenes.'

Although careful not to champion the site, Barratt did subscribe to DPR's belief that Silk Road was probably safer than an illegal face-to-face deal. 'Assuming they're buying from a reputable seller and it's someone who doesn't want to risk their rating by selling something that wasn't what they said it was, then you've got a system where the seller has a really strong imperative to do the right thing by the buyer.' She was impressed that Silk Road had an entire forum dedicated to drug safety, with advice on harm reduction and best practices.

In late 2012, a global drug survey was conducted by dance and clubbing magazine *Mixmag* in conjunction with *The Guardian*; the results were published in 2013. Over 15,000 people from around the world filled in the online survey, which took at least half an hour to complete and included a wide range of questions about drug use. It was the most extensive recreational drug use survey in history. Unlike the previous year's survey, this one included questions about Silk Road, at the urging of Barratt.

By 2012 Barratt had become the go-to person for all things Silk Road in Australia. Whilst not advocating use of the site, she didn't demonise it, either, saying, 'I think that it is an innovation that has the capacity to create ripples of changes in local drug markets and in behaviours around drug access.'

Dr Barratt and her colleagues published the findings from the global drug survey in relation to Silk Road in the academic journal *Addiction* in 2013, in a research report called 'Use of Silk Road, the online drug marketplace, in the UK, Australia and the USA'. They found that in November 2012, 65 per cent of American, 53 per cent of Australian, and 40 per cent of English respondents had heard of Silk Road, and 18 per cent of American, 10 per cent of English and 7 per cent of Australian respondents had consumed drugs purchased through Silk Road.

MDMA/ecstasy was the most popular drug purchased by Silk Road users in all three countries. For Australians, the next on the list was marijuana, followed by LSD. Cocaine, despite its high price even when purchased internationally (although significantly cheaper than purchasing it in Australia), came in fourth. In fifth place were amphetamines and sixth was occupied by NBOMe, a class of hallucinogen. These were followed by prescription drugs, especially Xanax and other antidepressants, then finally magic mushrooms and ketamine.

These statistics, which came from self-reporting of survey respondents, were empirically backed up some time later by researchers Judith Aldridge and David Décary-Hétu in a 2014 academic study. They collected data by trawling the visible listings on the Silk Road website. 'In annual revenue terms, the vast majority of sales were for cannabis ($24.8 million), ecstasy ($19.9 million) and psychedelics ($8.6 million),' they reported. 'Drugs associated with drug dependence, harmful use and chaotic lifestyles (heroin, methamphetamine and crack cocaine) do not much appear on Silk Road, and generate very little revenue.'

The *Addiction* report also outlined the reasons people chose to purchase from Silk Road. The most common reasons were the wider range of available drugs, better quality than otherwise available, greater convenience, and the use of vendor rating systems.

The survey also asked drug users who had heard of Silk Road but did not purchase from the website why they didn't. The most common reasons for avoiding Silk Road purchases were that the respondents had adequate drug access elsewhere and the fear of being caught.

The fear of being caught was discussed regularly on the Silk Road forums. The majority of buyers did not consider themselves criminals and were terrified of the prospect of a jail sentence or the effect of a conviction on their job.

Regarding marketing, I started a thread on the Bitcoin forum.
Everything else has been word of mouth.
– Dread Pirate Roberts forum post, October 2012

Karma, Journalists and Law Enforcement

The article Monica Barratt was interviewed for, 'The drug's in the mail', featured in Melbourne's *Age* and online in all Fairfax newspapers. It caused quite a stir and was picked up by conservative talkback radio and other news media and was a major feature on Network Ten's youth-focused current affairs show *The Project*.

Barratt was asked to appear on various news bulletins and to provide her opinion on talkback radio. The feature was well received and the comments by readers of the Fairfax news sites were non-inflammatory on the whole.

Many of the members of Silk Road detested journalists, viewing them all as sensation-seeking and hysterical. They could feel betrayed that there was a reporter among them, that somebody had infiltrated their private sanctuary and broadcast their secrets to the world. But this was one of the first pieces in a respected daily broadsheet that had not completely demonised the drug-dealing website. Once the article was posted in the Silk Road forums, members called it a 'great read' and 'more fair and balanced than the ones published in the UK'.

Dread Pirate Roberts also endorsed the article, which canvassed alternatives to the current approaches to drug policy. But then he immediately posted a lengthy, self-serving missive on the Silk Road forums about the dangers of lifting prohibition:

I keep hearing this argument come up when people talk about drug prohibition: legalize, regulate and tax it. On the surface it sounds like a good idea. No more drug war, more tax revenue, government regulators can make sure it is safe. Makes sense, right?

I can't help but think something is wrong though. Feels like the bastards that have been screwing everyone over all this time still win in this scenario. Now all that money can go to the state and to their cronies, right?

Here's the rub: the drug war is an acute symptom of a deeper problem, and that problem is the state. If they 'legalize, regulate and tax' it, it's just one more part of society under their thumb, another productive sector that they can leech off of.

If prohibition is lifted, most people here will go away. You'll go back to your lives and get your drugs from whatever state certified dispensaries are properly licensed to sell to you. Drug use will be as interesting as smoking and drinking.

Here's my point: Silk Road is about something much bigger than thumbing your nose at the man and getting your drugs anyway. It's about taking back our liberty and our dignity and demanding justice. If prohibition is lifted, and the drug industry is placed under the yoke of the state, then we won in a small way, but lost in a big way. Right now, drugs are ours. They aren't tainted by the government. We the people control their manufacture, distribution and consumption. We should be looking to expand that control, taking back our power, not giving what is ours to the very people that have been our enemies all along.

It's easy to justify though. Think of all the horrors the war on drugs has caused that will be gone, almost instantly. That pain could stop!

Don't be tempted by this short-term easy fix of 'let the government handle it.' Their time is coming to an end. The future is OUR time. Let us take this opportunity they've given us to gain a foothold from which we can throw that yoke off completely. We are NOT beasts of burden to be taxed and controlled and regulated. WE are free spirits! We DEMAND respect! The future can be a time where the human spirit flourishes, unbridled, wild and free! Don't be so quick to put on that harness and pull for the parasites.

If prohibition is lifted, where will you be? Will you forget about all this revolution stuff? Will you go back to ignoring that itching feeling that something isn't right, that men in uniforms and behind desks have just a bit too much control over your life, and are taking more and more of your sovereignty every day? Will you go back to thinking that taxes are as inevitable as death and the best you can do is to pull as hard as you can for them until your mind, body and spirit are all used up? Or will you feel the loss, as one more wild west frontier comes under the dominion of the enemy, and redouble your efforts to stop it?

I know where I'll be. I won't rest until children are born into a world where oppression, institutional violence and control, world war, and all the other hallmarks of the state are as ancient history as pharaohs commanding armies of slaves. The drug war merely brings to light their nature and shows us who they really are. Legalizing it won't change that and will only make them stronger.

Hold on to what you DO have, and stand for the freedom you deserve!

So Dread Pirate Roberts was not a champion for the lifting of prohibition and the end of the war on drugs. The more cynical of his readers thought perhaps his fear was more about the millions of dollars in commissions he would lose should prohibition be lifted.

And they were many millions indeed.

The Silk Road forums had a system of 'karma' – members could anonymously bestow positive and negative karma points with the click of a button depending on what they thought of a post or the member who made it. A member needed to have made at least 100 posts before they could do so, and could only give any other member karma once every seventy-two hours, to stop vindictive users from overloading negative karma on someone they didn't like. Vendors were notorious for smiting their competitors. The system was far from perfect, but the ratio of positive to negative karma became a reasonable yardstick by which to decide how much credibility to give to a particular member's post.

Journalists who posted on the forums inevitably amassed karma that put them firmly into the negative. The members of Silk Road were burned often when a reporter asked for information and stories via the forums and then ran a typical hatchet job, warning parents that their children could buy drugs, guns and hit men online from the privacy of their bedrooms. Rarely was a deeper analysis of the pros and cons of the site provided.

But a few journalists who persisted and carried through with more balanced articles were tolerated and eventually accepted as part of the community. Many members secretly wanted to tell their stories or provide information and would contact those reporters they trusted. Some were funny, some touching, some a little scary, like this one:

Hello,

Let me get to the point directly: I am Kais, i have worked in the illegal organ market for a few years and i am currently getting out. Thats why i contact you, i see a lot of parts of the web and its dark places are already exposed to the big community but my working area is not. I would have liked it this way, because extra attention is never good to blackmarkets, but like I said, i am getting out and i want to share my story and information on this subject. I can show you hidden message boards with vendings (protected but i can give you access) and share how things get shipped and personal experiences on this subject. I am willing to give a chat or email interview (i prefer e-mail) too. I expect a payment for this information, not because i am starving (i would not be getting out of this business then) but because i put myself and people i have worked with in danger. If you are interested we can discuss the rate, but that is not what this is about.

I am currently in contact with various parties to share my information, also pretty big ones, but i like your site because it is focussed on subjects like this, i have red [sic] a little myself before sending this mail too, good job.

Kind regards

A request for payment was a red flag that the author was ready to take the journalist for a ride. A response that there was either no money available, or it was unethical to accept any, would usually result in the writer ceasing correspondence. Such was the case with Kais.

People who provided the site or members with useful information about law enforcement efforts were heavily rewarded with good karma. Reports that were supposed to be classified were often leaked online by activists, hackers or thieves and such papers were uploaded to anonymous file-sharing sites, which allowed discreet downloading of documents that were quickly circulated among the members of the black markets. Members would dissect and discuss the contents ad nauseam and would be heartened by a repeated theme: the combined technologies of Tor, bitcoin and PGP encryption made law enforcement's task very difficult indeed.

One such report by the FBI, 'Bitcoin virtual currency: Unique features present distinct challenges for deterring illicit activity' (marked for official use only but leaked to the internet in early May 2012), claimed that bitcoin was ideal for facilitating illegal online trade and difficult to combat. It stated:

It stated that the traits of bitcoin – its anonymity, ease of use and lack of oversight by a centralised authority – made it nearly impossible to identify and track those using it for illegal activities. 'Bitcoin will likely continue to attract cyber criminals who view it as a means to move or steal funds as well as a means of making donations to illicit groups' the report said. The FBI was worried that if the currency stablised and grew in popularity, it would become 'an increasingly useful tool for various illegal activities beyond the cyber realm'.

The FBI estimated the bitcoin economy to be worth $35–45 million at the time of analysis. It was clear that international law enforcement authorities feared bitcoin and its role in the rise of black markets. It was also clear that there was absolutely nothing they could do about it.

Another report leaked around the same time had an Australian focus. According to gwern.net, a website providing a comprehensive history of Silk Road, a poster on the forums had written:

Recently, I gained access to an internal confidential report distributed to several Australia LE agencies and a few international anti-narcotic bodies regarding possible methods of combating illegal activities involving BC. Of course SR was a main feature of said report . . . So here are the nuts and bolts of the report, spread the information as far and wide as possible friends:

PGP is terrifying them, every new user who learns it and helps others learn, closes a possible loophole they were planning to exploit.

User ignorance of the technology being used (Tor, PGP etc) is their single best hope for any kind of serious action against the SR community.

Narcotic trade historically involves exploitation and violence. Users working together as a community for a greater good and towards the same goals has made all previous interdiction training basically obsolete. In other words, every user who helps newcomers learn how to be safe and secure especially through the use of PGP for all transactions and communication is a nail in LEO's coffin.

A total lack of violence and exploitation is very much working in our favor. So in other words, the idea of a community working together to protect the new and vulnerable has been identified as a huge obstacle for any kind of serious attempt to stop SR.

Their morale regarding fighting SR and BC is very low at the moment, mainly because very few LEO have the capacity to comprehend how the whole system works, but unfortunately, recent media coverage demands some kind of action, so they are going to have to show the public they are doing something to combat SR, they just aren't sure what yet.

The report was an extensive critique of and response to Silk Road, well researched and referenced. It described anonymity and encryption, darknets, PGP, Tor and peer-to-peer technologies. It explained what hidden services were and listed those that could be found on the Hidden Wiki at the time. It discussed the security features and vulnerabilities of Tor, illustrating these with the story of Anonymous' takedown of Lolita City. The report concluded that the main vulnerability of Tor and the hidden services was not the technology, but the user. Human error and a lack of understanding of the technology would be the best bet to bypass the anonymity provided by Tor and encryption.

'Other avenues to attack the Silk Road flagged in the report include social engineering, intersections between online transactions and the real world, and by targeting user error,' reported *iTnews*, which had viewed a copy. Some time later, an officer of the agency that commissioned the report pleaded guilty to contravening secrecy by allegedly providing the report to his son.

It was a recurring theme in reports by law enforcement agencies around the world that human error was their best chance for detecting crime. Silk Road's users could be comfortable that the technology, used correctly, would keep them safe. People in the forums often warned each other that human error and potential social engineering were the most useful ways law enforcement had of unmasking any major players or vendors on the market. Those who would be targets reassured each other that they had taken all necessary precautions.

Dread Pirate Roberts, the biggest target, was also confident his security measures meant nobody would find him through human error.

April 2012

A recently registered member of Silk Road, 'Nob', began private-messaging the Dread Pirate Roberts. He was a cocaine dealer and might be interested in selling on Silk Road. The two became quite chatty, in that way that drug czars do. It was the closest thing the Dread Pirate Roberts was able to have to a relationship.

Meet the Dealer

Silk Road was not only a boon for Australian recreational drug users, it was very lucrative for drug sellers as well. Those listed as being among the top 10 per cent of vendors were enthusiastic. 'I made it into the Top Ten, and let me just say, the money is GOOD!' said one. '[Silk Road] could take 50 per cent tax and I'd still be making a killing.'

Another claimed to turn over more than $4000 per day, 75 per cent of which was profit. A dealer who sold a variety of drugs said that his profit on cocaine alone was $20,000 per month. All of the vendors agreed that the commission structure charged by Silk Road was fair and reasonable.

One top Australian seller was an active member of Silk Road as both buyer and vendor. As a buyer, he spent over $360,000 in less than a year importing bulk cocaine and MDMA from overseas vendors in the USA and the Netherlands. Although he wouldn't provide exact figures of his income, it seemed safe to assume that his turnover was in the realm of $1 million in that time.

This vendor traded as 'AussieDomesticDrugs' and 'Natural Highs'. During the nine months that they vended, AussieDomestic-Drugs averaged in the top 7 per cent of Silk Road sellers, selling a variety of different substances. 'I've been selling drugs for about eight years now and am yet to be arrested or charged by the police for it,' said 'Blake', a man in his twenties and the online presence of AussieDomesticDrugs. Originally selling person-to-person in clubs, he had moved his business online when he discovered Silk Road:

> Online markets have completely revolutionized the drug trade. The war on drugs has well and truly been lost by the government, and every year this is becoming painfully more obvious. Now anyone who wants any drug can go online and get it, and if they are smart they can do it without the risk of arrest or being ripped off.
>
> I won't go into detail about how much money I have made, but it would be significant by most people's standards. I'll just say there's not much I want that I couldn't afford and I don't think I'll be short of money for many years to come regardless of what happens to me.

Blake, of course, was another anonymous character who wrote up his Silk Road story in his own words and published it through the Tor anonymising network. So although it was easy to confirm that the tale came from a prominent Silk Road vendor making a very tidy income, it wasn't possible to verify all the details of the story of AussieDomesticDrugs' rise in Silk Road. Some of what Blake claimed may well have been him spinning a yarn. But it is similar to the typical tale of many a Silk Road vendor, so either they have all been watching the same gangster movies, or there is a shred of truth to it.

Blake said he grew up in a poor household. 'Although my upbringing was happy and free of any abuse I never had any of the comforts most children take for granted,' he said. 'Sometimes there was not much food in the cupboard and I had to live off tinned beans, Weetbix with water or whatever I could pinch from the local shops, and new clothes, trips to the movies and other such luxuries were non-existent.'

When he got to an age where he could leave school, he held down a range of minimum-wage positions where he would slave away for forty hours or so a week, being told what to do and following orders, in exchange for a pay cheque that would keep him fed and give him a small amount of disposable income to get a nice shirt, eat out on Friday night or maybe go clubbing and get drunk if he didn't have any bills to pay that week. He laid on the story of his desperate poverty thickly: 'I would always look at the wealthy people I met while socializing like they were from a different class to me. Their lifestyle of being able to eat out whenever they wanted, buy designer clothing and go on holidays regularly seemed alien and unachievable. Over the first couple of years of my working career I grew steadily more and more depressed as I started to feel like my place in life was just to slave away, nine to five, in the hope of being able to retire with some small degree of comfort.'

Like many young men, Blake liked to smoke weed and take ecstasy pills from time to time, and he soon fell into a group of friends who shared his interests. They would go clubbing or to festivals together and then spend the weekend hanging out. 'Some of the guys in my group sold pills and it never seemed like a big deal at the time as they never talked about what they were doing with me and I never asked many questions. They were just friends to me although being shouted free pills when we went to festivals was always a welcome bonus.'

Those friends always had a lot of disposable income and were extremely generous with their money. 'As time went on I started wanting what they had, but I had no idea where to start as I had no experience selling drugs and had only ever bought drugs from a small amount of people I socialized with.'

A turning point for Blake came after a bender where he spent every last cent of his pay cheque. He woke up in the house of Tom, the most successful pill dealer of the group. 'A sinking feeling hit me like a ton of bricks as I realised I was going to have no money whatsoever for petrol, food or to pay the bills for the next six days,' he said.

'No worries,' Tom told him. 'Today is on me!'

Tom spent the day showing Blake how the other half lived, splashing out cash on restaurants for all of their friends, a mammoth session on Time Zone games and clothes for both Blake and himself. That night they went clubbing again, all on Tom's dime. Blake was impressed that Tom could do what he wanted, when he wanted and with whom he wanted. And he wanted to be able to do the same.

'I remember sitting down on a couch and thinking this is what I want out of life. What I've been doing for money is just making me miserable,' he said. He was tired of being poor and constantly stressing about his finances. It was time to have a private chat with his friend.

'Tom,' he said, 'I want to sell. Can you help me get started?'

'Don't worry, mate,' he replied, giving Blake a huge grin, 'I'll hook you up and show you what to do.' The following weekend, before the usual group of friends were due to meet and imbibe before heading out to the clubs, Tom and Blake sat on Tom's bed. Tom produced Tic Tac containers filled with pills – more than Blake had ever seen in his life.

'There's 100 pills in there, they are all good quality and people will love them,' Tom confided. He didn't want any money up-front, but he wanted Blake to take over selling small amounts. He said he would charge Blake $15 per pill and recommended he sell them for $30. 'As soon as you have $1500 you come and give it to me. The rest is yours, sweet?'

Tom schooled Blake in the art of small-time club dealing; how to make the exchange without looking suspicious. Within two hours Blake was able to repay Tom, and by 3 am he had sold out of his stock. 'I went into a toilet cubicle to count my money on the seat. I had just over a grand, all profit. I had just made more in four hours than I'd ever made in a week in my entire life. I felt on top of the moon,' he said. He repaid Tom one of the many drinks he owed him, and a business relationship was born.

Soon Blake was earning $3000 a week selling ecstasy to clubbers. He revelled in not only the income, but also his new status as the go-to guy for good drugs. And it didn't take long before, like Tom, he was getting sick of doing deals for small numbers of pills. He enlisted his friend Mike to sell at another club. Blake, now paying only $14 per pill, would give Mike 100 pills for $1700, making a $300 profit in minutes. He needed more friends like Mike.

At this point, Blake's story ventured into *Underbelly* territory, with the introduction of a 'friend's cousin's friend' who was looking to provide bulk customers for a shady big-time dealer. 'He was a very cagey guy and didn't trust many people, but he trusted my friend's judgment and my friend trusted me,' Blake said.

He met Steve – resplendent in a Rolex watch, gold jewellery and a well-cut suit – in a cocktail bar where they could talk without being overheard. Steve had a large scar on his head. 'I was told later that he got it from a group of bikies who broke into his home, tied him up and slashed him up with a machete to find out where he kept his drugs and money. After that he always chose to live in secured apartment complexes with a video intercom system,' Blake said.

Steve was not the warmest chap to get to know. 'How do I know you're not a cop?' he demanded. 'You don't look like you've ever popped a pill in your life.'

'I don't know what to say, but you can always come back to the club with me and watch me sell pills,' Blake suggested. 'I don't think cops are allowed to do that.'

Steve decided to drive him around and grill him for several hours. 'I could tell he was a smart guy, but extremely paranoid and potentially dangerous if I got on the wrong side of him. I was more than a little nervous but he wasn't threatening or aggressive and I could tell he was warming to me,' Blake said, with the air of someone who was also warming to his story.

Eventually Steve indicated his satisfaction with his new associate with a speech straight from a tough-guy character in a movie: 'I'm gonna put my trust in you, mate. You don't look the type but you've been vouched for and you've got a head on your shoulders, which is more than I can say for most of the halfwits I know. Don't ever fuck me around or lie to me and I'll look after you. If you ever snitch on me, I'll have someone track you down when you least expect it and burn your face off with acid as well as your friend who vouched for you. If you're loyal to me, and anyone rips you off, I will make them wish they didn't. I'll only ever give you the best pills and the best prices, but you've got one month of tick to get started and then I expect you to have cash for everything you buy from me. Now wait here and don't go anywhere.'

Blake waited and was rewarded with 1000 pills at $10 each and a burner phone – a cheap Nokia mobile that could not be traced to any particular person and could not provide the wealth of information newer smartphones are wont to do about their owners. The phone was to be used only to contact Steve via text message, always in code.

By now Blake wouldn't sell any less than 100 pills at a time, and he became Steve's best customer. The two became friends and Steve – who had all the trappings of success and no criminal record – taught him how to move in the big time. He was, Blake thought, the epitome of a successful drug dealer.

'One time I met up with him just after he met his supplier, and he pulled out a luggage bag with a huge plastic bag inside absolutely full of pills, easily over 50,000 in total,' Blake recalled. 'I was in awe as he started weighing them into 1000 bags on scales. He told me he got the pills straight off the guys pressing them and bought about a month's supply at a time.'

One day, Steve simply stopped dealing. He had enough money and a legal business he could attribute it to. Tom got in trouble with the police and went on the run. Blake was on his own and no longer had a steady supply to pass on to his customers. He resorted to smuggling mephedrone from the UK in his stomach, which made him anxious and depressed, and eventually settled on importing various research chemicals directly from Chinese factories that he contacted through the internet. The life of a drug dealer wasn't looking as glamorous as it had previously.

And then he stumbled across the Wikipedia entry for Silk Road.

Downloading Tor, Blake had the same thoughts that everyone had the first time they heard about Silk Road: this couldn't be real. But there they were – a bunch of drug listings, complete with advertisements and accompanying pictures.

Not sure what to make of it all, he filtered the thousands of listings to those being sold by Australians. What he discovered astounded him. 'I did a bit of maths and thought, wow, these guys are paying ridiculous prices for their drugs, there's definitely profit to be made here!' he said. Joining forces with Mike, with whom he was still friends, Blake started AussieDomesticDrugs and later a separate shop called Natural Highs.

The obvious place for them to start was ecstasy. 'Within twenty-four hours of my listings being up I had orders for over 100 pills, and within two weeks I had sold the entire 1000 pills I originally listed,' he said. Soon his whole business was online, when he realised he could buy overseas, bang on a 400 per cent mark-up in price and sell domestically.

Before long, the enterprise saw Blake and Mike putting on two employees responsible for packaging and posting all orders. 'I try and keep as much distance between myself and the handling of the drugs as possible,' said Blake, 'as possession is nine-tenths of the law.'

Determined not to become a jail statistic, Blake studied online security furiously, learning all the technologies that worked together to make online vending as safe as possible. He used a dedicated computer running open-source applications only, and conducted all his online business through Tor. 'My day-to-day tactic for staying free from the law is to avoid being in physical possession of drugs at all times except when absolutely necessary. I pay other people to send and receive any illegal substances for me and I never, ever have anything stored at my house or in a place that could be linked to me. If the police ever raided my house or pulled me over to search my car, their efforts would be in vain,' he said.

Blake stopped using drugs himself, not even imbibing alcohol or caffeine. His motivation for working in the world of drugs was now completely financial. He became a typical everyman, dressing down and not drawing attention to himself. 'I only associate with a very small amount of people who use drugs themselves – most of my friends are what you would call "cleanskins" who have no idea what I do,' he said. 'I dress normally, appear very clean-cut and I can blend into a crowd without being noticed or walk right by police without them giving me a second glance. This is something I pride myself on as I believe that only stupid drug dealers draw attention to themselves in real life. Once you become too high profile, by committing public acts of violence like many real-life dealers, or by driving a flashy car and buying too many unexplainably expensive assets, you are putting a time limit on how long you can stay free for.'

He thought the online drugs markets like Silk Road were the way of the future. Having witnessed the violence that can occur in real-life deals, he revelled in the anonymity Silk Road provided him. 'I believe as the years go on the middlemen will be cut out more and more, until people can use the internet to source drugs directly from the producers or from an importer who sources directly from the producer. Drugs online will become cheaper and purer, and anonymity will reduce the violence.

'Right now the market for sourcing multi-kilogram quantities of many drugs online is not there, but this will change as bitcoin becomes more and more mainstream. When there are wholesale dealers and producers selling online in the future, that's when we will really start to see the effect of online drugs marketplaces on the narcotics industry. My long-term goal is to leave Australia and move to a Scandinavian country in Europe whose government I can trust and believe in – maybe the Netherlands, Belgium, Sweden or Switzerland – and start a new life with a nice house and a comfortable, legitimate job; and free myself from the paranoia that I have had to live with for so many years now,' he said.

Blake's tale sounded a bit too much like the plot of a novel or *Underbelly* series to be completely believable. But one thing was certain: AussieDomesticDrugs and Natural Highs did a very comfortable business on Silk Road.

Follow the Money

The top vendors on Silk Road changed from time to time, but they were always vendors of ecstasy, LSD and similar 'party' drugs. While heroin and crystal meth dealers did well, it seemed most people came to the online markets for party drugs rather than drugs of addiction. As a general rule, the most severe addicts – those we often call 'junkies' – did not use Silk Road. Junkies need an immediate fix and their lives revolve around obtaining money, getting heroin, wash, rinse, repeat. They are unlikely to go through the process of obtaining money, exchanging it for bitcoin, going online, doing their research and waiting a couple of weeks for their drugs to arrive.

'Silk Road seems predominantly (although not exclusively) to cater to the sales of drugs typically associated with "recreational" use – cannabis, ecstasy and psychedelics,' wrote academics Aldridge and Décary-Hétu. Analysing why this may be the case, they said, 'The site may therefore have suited purchases by recreational users with the resources and time to place orders and wait for deliveries; dependent users with chaotic lifestyles, in contrast, were likely to have neither.'

Although Silk Road did not mind publicity in general, the site and Dread Pirate Roberts always jealously guarded any real statistics or data about their activities. Anecdotally, it was clear that income was healthy for both the site owner and the many dealers. But there was a dearth of hard data that could put any sort of figures to the earnings. At one point 'Supertrips', who had been one of the Road's top three vendors for a long time, boasted that 1 per cent of the world's bitcoin passed through their account.

On 22 May 2012, a contributor to the Bitcointalk forum, 'Arkanos', provided a link to a bitcoin account that held a very large stash worth over $2 million. He claimed he had uncovered Silk Road's wallet. 'I sent btc to silk road and then I tracked the funds. They immediately went to that address. That is Silk Road's main storage. Nearly two million USD is tied up in the Silk Road Marketplace,' he said. 'This account will now be thrown away.'

This was the last post from this member who true to his word disappeared from the forum immediately after posting, but the internet sleuths jumped on the information and began their own digging. They signed up for Silk Road accounts into which they deposited bitcoin, then followed the blockchain trail to see what happened.

Although every transaction made with bitcoin is public and visible, the use of tumbling services to 'wash' coins as they pass through wallets and the sometimes apparently endless paths that need to be followed and that split off into an ever-increasing number of directions can make following the trail very difficult. But some of these internet detectives had a lot of time on their hands, and after thirty-four pages of posts on the forum, the community found compelling – if not completely conclusive – evidence that the wallet was indeed owned by Silk Road, or by somebody who had a very close connection to it.

It was fascinating, and people speculated that all anyone needed to do was to keep an eye on any attempts to move bitcoin from that wallet to an exchange where it would be cashed out for fiat currency and they would find Dread Pirate Roberts.

At its height, the wallet contained 5 per cent of all bitcoin. But in August, the 500,000 bitcoins – worth by this time closer to US$5 million thanks to an increase in the bitcoin price – disappeared from the wallet. The trail ran cold on the Bitcointalk forum until it was picked up again by a group of researchers at the University of California, who later published a paper called 'A fistful of bitcoins'.

The university paper theorised: 'While it is largely agreed that the address is associated with Silk Road (and indeed our clustering heuristic did tag this address as being controlled by Silk Road), some have theorized that it was the "hot" (i.e. active) wallet for Silk Road, and that its dissipation represents a changing storage structure for the service.'

The researchers decided to try to trace where the funds went. They claimed it was clear that when the address was dissipated, the resulting funds were not sent en masse to any major services. They traced the coins into a number of services, mainly exchanges, but again the trail went cold. Dread Pirate Roberts had found somewhere else to store his bitcoins.

But now the world had some idea of the magnitude of the little start-up Silk Road.

In August 2012, unassuming security professor Nicolas Christin quietly released an academic paper in which he described trawling the available data of Silk Road. The paper, 'Traveling the Silk Road: A measurement analysis of a large anonymous online market-place', created a convincing picture of the site's sales activity, which Christin conservatively estimated at $22 million per year and growing exponentially. Dread Pirate Roberts was taking about 10 per cent of this in commissions.

The paper sat unnoticed on the university's server until it was mentioned on the Silk Road forums and the Silk Road sub-Reddit. It didn't take long before it was referenced on sites with more traffic, and soon Christin was being interviewed by IT and business maga-zines around the world, including such luminaries as *Forbes*. 'It is quite surreal having more than half a dozen people read one of my papers,' he quipped when questioned about his sudden fame.

Christin's paper became the subject of much debate. He was careful to note that he was not working with the full range of data; for example, any vendors who were operating in 'stealth' mode (i.e. not visible to anyone other than selected buyers) or custom list-ings for specific buyers were not included in his trawled data. As such, his work could only represent an estimate, and not actual verified volumes of sales – but he believed the estimates to be on the conservative side.

Christin's paper was the most reliable indicator to date of the sort of volume Silk Road was turning over and the kind of profits the Dread Pirate Roberts might be enjoying. Christin concluded Silk Road was taking in slightly over $1.2 million per month for the entire marketplace, which in turn represented around $92,000 per month in commissions for the Dread Pirate Roberts.

If DPR was keeping his commissions in bitcoin – which seemed likely, as holding bitcoin could be done with relative anonymity, while cashing out in such volumes could create many problems – most of any fortune amassed would come from the steady rise in the value of bitcoin rather than the volume of drug sales themselves.

As well as his quantitative analysis, Christin also made observations about customer satisfaction and trust in black-market transactions. 'On a site like Silk Road, where . . . most of the goods sold are illicit, one would expect a certain amount of deception to occur. Indeed, a buyer choosing, for instance, to purchase heroin from an anonymous seller would have very little recourse if the goods promised are not delivered,' he said, noting that 97.8 per cent of customers gave sellers positive reviews.

Members of the Bitcointalk forum debated how much of the bitcoin economy Silk Road accounted for. Around that time, estimates of Silk Road as a percentage of the bitcoin economy were ranging from a sixth to a third. The arguments about whether it was the backbone of the market or would be its downfall continued.

Movements in the value of bitcoin still seemed to correlate with what was happening on the Silk Road market. When Silk Road suffered a series of DDoS attacks, destabilising the site, bitcoin reacted with a drop in price. But market observers pointed out that the drop, which after a sharp dip levelled out at around a 25 per cent loss, was considerably less than drops that had previously occurred upon negative Silk Road news.

It seemed that bitcoin was beginning to have a life of its own, relying less on the black market for its value. Each time Silk Road came under threat, the impact on the value of bitcoin was less than the previous time.

Right now we are reading Defending the Undefendable . . . The author is biased in favor of defending the drug pushers and addicts, downplaying for example the negative effects of heroin use in [and] of itself, but overall I think he paints a vivid picture of why we have nothing to be ashamed of in what we are doing here at Silk Road, and in some cases should even be proud.
– Dread Pirate Roberts post in 'DPR's Book Club' forum
thread, 26 November 2012

Nice Guys

By the end of 2012, it was clear that, more than just a market-place, Silk Road had become a close-knit community of people from all around the world with one thing in common: illicit drugs.

In 1.2 million posts in over 70,000 topics, discussions on the site's forums covered everything from sophisticated methods of evading law enforcement to favourite movies to watch when stoned. But they covered much more than that.

One thing that continually struck newcomers, journalists and researchers alike was how civil and intelligent the majority of contributors to the Silk Road forums were. For a place that prided itself on libertarianism and free speech, it remained remarkably troll-free much of the time. And some of the most popular threads were the particularly warm and fuzzy ones.

For one thing, the users of the site were surprisingly charitable. One of the lengthiest and longest-running threads was 'The Spare Coins Thread'. People would often miscalculate the amount of bitcoin they needed to transfer into their accounts for a purchase, forgetting about the minuscule transaction fees or being caught by an unexpected shift in the exchange rate against their currency of origin. They would find themselves unable to place an order due to a deficit of sometimes just a few cents.

As this was a reasonably regular occurrence, one of the members started a thread in which such people could ask for a loan or donation of bitcoin that could be transferred instantly between members, rather than having to wait for currency deposits to appear in their account, which could on occasion take twenty-four hours. It was similar to the 'take a penny, leave a penny' movement seen at some shops, with a 'pay it forward' vibe. The thread became a lovefest that ran to 12,500 posts. Although some people were put on the shit list when they failed to repay their loans, the vast majority of people who took advantage of the good nature of their forum buddies did so in good faith.

Even Dread Pirate Roberts couldn't explain why a community that could be a den of conniving drug dealers and desperate addicts worked so well with little oversight. 'Honestly I don't know,' Roberts said. 'It could have something to do with camaraderie. While there is some infighting, most people understand that our best chance is to stick together and help each other out.'

Dread Pirate Roberts may have been at a loss, but most of the community attributed the warmth and comradeship to the site's founder and the steadily growing moderating team, a group of members hand-picked by Dread Pirate Roberts to keep the forums tidy and on-topic and to guide new members through the process. Moderators were appointed from the various time zones, ensuring that they could respond to the forum's needs around the clock.

It made sense that Australia, having a strong presence in the discussion forums, got its own Australian moderator. DPR appointed long-time contributor 'Samesamebutdifferent', known as SSBD for short. He became a constant presence and was almost universally admired for his level-headed, respectful approach to the community.

DPR looked for moderators – who were not supposed to censor anything but spam, scams, personal information and links to child porn – who were articulate, fair, warm and helpful. 'People look to them for guidance and it is important that they represent Silk Road well,' he said. There was no ban on trolling or personal attacks, but rogue posters were publicly challenged by mods and senior members alike.

Some members took it upon themselves to educate others on drug safety, legal rights and security. Two of Silk Road's best security authorities, 'Pine' and 'Guru', would spend hours of their time providing tutorials in PGP encryption. One thing law enforcement investigations had repeatedly reported was that PGP was one of the strongest weapons those trading on black markets had with which to protect themselves. Despite this, Silk Road vendors claimed that fewer than 10 per cent of customers actually used PGP; some customers simply weren't concerned enough to take the time.

'Even if Silk Road is compromised, the Feds are hardly going to come after every small-time buyer,' one user defending their decision not to encrypt their information said. Many agreed that a lack of resources would prevent authorities from targeting everyone.

Pine, especially, established herself as a Silk Road legend (she held herself out to be female, although whether she was or not was hotly debated in the forums – some people simply couldn't believe that anyone with that amount of technical knowledge could lack a penis). She joined in January 2012 and became a self-styled resident security expert. She was quick to admonish those who didn't take their security seriously (which meant to the level of extreme paranoia). Aghast at the apparent lack of self-preservation among the site's users, Pine set up how-to guides and a 'PGP Club' that provided advice, guidance and testing for those new to encryption. She amassed thousands of posts assisting Silk Road members with technical security queries, provided extensive explanations for all sorts of technical issues and collected a fan base of overwhelmingly male geeks who chose to believe the attractive picture used as her avatar was really Pine, even though her own paranoia over privacy meant that was simply not possible.

At other times, vendors would announce that they were donating a certain percentage of their sales for a day or a week to a charity. Vendor 'FiberOptic' stated that he/she felt like 'it's time to pass on a bit of the good fortune to others' and promised to donate 30 per cent of one week's sales to charity. Half was to be donated to Erowid, a drugs harm reduction organisation, and the other half to Sean's Outpost, a charity that helps the homeless. FiberOptic urged others to do likewise. Two more vendors offered to donate a percentage of profits to charities of their choice.

Dread Pirate Roberts chimed in with his thoughts on the efforts of his flock to raise money to make charitable donations:

It warms my heart to see everyone's generosity. There are a couple of points I'd like to mention about giving to charity.

For one, I think it is an important pillar of civil society. Our capacity for empathy and wanting others to succeed should not be ignored or downplayed. A lack of charitable spirit is often used as a point in favor of a central authority with the power to take from the rich and give to the poor. It is said that, absent government intervention, no one would have the incentive to help those who are in need and have little to give in return. You are proving them wrong right now.

Second, you must be responsible for the effect of money on your fellow man. Money encourages and motivates people to do whatever they have to in order to get that money. For an employee, that's doing a good job and pleasing their boss, or maybe blending in and not risking a visible mistake, or maybe lying on their resume. For a businessman, that can mean serving their customers, or brib[ing] the authorities to enact laws that hurt their competition, among many other things. A dictator/politician will murder thousands, even millions, to keep their, or their party's control of tax revenue. Con artists and thieves have their way of getting money. For beggars, often being helpless and/or destitute gets a good return. In other words, money shapes people's behavior, which in turn shapes who they are, and it is not the case that giving someone money always has the effect you hope it does.

So, don't ignore your desire to help people, but strive always to give in such a way that people are empowered to rise up out of their conditions and transform their lives. Just be careful you aren't creating an incentive for people to become needy and destitute in order to win your charity.

This seemed to be a very hardline position to take and came as a surprise to many who considered DPR compassionate and loving. But it fit within his agorist and libertarian philosophies.

There were also some more practical efforts at harm reduction among drug users. A group calling itself 'The Avengers' took it upon itself to order and provide independent reviews of LSD from every vendor on Silk Road:

> We are a group of people who have decades of experience with tripping, vending, laying [transferring liquid LSD on to a paper blotter] and general cyber-crime. We, both as a group and as individuals, have extensive knowledge about the manufacturing, distribution processes, and general market frameworking. We created this group in this community with a common goal of providing a better view of the LSD landscape here on SR.

They took their job seriously, providing trip testing and reports, chemical and lab testing, and evaluating vendors on packaging, stealth, shipping time, communication and quality of customer service. Initially self-funded by the testers, as the thread containing their reports became a must-visit area of Silk Road, vendors soon began providing them with free samples of acid to review. It was probably a very clever ploy to get a steady supply of free drugs, but they did provide a great service to the community.

There were also dealers who were determined to offer customer service to rival the best. One Silk Road user recounted a story of an order of 7 grams of meth that went awry. The package was delivered, but held at the post office because of insufficient postage. 'I was shitting my pants,' the buyer said. But not so much that he didn't still want his package. 'I talked to a mailman. He assured me it was safe to pick up the package, but it was going to be returned to sender early the next morning so I had to get there early. I went to the post office, had to pay $14 postage, and fill out and sign a form.' He left a positive review for the vendor, but sent them a private message admonishing them for the sloppiness that led to his hassle. 'A little over a week later I get a package. He sent me 7 grams for Christmas. It came out of nowhere, was a complete surprise.'

Then there were the people who credited the site as practically lifesaving. One member, 'Arlingtonbridge', who claimed to have terminal cancer, wrote this touching missive:

Hello all,

Recently, I placed an order for an ounce of weed from the vendor Incoming. FE'd [finalised early] for him because the site was going down, and he asked nicely. Did it without thinking and got ripped off. (note: I'm still not sure, if he does actually come through, I will update this to save Incoming's rep). The reason I bought this ounce was because I have cancer, leukemia to be exact. I was diagnosed a year ago, and this will be my last Christmas . . . ever. It's a sickly sweet time in my life. I use marijuana to control nausea and pain, and it's the only thing at times that can get me through the pain i'm going through.

What I'm trying to say is, even though I got ripped off, and my life seems to really be falling apart as I am dying, something really weird happened.

A tiny little gift from the universe, a token, a bitcoin to say everything will be alright.

I deposited .1 bitcoin into bitcoin fog [an online bitcoin wallet], all I could really afford at this time, as I wanted to buy before SR shut down now that i'm not getting my order from

Incoming, and didn't want to suffer over christmas/be sick. I withdrew them into my wallet, and what do you know, bitcoin fog fucked up. I was given .9328btc in return for the .1btc I deposited. While I feel bad for bitcoin fog, I can't help but try and take this as a sign that even though my time is coming to an end, things will always be alright, and there is always a tiny light at the end of the tunnel. For everyone. I thought nothing could ever get better for me, but something did.

Have a merry Christmas everyone. Thank you Silk Road and DPR for everything you have done for me, personally. I wouldn't be able to have quality of life without you people. The FBI and DEA may see this place as criminal, but it has made my life a lot better, and has done more for me than I could ever imagine. For that, I thank you all from the bottom of my heart. The trustworthy users of SR, buyers and sellers are what will keep this idea alive. The dishonest people who scam others, are what will truely [sic] kill the idea Roberts created. Please don't let this die, it must stay for the greater good. Which I believe this site is now for. It's something that needs to stay forever.

Doesn't matter if your [sic] an opiate addict or a cancer patient just like me. The safety you provide me and others, in exchange for your own is amazing. You give your freedom for us, anonymous people you will never see. While i'm not religious myself, Jesus did something similar in that fancy book of his. You might not realize it DPR, or Sarge, or anyone else at SR. But you are a piece of history, and someone I hope to see on the other side. This is the meaning of humanity, this community is a pure form of human nature, not bound by rules of society or government.

I'm proud to be a part of you all. Stay strong and stay free. Live your lives happy, and enjoy everything while you can. I'd never imagine i'd die this young, you don't know when you will either.

Merry Christmas everyone. :)

The Doctor

For most members of the site, anonymity was paramount, although a surprising number offered to speak to or even meet with journalists to tell their stories, trusting they would not expose them or reveal sources of sensitive information.

And then there were the select few who were open about who they were and what they were doing there.

One such person was Dr Fernando Caudevilla, a Spanish physician and an authority on drugs of addiction. In between running his busy practice and working for harm reduction associations and a Spanish NGO, the 39-year-old provided expert personal advice on drug use and abuse to Silk Road's anonymous membership.

His username was, appropriately, 'DoctorX'. He started a thread in the drug safety forum called 'Ask a Drug Expert Physician about Drugs & Health' in April 2013, inviting Silk Road's users to post or message specific questions and saying he would do his best to help them. He would sign off his posts with a link to his site and contact details so that potential patients could check his credentials.

DoctorX's thread became one of the most visited on the Silk Road forums and one of the few member-created threads to become 'stickied' to the top of the drug safety forum so that it was the first thing any visitor to that section would see.

Dread Pirate Roberts provided his full endorsement for DoctorX's work and was happy to talk about the work done by the professionals such as DoctorX on his site. DPR claimed drug safety and responsible use were 'incredibly important' to him and his team. 'I care very much about the community of people that surround Silk Road,' he said. 'Many of the substances sold on Silk Road are quite powerful and if not used responsibly could lead to addiction, injury or even death. Not surprisingly, most people don't want these things for themselves.'

Like researcher Dr Monica Barratt, a dedication to harm reduction was the motivation for Caudevilla's involvement in Silk Road. 'Drug users try to take care of their health, the same as the rest of the population,' he said. He made a quote in the forums that Dread Pirate Roberts used as his signature for some time: 'All drugs are absolutely harmless. If you leave cocaine, MDMA, meth or 4-AcODMT on a table, they won't try to assault you, rape you or hit your balls.' He did, of course, acknowledge that some drugs could be harmful or deadly if used to excess, or if they were mixed with other, more toxic substances.

DoctorX started his free service on Silk Road partly because he is a bit of a rabble-rousing activist at heart but mostly because he felt that information about drugs was limited to the negative aspects of use, such as the risk of addiction or overdose, with the intention of scaring people and preventing the use of any illegal psychoactive. 'But drug users need more than that,' he said. 'They need answers. That is what I try to do. There is a lack of attention to recreational drug users.'

He was not, however, prepared for the overwhelming response to his health advice initiative. 'I didn't think that my thread would become so popular,' he said. 'I have reached more than 8000 visits, 150 public queries and more than 100 personal messages.' The site's members bombarded him with questions about dosage and patterns of use; addiction and withdrawal issues; considerations for sufferers of diabetes, asthma and depression; risks of specific substances; and pharmacological interactions between illegal and prescription drugs. DoctorX endeavoured to answer all of them with a refreshing, straightforward holistic approach to illicit drug use.

He did urge some people to seek more hands-on help than he could provide in an online forum, particularly when they were experiencing symptoms that were unusual or not normal reactions to the drugs they were taking. Unfortunately he knew most users would not take that advice. Many drug users are reluctant to visit a doctor either because they fear legal repercussions or because they know the doctor's response will be to tell them to stop using their drug of choice, rather than advice on how to minimise the risks while continuing to indulge. DoctorX would provide links to research that showed dosages of drugs that were generally considered to be non-toxic. If he saw evidence from a member that their life was being negatively impacted by their addiction, he would gently point out that many opiate addicts did not realise or accept that their use was a problem. He would warn people about the danger of mixing certain drugs, such as ketamine and alcohol. Once he told a lactating mother to abstain altogether when she asked if it was safe to use MDMA while breastfeeding.

Caudevilla didn't use scare tactics. Instead, he used information about an inquirer's particular circumstances, such as age, sex, motivation, as well as the type of drug and patterns, context and frequency of use, to tailor his responses. 'Classical prevention methods exaggerate the dangers of drugs instead of giving concrete answers to specific questions,' said Caudevilla. 'I try to change things with my modest work.'

Sometimes he took an unusual path to encourage moderation, such as pointing out the diminishing returns and thus escalating monetary costs of increasing doses of certain drugs. This sort of realistic advice earned him the respect of members with such accolades as: 'How cool, the good Doctor is against overdosing since it is a waste of product. How often does this happen?'

Caudevilla was not surprised at the camaraderie within the Silk Road community. 'The fact that there is a considerable freedom of speech doesn't mean that people have to behave in a bad way,' he said. 'The general idea is that people involved with illegal drugs – both dealers and drug users – are evil in nature, people not to be trusted. But Silk Road is an anonymous market based in trust, loyalty and confidence. And it works.'

Caudevilla was frustrated that some of his fellow medical professionals refused to provide information to drug users from a risk reduction perspective and recommended only abstinence, a tactic that rarely worked. He attributed this traditional approach largely to former US president Richard Nixon's 'war on drugs'. 'The war on drugs has been a disaster for public health and human rights,' he said. 'Prohibition has not succeeded in its objective to make drugs unavailable and has produced terrible consequences at all levels – political, economic, social and medical. I hope we will see soon significant changes, as the actual situation is a huge failure. The question is not if prohibition will continue or not, but when and how [to] shut down this big monster.'

DoctorX was particularly scathing about the new 'legal highs' that started flooding the market in 2012 and 2013, believing them to be significantly more dangerous than the drugs they purported to mimic. They were manufactured to imitate the effects of the most popular recreational drugs – marijuana, ecstasy, LSD and cocaine – while circumventing laws prohibiting the original drugs' use.

'They are extremely dangerous and unsafe,' said Caudevilla. 'Let's take the example of cannabis. Cannabis has coexisted with humankind during the last 7000 years. We know absolutely everything about its possible risks and problems. Same with LSD, cocaine or MDMA that have been widely studied in humans during decades. If someone takes cannabis we can predict or estimate what kind of problems can appear. But most of the synthetic cannabinoids have been designed in the last decade and have not been proved in humans. There is a lack of experience about their risks and people using them are behaving as guinea pigs. Lack of reliable information means that some people are using 25-I-NBOMe, a new psychedelic with no studies on humans and responsible for some deaths.'

This example of the more problematic 'new' drugs to hit the market, 25-I-NBOMe (25i), had become much reported in the media. Designed to impersonate the effects of LSD, it was sometimes sold to unsuspecting users as acid but could become toxic at higher levels in a way that LSD did not, resulting in overdoses or other unexpected consequences.

Online drug dealing was a full-time job for many of the vendors on Silk Road. Drug users can be highly suspicious of anyone nosing around asking questions, and researchers can face the sort of overt hostility usually reserved for journalists. Caudevilla, however, was one of the elite who amassed huge 'positive karma' without receiving a single hit of 'negative karma' – something not even Dread Pirate Roberts could lay claim to. DoctorX reached almost rock-star status on the forums, with anonymous drug users around the world singing his praises.

Although he never sought out the participation of drug experts such as Barratt and Caudevilla, and rarely communicated privately with them, Dread Pirate Roberts was aware of their presence and appreciated their input. 'These professionals are an asset to us and I am grateful for them,' he wrote. 'It's remarkable how people are willing to step up when they see a need. I think the desire to contribute to others is a basic motivation for many people, myself included.'

One member, who had weaned himself off heroin, credited DoctorX with 'literally' saving his life:

After several years using heroine [sic], last August I decided quitting. It has been very hard. If you live in an Eastern European country as I do you cannot expect too much help from doctors. They do not see drug addicts as ill persons or people who need help, but scum, shit and vicious people. So when I first felt that abstinence symptoms lasted more than usual I went to my doctor but he did not even listen to me and say, without doing any exam, that it was normal.

Then I asked here, in the Drug Safety forum to good DoctorX and he told me that, with no doubts, my symptoms were not related to abstinence. He suspected a disease in blood and insisted that I should have blood tests. He even PM me to insist and discuss on the issue and explained me how to proceed if my doctor does not want to make blood tests.

Today I have my results. I have leukemia. The doctor who made exams was not the usual, she was kind and told me that the stage is not very advanced and, probably, with treatment will work. But it seems aggresive [sic] and she told me that if I had waited more things would be very worse.

So I want to express my infinite gratitude to this good man, DoctorX, who has behaved as a real doctor, providing help and information. Thank you very much, you will be always in my heart.

DoctorX provided a bitcoin address in his forum signature, inviting donations from anyone who thought his work was worthwhile. Several donations came in, including some that were particularly healthy – certainly worth more than a few consultations. It was impossible to tell where the donations came from, and they could not be returned. But it would not be surprising to learn that they came from Dread Pirate Roberts, who made no secret that he believed the doctor to be an asset to his little empire.

You've been hacked, really hacked for the first time ever and I'm sorry but you just don't seem concerned enough for me. Apart from Leo [law enforcement] closing you down this is as bad as things can get.

− Silk Road vendor's message to Dread Pirate Roberts,
December 2012

Turbulence

By late 2012, Silk Road had become, if not a household name, fairly common knowledge. Articles would pop up online from time to time – usually in specialist IT magazines or on edgier non-mainstream sites – and the site's membership grew exponentially as more people took the plunge and risked an order.

As membership grew, the servers strained under the enormous amount of traffic and Silk Road became the target of malicious hackers and, some suspected, law enforcement attempting to bring the website down. It wasn't difficult to imagine what law enforcement thought of the technologies that allowed black markets to thrive openly and in defiance of politicians, police and outraged talkback callers. Tor, PGP and bitcoin had made their lives very difficult. When whistleblower Edward Snowden released his barrage of documents in 2013, purportedly among them was a top-secret National Security Agency (NSA) presentation from June 2012 about Tor. The leaked document described the ways in which

NSA had been frustrated by Tor and the agency's acknowledgment that Tor was really quite secure. One of the slides emphatically stated 'Tor Stinks', which is funny when you think that Tor was developed and funded by the US military. The presentation stated that, using manual analysis, it was possible to de-anonymise a 'very small fraction' of Tor users, but it was not possible to locate a suspect on demand. 'We will never be able to de-anonymize all Tor users all the time,' the presentation said.

Similarly, a leaked FBI report on bitcoin revealed the frustration law enforcement felt in trying to trace the funds of people and organisations that used the cryptocurrency for nefarious activities.

But the technologies were not impervious to attack. In late 2012 Silk Road seemed to be under sustained assault. In one three-week period, users of the site found themselves unable to log into the site more often than not, and when they could, the site ran so slowly as to be almost unusable. Reports flooded in of timeouts, missing CAPTCHAs (the visual tests that require a user to retype distorted letters to prove they are human and not a computer or bot; the word is an acronym of Completely Automated Public Turing test to tell Computers and Humans Apart) and other difficulties.

Dread Pirate Roberts posted an update titled 'Explosive Growth':

Just want to keep everyone in the loop. We are in uncharted territory in terms of the number of users accessing Silk Road. Most of the time we've been able to keep up with the demand, but we ARE behind the curve right now. Being the largest hidden service ever to exist and having limited options for expanding infrastructure due to the need for security means we may stay behind the curve until we can find a way to accommodate the

192

demand. There are several paths we are currently pursuing and we hope to be back on track very soon. Please be patient and try using the site during off-peak times.

He also posted a message stating that he intended to change his writing style to a more bland approach to beat identification by stylometric techniques, which match different passages of prose to discern whether they are likely to have been written by the same person. After all, as was continuously reinforced by DPR and other security experts on the forums, it was real-world policing combined with human error that would be a Silk Road member's undoing – not the technologies that underpinned the black market.

Things only got worse after that update. A short while after making the 'Explosive Growth' announcement and knowing that the site was experiencing issues, DPR inexplicably 'went away' for twenty-four hours, becoming completely incommunicado even from his administrators. Few people reported being able to log into their accounts at all. It was the longest period of site inaccessibility since Silk Road had closed for maintenance right after the Gawker article. Millions of dollars in bitcoin were tied up in the escrow system as trading halted and neither buyers nor sellers could access their funds or complete orders.

The community had become a little complacent by this time. Surely, if it were possible to shut the site down, the authorities would have done so by now. It seemed that the technologies were holding up and the website could continue to operate flagrantly and with impunity. People had become used to how smoothly it cruised along. If you deposited bitcoin, you could expect it to be available for you to place an order at your leisure, which would turn up and the seller would receive his funds, hedged against inflation, as soon as the satisfied buyer released them and provided glowing feedback. It was easy to forget that you were actually shopping for illicit substances.

So when the site suddenly became unavailable, and updates from administration unsatisfactory, Silk Road users started to panic. The reactions of the community ran the gamut from hopeful acceptance to threats of violence against Dread Pirate Roberts, administration and other random anonymous people.

Upon his return from his hiatus, Dread Pirate Roberts went into damage control, posting on 12 November:

Hello everyone,

I'm alive, I'm safe. Luck would have it that the first time I'm away for more than 24 hours, the site goes down and I'm the only one that can bring it back up. As soon as we are sure there haven't been any security breaches and taken all of the necessary precautions, we will get back up and running. If anyone's orders get messed up because of this (auto-finalizing, etc), we will take full responsibility and make things right, just contact support once we're back up. I'm terribly sorry for this and all of the recent problems. I promise it is my top priority to get things running smoothly again.

Despite assurances by moderators and staff that the site was simply experiencing technical issues that needed to be sorted out and stability and security tested before the site could be made available to members again, all sorts of theories started cropping up.

Some were simple: the devastating Hurricane Sandy, for example, had left a path of obliteration in its wake and users pointed out that the aftermath could be to blame. This was pure speculation, as there was no evidence that the Silk Road server was anywhere in the hurricane's path; in fact, it was doubtful it was even in North America.

Infiltration by law enforcement was a major theory. Some users panicked, thinking the authorities had finally cracked Silk Road and were busy setting up a massive honeypot. After all, Silk Road had become a high-profile problem, making a mockery out of politicians and law enforcement as it not only operated but flourished quite openly. Merely closing down the site would not be enough to satisfy the blood lust of the conservatives: they would want arrests – preferably worldwide arrests and hyperbolic announcements claiming it was a battle win in the war on drugs.

In mid-2012, a law enforcement discussion paper had been circulated and reported on by some technical websites, which flagged the law enforcement strategy users were now speculating about. In particular, the report had suggested a tactic of undermining user trust and the reputation of the market, the forums or specific members. The paper recommended that law enforcement officers become active on the site, establishing themselves as respected participants and 'later undermining confidence and trust in a particular area'. As panic intensified, someone took advantage of the chaos by making several posts on 14 November with topic names like 'DPR has been caught by NZ police. See pictures here.' The links within contained Trojan horse malicious malware. Naturally, the main suspect was law enforcement.

The law enforcement infiltration brigade believed that either the server or Dread Pirate Roberts had been compromised and a sting was underway to gather intelligence for worldwide arrests.

They noted that the accounts of some administrators had been disabled without notification. And, they reported, new vendors had mysteriously popped up during the blackout. How had they had access when nobody else had?

Others were sceptical of this theory for the downtime. While $22 million per year (the figure reached by Nicolas Christin) might seem like a lot, in the context of the worldwide illicit drug trade, which amounted to hundreds of billions of dollars, it was minuscule. What's more, the $22 million was spread across thousands of vendors in dozens of countries. Silk Road was operating peacefully and could be argued to be working to reduce drug-related crime by cutting out many of the criminal middlemen usually involved in getting drugs to an end user (though clearly not cutting out the crimes committed at the top of the drug chain by the cartels who produced them). The chance of any law enforcement agency having the resources to commit to such a sting, especially a cross-border sting, seemed remote. And even if they infiltrated the Road, any vendor practising basic safety precautions would not be at risk of identification.

For the first time another theory started to circulate: what would prevent the site's owner, Dread Pirate Roberts, from simply walking away, taking all the money in the accounts with him? The bitcoin sitting in the tens of thousands of users' accounts at any one time, as well as all that tied up in escrow, would certainly be in the tens, if not hundreds, of millions of dollars.

Despite the growing complacency, nobody had really thought that Silk Road could last forever. Users now had evidence that DPR had earned millions of dollars over the past year and could probably retire quite comfortably – especially if, on top of his commissions, he had access to all the money sitting in escrow and vendors' and buyers' accounts. If he had not been cashing out, the bitcoin he had earned in the early days would have increased in value tenfold from the time of the site's launch.

What if the Pirate had been inspired by the success of Tony76's mega scam? How tempting would it be to simply walk away with millions of dollars from people who were unlikely to report the theft to the police? After all, the Dread Pirate Roberts of *The Princess Bride* scarpered once he had enough loot to retire on. Doing so would run counter to all of the philosophies Dread Pirate Roberts had espoused, but that could simply be a cover, too.

If this theory were true, there would be the problem of converting all that bitcoin into currency that could be used in the real world. Cashing out that sort of money would not only be extremely difficult without alerting the authorities but, as Silk Road accounted for the single largest wallet in the blockchain at the time, dumping the coins would cause the value of the bitcoin to nosedive.

In any event, Silk Road provided semi-regular updates to the membership about the blackout, and when the site was restored for a short time, several vendors reported being able to withdraw from their accounts. So the idea that Dread Pirate Roberts had robbed everyone seemed unlikely.

Another theory that had a ring of plausibility was that Dread Pirate Roberts had sold Silk Road as a going concern and the downtime was due to issues with migrating the server. Silk Road was a valuable asset with no real competition and there would be no shortage of buyers for the infrastructure and goodwill. The name chosen by the site's owner – Dread Pirate Roberts – suggested that he had the intention of passing on the mantle at some point. This could also account for his recent declaration saying he was sorry for sounding different but 'It's safer to make my writing style bland so it is less identifiable'.

It could take months or years before anyone realised such a sale had happened, so nobody – neither ripped-off site users nor law enforcement – would be looking for the fugitive. But making such a sale would invariably require some real-life dealings, which would be fraught with danger. Why would anyone take such a risk to get rid of something so profitable?

In the end, a more banal theory emerged triumphant: that a hacker had attacked Silk Road. Dread Pirate Roberts later claimed this was the case, but he had fixed the problem. That should have been the end of it. He wrote a lengthy missive on 18 November thanking those who had stood by him and apologising to those who thought he had betrayed them. He finished with:

Especially you old hats that have been around since the beginning, but this goes for everyone, you all are like family to me.

Sure we have some crazy cousins floating around, but they just add character, right? Doesn't matter though, I love you all. Of all the people in the world, you are the ones who are here, in the early stages of this revolution. You are the ones getting this thing off the ground and driving it forward. It is a privilege to have you by my side. Thank you for your trust, faith, camaraderie and love.

But it wasn't the end of it. The problems kept on coming, one on top of the other.

The Silk Road forums had been under attack from a scammer spammer for some time. Hundreds of posts per day filled the forums with repetitive, too-good-to-be-true offers of bitcoin exchange. A number of 'spam busters' were appointed – forum moderators with the limited power of deleting useless posts. But when the strange blackout of November occurred, all moderators and administrators were unexpectedly stripped of their powers. No explanation was given other than that the spam was under control so their services were no longer required. Only this wasn't exactly true, as the spam kept ramping up.

Amazingly, some people fell for the scammer's con despite the spam looking and sounding like it was straight from a Nigerian scammer's playbook. Those people lost their money and some blamed Silk Road's administration for not doing enough to stop the spammer. In an attempt to combat the spam, Silk Road implemented a 'Newbies Forum'. Members with fewer than fifty posts were restricted to posting in that forum, much to their chagrin. This had some effect on slowing down the spammer, but it still managed to spam its way out of the Newbies Forum several times.

A more successful ongoing scam involved someone changing the URL for Silk Road in the Wikipedia entry. It looked enough like the real site address to fool many people. Entering that URL into the Tor browser brought the user to a login page that looked just like Silk Road's except that it requested the user's PIN (which the legitimate site did not require) as well as their password. The PIN was only required when a user wanted to withdraw bitcoin from the site rather than use it to make a purchase. This scam was a classic example of a phishing trick. 'Phishing' is the act of fraudulently enticing people to enter details into a fake website, thus revealing personal information such as usernames, passwords, credit card details or PINs. Because dark web URLs are difficult to remember, and because anyone can edit a Wikipedia page, it was a simple matter for fraudsters to change the address to one that had a look and feel almost identical to the legitimate Silk Road site. When users entered their details, these were captured by the scammers, who could then use them to log into the real Silk Road. Users who fell for the scam had their passwords changed and their accounts cleared out. Several members claimed to have lost thousands of dollars worth of bitcoin.

One who was caught by this scam was Blake of Aussie-DomesticDrugs, when he was first setting up shop. He lost control of his account and the $500 he had deposited to pay for a vendor account. 'It was a rookie mistake but I'd learned my lesson and I was much more careful from that point on,' he said.

Wikipedia combated the phishing attack by blacklisting all dark-web (i.e. .onion) URLs except for those specifically whitelisted (allowed), such as the Silk Road address. This prevented anyone from being able to replace the Silk Road URL with another. The Hidden Wiki, however, continued to be a source of phishing links. Silk Road warned all visitors to the forums that clicking on the URL provided by the Hidden Wiki would almost certainly result in their accounts being ransacked.

The attacks didn't stop. In December 2012 hackers placed an image on vendors' product listings claiming it was a 'Silk Road Quickbuy' button. It had a fake bitcoin address for payment. They also disabled shipping options so that buyers could no longer make purchases in the usual way and were forced to copy and paste the fake 'Quickbuy' address.

Apparently only a few members were caught by this scam as it was a poorly executed image and the fake bitcoin address needed to be manually cut and pasted rather than simply clicked on. The vulnerability was patched within twenty-four hours. However, the administrators of the site were unable to fix the hacked images.

On 19 December, Dread Pirate Roberts wrote:

The issue has been resolved. The hole that lead [sic] to the hacker gaining access to other vendors' images and postage options has been plugged. I've sent a message to all vendors asking them to update their images and postage options if their listings were affected, so hopefully the listings will be back to normal soon. I've turned off incognito mode on all accounts, so if you were using incognito browsing before, you'll need to re-enable it on your setting page.

The message that was sent to vendors was:

Dear xxxxxxxxxx,
This is an automated message to all sellers at Silk Road:
Many of your listings were recently altered without your consent. Postage options were deleted, and images were changed. We've corrected the problem that allowed this to happen, but we cannot restore your listings to their former state. Please take a look at your current listings and be sure to add back in any missing postage options, and update any altered images.
Best regards,
Silk Road Vendor Support

Neither vendors nor buyers were very happy, one vendor saying: 'You've been hacked, really hacked for the first time ever and I'm sorry but you just don't seem concerned enough for me. Apart from Leo [law enforcement] closing you down this is as bad as things can get.'

People also noticed that nearly all of the forum moderators were gone. One of these, Guru, was among the most respected and loved moderators to have graced the site. He was not a drug user, but believed in the philosophies of Silk Road. But he was suddenly demoted without warning or explanation, as were at least two other moderators.

Another member confirmed that Guru had been demoted without any warning or reason given. To that member Guru wrote:

I'm leaving and not coming back. Why? Well, there has been a LOT of weird shit going on around here over the last little while, with moderators being stripped of their positions, without so much as a by-your-leave. I wrote DPR asking about this, trying to get some clarification as to what the hell is going on, and I never received even so much as an acknowledgement. Now this has happened to me.

Nomad_Bloodbath was a Global Moderator on here; he literally was with SR since Day 1, and he was stripped of his position. He claims it was due to a 'hacker' who had it in for him. I don't know how one could ever verify that, but there has been some weirdness over the last while, and just in the last 24h or so, someone asked if the hidden moderators could take care of a problem – a vendor had posted an image with his GPS coordinates in it.

You could use Google Maps and be looking at the guy's front door. I did what I could to fix this, and within a few hours of that, I essentially find myself booted as a moderator. No rhyme, no reason, no notice.

I won't lie to you . . . I've lost count of the hours I've spent helping people on here over the last 7 months or so, and being treated like this is just a slap in the face.

Frankly, I don't need this shit, and I've made up my mind to leave and not come back.

Thank you again for your kindness.

Guru

Many members were unhappy with the secret-squirrel changing of the guard. 'This place has not been the same since the big November debacle – weird shit IS going on,' said one, echoing the sentiments of many.

Security expert Pine pointed to the fiasco that was movie night. Dread Pirate Roberts had directed interested members to all watch *V for Vendetta* at the same time and discuss it in the Book Club forum. He had even provided a link to a torrent to download the movie – something immediately decried by the security-conscious membership as an appalling lack of judgment.

'My new tinfoil hat theory is that the "Dread Pirate Roberts" theory is correct and what's actually going on, we're witnessing a change of control,' said one member. The theory of Dread Pirate Roberts living up to his name was gaining traction.

But after several weeks of turbulence, the site returned to normal and DPR assured everybody that they had nothing to worry about, security hadn't been compromised and everything could be explained by a DDoS attack by a competitor. He didn't elaborate on which competitor he thought it was.

It was the online equivalent of a drug cartel war. Instead of guns and machetes, the competitors were attacking each other with technology. And it seemed to be working.

Everyone take some time to appreciate that instead of giant Cartel gang wars, SR has managed to reduce drug conflict into nerds sending virtual 'fuck you's' through the internet.

— Silk Road user 'Tabit', post on the Silk Road forums

A Blip

In December 2012, drug dealer Nob, who had been chatting to Dread Pirate Roberts quietly for months, began to complain to him about the small-time nature of most deals on Silk Road. 'It really isn't worth it for me to do below ten kilos,' he wrote in a private message exchange between the two drug barons.

The vast majority of deals on Silk Road were between dealer/ manufacturer and end user. That is, they were for personal amounts of a gram or two, though some dealers sold in bulk to smaller dealers to pass on to end users. But ten kilos of cocaine or heroin was well beyond the size of any deal usually made on the Silk Road website.

For reasons known only to him, Dread Pirate Roberts offered to help Nob find a buyer who would be willing to purchase such massive quantities of drugs. He suggested the services of one of his most trusted administrators, Chronicpain, to speak to the top dealers on the site on Nob's behalf. Chronicpain duly began canvassing interest from those who had the capacity to deal in kilograms, eventually securing the interest of vendor Googleyed1.

'Hey,' DPR wrote to Nob, 'I think we have a buyer for you. One of my staff is sending the details.'

Chronicpain acted as a go-between between Nob and Googleyed1, and by mid-January 2013 had brokered a deal for a kilogram of cocaine. He duly reported this to his boss, Dread Pirate Roberts, who was enthusiastic. 'Congrats on sale!' he wrote to his friend Nob.

Nob wasn't keen on using the US postal service to ship the cocaine, though. 'I'm sending my goons instead, ok?' he said.

Nob's goons delivered the cocaine but, unbeknown to Dread Pirate Roberts, Chronicpain had decided to act as an intermediary, taking delivery on behalf of Googleyed1 at his own house. Upon receiving confirmation of the delivery, Googleyed1 sent Nob approximately $27,000 worth of bitcoin. Everyone was happy. It was perhaps the largest single transaction made through Silk Road to that time.

A week later, Dread Pirate Roberts had word that Chronicpain had been busted on drugs charges. He turned on his computer and wrote to Nob. He trusted Nob now. Maybe Nob had an idea of what to do about it.

Assuming great success for Silk Road, how easily could it become another bloodthirsty cartel seeking profit at all costs? We must maintain our integrity and be true to our principles, the opportunity to make a lasting difference is too great not to.
— Dread Pirate Roberts forum post, October 2012

Silk Road Arrests

'**M**ost people who are caught are done in through the same basic mistakes: trusting the wrong people, having drugs in their house or in their car or having incriminating things in their possession that suggest they are dealing, like text messages or other records,' Blake of AussieDomesticDrugs had written. Nowhere did this become more apparent than in the story of Paul Leslie Howard, the first Australian Silk Road bust.

Howard was an Australian drug dealer who registered on Silk Road on 20 April 2012 under the username 'Shadh1'. He sold pills, MDMA, LSD, marijuana, crystal meth, DMT and speed to Australian customers both on Silk Road and in real life. He was a low-level dealer, supplementing his job as a nightclub bouncer by selling pills and coke to his clientele and friends. Unfortunately, he wasn't very good at one of the most important factors of his job: staying off the radar of law enforcement authorities.

Shadh1 failed miserably at the whole stealth thing. He allowed customers to pass on his phone number – not a burner phone but his regular-use phone – to complete strangers for the purposes of ordering drugs, and he kept every single incriminating text message ever sent or received. He left all the paraphernalia that screams 'drug dealer' strewn around his house. He created a vendor account on Silk Road with an unusual username – the only other place it could be found was on his BMW's numberplate.

Shadh1 used the proven method of ordering drugs in substantial quantities from overseas – especially the Netherlands – then marking them up to Australian-level prices and reselling them. He used the cunning strategy of having everything sent to his own home and in his own name. When twelve pieces of mail went missing, he just kept ordering more – to the same name and the same address – without stopping to wonder what had happened to the ones that never showed.

So it wasn't altogether surprising that he got busted a few months into his new career. Those twelve missing pieces of mail weren't due to scamming black-market sellers, but interceptions by the police after customs discovered the first one. Of the twelve items seized by Sydney and Melbourne customs, ten came from the Netherlands and two came from Germany. The substances inside were packaged in a variety of ways – within greeting cards or DVD cases, in baggies (small plastic bags commonly used to store drugs for sale) flattened inside cardboard, and inside a thermometer.

Shadh1 was the poster child for the notion that it would be human error, rather than failures in technologies, that would lead to the arrest of a Silk Road user.

On 18 July 2012, the Australian Federal Police raided Howard's home, finding close to a kilo of marijuana, envelopes from Canada and the Netherlands that had made it through despite his address having been flagged, a variety of drugs including DMT, $2300 in cash, a money-counting machine, scales and baggies, and what appeared to be an order book with the names and purchase details of his customers.

The police also seized three computers and two phones. The phones contained thousands of messages from apparent customers requesting goods, and messages from Howard such as 'I've got 5 grand worth if you want it', 'promote the LSD' and 'I'm at the mercy of Australia Post'. The computer housed pictures of drugs sitting on a piece of paper saying 'Shadh1', kept in a Dropbox folder called 'SR'. These matched the photographs advertising his wares on Silk Road. His Google search history included 'Does Australia Post record tracking' and 'Silk Road Tor address'.

Caught red-handed with overwhelming evidence, Howard showed police how Silk Road worked and provided access to his account, registered in the name Shadh1.

Howard's arrest was reported in the news as the first Australian 'Silk Road bust' but with few details. The website's forums became abuzz with speculation as to which of their members it was who had been arrested, as Howard's Silk Road username hadn't been reported. They soon deduced who it was and dissected his prior postings. His customers feared their own security had been compromised and were urged to 'clean house' to rid themselves of drugs and any other incriminating items.

At his committal hearing in early 2013, Howard pleaded guilty to two charges of importing a marketable quantity of a controlled substance (MDMA and cocaine in a total of eleven packages) and one charge of trafficking (encompassing MDMA, cocaine, LSD, speed, ice and weed). The hearing lasted only a few minutes and he was set free until his sentencing hearing in the County Court in the first week of February 2013.

A few months after Howard's arrest, in September and October 2012, local police started Operation Cinder after two brothers aged fifteen and seventeen from the small town of Esperance in Western Australia were hit with possession and importation charges when their parents turned them in after intercepting their mail. Operation Cinder resulted in the interception of over thirty packages containing cannabis, crystal meth, cocaine, LSD and ecstasy.

The teenagers were subsequently jailed for eight months and twelve months respectively and a 26-year-old man, who was charged with five counts of Attempt to Possess a Prohibited Drug, was fined $1000 over the drugs seizure. In a town as small as Esperance, it was easy for postal workers to spot an unusual pattern of mail.

The sentencing hearing is where a judge hears the prosecution's case and the defence's case and decides on the appropriate punishment for the defendant. As well as the charges of importation of marketable quantities of MDMA and cocaine, and trafficking of cocaine, MDMA, LSD, marijuana, methamphetamine and speed, Howard was charged with the possession of thirty-two prohibited weapons, which turned out to be stun guns.

The court heard evidence of twelve parcels containing drugs that had been intercepted between 27 March and 29 June 2012. In his opening, the defence barrister said he would be tendering a news article into evidence that he claimed led his client to discover Silk Road.

The prosecution tendered all of Shadh1's posts to the Silk Road forums in evidence. His account had been registered on 20 April 2012, the day of the Great 420 Sale and Giveaway. He had started a thread called 'New Aus vendor, thought i'd say HI' on that day:

Hey guys, I'm just starting out here. I'm Aus based and only shipping to Aus so as not to roach on anyone's turf :). I'll be basically doing dutch speed and peruvian charlie to start and branch into more as I get coin back in my pocket. I source from both sr and non sr vendors but I prefer the sr system as far as selling securely is concerned! So yeh that's me story and I'm keen for any tips or just some chat from you guys as I'm still learning!

One by one, Shadh1's dozen or so forum posts were read out in court, further incriminating Howard, who had admitted to police that he posted under that username on Silk Road. For example, he vouched for a vendor from the Netherlands from whom he bought in bulk:

Ive bought off aakoven in the past and its always been good, albeit sometimes a little underweight but ive received 5–50 g lots off him so far and just awaiting the 6th.

213

The implication in this message was that Howard had imported 250 grams of MDMA from this vendor alone (and was waiting on the next 50 grams): considerably more than what he was charged with, which was a 'marketable quantity' of a little under 50 grams.

After the recess, events took a turn for the surreal. The defence barrister tendered the article he had flagged earlier, with a 'mitigating circumstances' argument along the lines of (paraphrased): 'My client was down to his last cent and his marriage was on the rocks. He found this article describing how to get on to Silk Road and how cheap drugs could be bought there. He followed the instructions and was overcome by the temptation of the smorgasbord of cheap drugs available to him.'

'The author of the article is in court today, Your Honour,' defence counsel said, pointing towards the back of the courtroom, where I was sitting.

The judge peered where he had indicated, then back at the article before him. 'Her website is called "All Things Vice"?'

There were some snickers of agreement.

'Is she under a code of conduct?'

'She also writes for *The Age*, Your Honour.'

His Honour nodded. As he skim-read he muttered things like 'Extraordinary'.

Paul Howard was convicted of all crimes other than the possession of the thirty-five stun guns, which the defence argued were for the personal safety of his wife. It seemed unlikely that the court really bought this explanation, but the prosecution also mentioned that they were cheap imports from China, most of which didn't work anyway, and didn't seem overly concerned with pressing to prosecute.

Much to the shock of his family, Howard received a sentence of two and a half years on the 'importing a marketable quantity' charges, and eighteen months on the trafficking charge (to begin when the importing sentence had six months to go), for a total of three and a half years (non-parole period of one year nine months).

This seemed harsh, especially the sentence for buying the drugs, which was more than the sentence for selling them. It smacked of there being an example made of the 'first Silk Road case'.

The next day, an article appeared in *The Age* recounting the events of the hearing. The reporter mentioned that the article tendered – the one by me that purportedly had led Shadh1 into the temptation of dealing drugs – had been published in October, a good six months after he had registered his account on Silk Road.

The piece was picked up on the wires, and the myth that my article was somehow responsible for the defendant's decision to deal drugs was perpetuated over Twitter, Reddit, Wired, Ars Technica and numerous blogs, forums and lesser-known websites. The bizarre thing was that it was simply not possible that my piece had led Howard to Silk Road. The typical paragraph went:

> During the trial he said that he had been drawn to the site after reading an article by a journalist called Eileen Ormsby, who regularly covers the Silk Road in Australian newspapers. Since Howard's conviction, the Silk Road has warned its users via its Twitter account not to follow their feed nor the feed of Ormsby with their real names.

No doubt the defendant was led to Silk Road by an article, but it wasn't the article tendered. And when the reasons for sentencing were published several months later, the judge didn't even mention my article.

After Howard's conviction, the Australian Federal Police released a statement promising there would be a crackdown on Australian Silk Road users, but few arrests directly related to the website followed in the next year or so. Six people were reportedly arrested in March 2013 after an AFP operation targeting Silk Road users, but no further details were supplied.

One thing was clear: any 'Silk Road arrests' made in Australia were not the result of cybercrime officials cracking Tor or tracing bitcoin transactions. They were simply the result of dumb crooks being dumb. As law enforcement reports had stated, anonymity and encryption were strengthening. Their best bet was to exploit human error rather than try to tackle the technicalities of hidden services.

Scammers, Cheats and Scoundrels

It may by now sound like Silk Road was a utopia filled with kind, peace-loving souls. But the truth was that the website was never short of scammers, cheats and scoundrels.

The feedback and escrow system could only go so far to protect those who used the website, and there were always some who were keen to figure out an even easier way to make a buck. Silk Road would try to deal with scammers, but often kept the scams a secret from its customers: scammers were bad for business.

Most scams were small-time, nabbing a few unwary newbies and the perpetrators disappearing soon after. An example of this was a simple lottery scam (vendors often ran lotteries, as lottery 'tickets' could be bought cheaply and could bump up the number of sales for a seller, ensuring them higher search rankings). Some vendors would run a lottery and would not pay the winner, whilst retaining the losers' funds. Complaints to Silk Road went unheeded with SR Support responding to complainants: 'We don't provide support for lotteries'. Some scams were carried out by vendors who claimed to have sent goods they never had, and then recovered at least 50 per cent of the funds in escrow through the dispute resolution system. This worked especially well for vendors with otherwise excellent statistics, who could selectively scam newcomers. The verified vendor would inevitably win over the newbie who had no stats. Buyers similarly scammed vendors by claiming no-shows and demanding a resend. Others would hold newer sellers to ransom by threatening them with bad feedback, which could cripple the ranking of a seller with few sales.

In the Vendors' Roundtable, moderator Nomad Bloodbath started a thread called 'The Elephant in the Room'. He said, 'It seems to me that the scammer(s) are taking money out of reputable vendors pockets and i'm tired of it in particular one very annoying one that keeps popping up every 3 weeks. Makes 8–13k and gets banned.'

The general membership were never told of this scammer, who was apparently making a tidy sum by offering to exchange money-paks (reloadable prepaid debit cards) for bitcoin in deals that never eventuated.

'Scammers have absolutely ZERO repercussion on this website,' agreed vendor 'dankology'. 'Which is why one keeps coming back over and over.'

Dankology (who, incidentally, was arrested and jailed in 2012 on charges unrelated to Silk Road, and subsequently gave up vending online) was all for exposing the scamming buyers' personal details in the main forums, but others thought this was a bad idea. 'I love the idea of this in a perfect world . . . but it simply is too over the top,' he was told. 'LEO would be on him like fleas on a dog . . . and what's to prevent people from forming fake scam reports just to SWAT a member they dislike?'

The vendors were right to be concerned about scamming members of the community, as they were always present. Many followed tried and tested methods with slight variations to catch new or naive members.

The most famous scam in Silk Road's history had been pulled off by Tony76 during the Great 420 Sale and Giveaway in April 2012. The idea that he'd stolen $250,000 had seemed fanciful at the time, but by the time users discovered the sort of money that was being passed through Silk Road, it was not so unbelievable after all.

After that, as if to prove that drug users have short memories, history repeated itself with a member going by the name of 'Lucydrop' in 2013. Following a remarkably similar pattern to Tony76, Lucydrop offered North American customers high-quality LSD at reasonable prices, provided excellent customer service, freebies and extras when things went wrong, and built up a reputation. Lucy received glowing reports from the Avengers, the self-styled LSD-testing group on Silk Road. You can guess the rest: one day, Lucydrop disappeared with around $100,000 of users' money.

During the post-mortem of the event, some users pointed out similarities between the writing styles of Lucydrop and Tony76 – odd capitalisations, overuse of ellipses, certain turns of phrase. Many believed that Tony76 had simply waited a while and then pulled the exact same scam all over again. He had the infrastructure, he had the know-how and he had the six-figure incentive.

But there was a new twist to this scam. A little while after Lucydrop disappeared with the money, a new member posted to the Silk Road forums. 'RealLucyDrop' claimed that his partner had taken advantage of him being in prison, taken over his account and ripped off his customers. They wrote a warning in the forums:

DO NOT BUY FROM LUCYDROP ON SR

I can't talk about specifics for security reasons, but I was in jail for more than 2 months but less than 7. I got released very recently. LucyDrop on SilkRoad is NOT ME. DO NOT BUY FROM THAT ACCOUNT. My partner completely fucked me over. I went to our spot . . . there is nothing there and he won't answer my phone calls. He took the work computer and everything else. He took my entire savings with him that was being used to keep supply up. He took my entire life.

RealLucyDrop desperately wanted to get in touch with Dread Pirate Roberts.

'I need to get the Lucydrop account shut down immediately and freeze all the funds in the account,' RealLucyDrop wrote. He eventually claimed to have sorted things out with DPR, but no official announcement was ever made and the customers remained out of pocket.

Unbeknown to the Silk Road users at the time, RealLucyDrop's story had credibility. Someone calling himself 'FriendlyChemist' had contacted Dread Pirate Roberts and was threatening the security of Silk Road and its most loyal customers. FriendlyChemist told Roberts he had a long list of real names and addresses of Silk Road vendors and customers that he had obtained from hacking into the computer of another major Silk Road vendor. '[W]hat do u . . . think will happen if thousands of usernames, order amounts, addresses get leaked?' demanded the not-so-friendly vendor. '[A]ll those people will leave sr and be scared to use it again. those vendors will all be busted and all there [sic] customers will be exposed too and never go back to sr.'

The threats were accompanied by a sample of the information FriendlyChemist intended to leak unless DPR paid him $500,000, an amount FriendlyChemist said he owed to his suppliers. As proof that he had obtained the data from the vendor whose computer he claimed to have hacked, FriendlyChemist supplied the vendor's username and password on Silk Road. He was the rogue 'partner' RealLucyDrop claimed had hijacked his account. RealLucyDrop's story had credibility.

Dread Pirate Roberts was convinced that the threat was real. 'Being blackmailed with user info,' he wrote in his journal on 28 March 2013.

Australia had its very own Tony76 with a user by the name of 'EnterTheMatrix'. Aussie vendor EnterTheMatrix, or ETM as they became known, was one of the earlier sellers on Silk Road. In September 2011 they wrote: 'We have an associate in Australia who deals with our orders there, we also have a runner in Thailand and we are expanding at a moderate pace to other locations. We have a 100 per cent satisfaction 5 out [of] 5 rating and with over 49 transactions, we are proud of this!'

Six months and hundreds of cheerful, helpful posts later, they had become one of the most admired forum members, as well as one of the most popular Australian sellers. They were just one of the gang. 'Thanks to all the new and old customers ordering during this AMAZING weekend sale!' they gushed. 'We are so happy to serve the Australian community and hope everyone had a great weekend. :)'

ETM's business model was the same as other Australian vendors. Purchase Australia's most popular party drugs from overseas vendors on Silk Road, add a 300–400 per cent mark-up and resell them to Aussie Silk Road customers. Although there were plenty of grumbles about the prices, those who wanted their drugs quickly (ETM sent by Express Post) and did not want to take the risk of importing via customs begrudgingly paid a premium. After all, it was around the same as street prices, and at least the quality of the goods tended to be consistently high.

The public face of EnterTheMatrix – the person who posted on the forums – was always cheerful and helpful. ETM was a master of self-promotion, building up the business over more than a year and eventually becoming one of the top 1 per cent of Silk Road sellers with over 99 per cent positive feedback. Despite the high prices, users lavished praise on the service and the quality of the product.

'You are SR's marketing man of the year ETM,' said one of the more visible Australian posters, as ETM advertised yet another special:

******** BLACK KISS MICRODOTS RAFFLE ********
Every purchase of Matrix™ 25i-NBOMe Blotter Tab's will entitle you to FREE ENTRY to the Black Kiss LSD Microdot DOUBLE PACK Raffle! Drawn 10/4/2012
Winner announced in forum.
******** BLACK KISS MICRODOTS RAFFLE ********

'I'm in! Gonna load up about a million BTC this week and fuck myself to pieces next week!!!' was a typical response to their promotions.

Unlike Shadh1, who had been caught with a notebook full of the names and addresses of his best clients, ETM assured customers they took great precautions on their behalf. 'We cannot speak for other vendors however our customers [sic] security is our top priority,' they promised. 'No personal identifying information is kept of previous buyers. In fact, we have weekly regular buyers who must provide their address EVERY time they order with us, because we have no such details of their address or previous orders.'

By February 2013, ETM was easily the most successful and trusted Australian vendor on the Road. That's when they offered a new product. 'Matrix Secrets! Learn from the Top 1% of SR' promised to reveal all the tips and tricks necessary to run a Silk Road business safely and profitably. The price tag – 86 bitcoins, which at the prevailing exchange rate was over $2000 – was too steep for many, but five potential Escobars ponied up with the money.

Then EnterTheMatrix was feeling the love on Valentine's Day and announced a sale, offering tempting discounts on their usual prices for MDMA, LSD and other goodies. Everyone assumed this was in response to a couple of new Aussie vendors who had popped up in recent months, offering similar-quality drugs at slightly lower prices. Orders flooded in for the 'one day only' sale, which was soon pushed out to two, then three days by the generous ETM to loyal customers.

A couple of buyers expressed surprise that ETM told them that the 'small print' of the sale required them to finalise early on the cheap products to keep the cash flow going. 'They could stay in escrow if they wanted, but they would get the product at the regular prices. Knowing they were dealing with the top-rated and most highly respected Australian seller on the Road, most finalised as requested.

By Friday that week there were a few pissed-off customers – the Express Post hadn't arrived and ETM wasn't responding to messages. It was all sounding very familiar to those who had been on the Road for a year or more. The modus operandi was identical to that of Tony76.

Apparently ETM had decided to retire and go out with a bang and wanted everyone to know about it. Just before they disappeared they added an ASCII 'up yours' finger made out of number 5 digits (5555 translates to 'LOL' in Thai) to their seller's page. A little later, a quote appeared: 'The game's out there, and it's play or get played. That simple.' This was a famous quote from the TV series *The Wire*, uttered by the character Omar Little, who was known for double-crossing and outsmarting drug dealers.

Nobody really knew how much money Australian customers lost to ETM before the website pulled their listings, but it was certainly well within the tens of thousands of dollars; it may have reached six figures.

ETM had been such a popular and respected member of the website that it was surprising they had gone rogue. Had they always planned the long con once they had earned enough money, or was it a crime of opportunity? Perhaps the sentence handed down to Paul Howard – Shadh1 – a couple of weeks earlier had spooked them, accelerating their exit. If a judge were willing to sentence such a small-time dealer to three and a half years, what might he do to the person who could boast a year-long ranking of number-one Australian vendor?

Not surprisingly, ETM resisted any attempts to contact them. Not only would law enforcement be very interested in any correspondence, there were many people who had lost money by finalising early who would have liked details of where to find them. Some wanted those behind the scam killed. The usually warm and fuzzy Silk Road was calling for blood.

The beginning of 2013 brought more sinister attacks. Silk Road was a booming commercial enterprise by this time, with tens of thousands of drug listings. There was incentive from rival markets, law enforcement and hackers wanting to make a name for themselves to bring down the site.

Most frightening for many on Silk Road were the threats to supply identifying information of members – known as 'doxing' in the online world. A vendor could threaten to expose the address of a recalcitrant customer online or by sending an anonymous tip to their local law enforcement representatives or post office. A poster could claim to have discovered details of a vendor or their customer base and demand money. Doxing is considered one of the most heinous crimes a person can commit on the dark web – worse than scamming, worse than stealing, worse than death threats. Those who use Tor do so to protect their identity, and anonymity is sacrosanct.

Sometimes a doxing threat on Silk Road was part of a blackmail scheme, but other times the motives were less clear. Such was the case with user 'Infowars', who pounded the forums for two days with repeats of the same post: a list of names and addresses, along with alleged drugs orders delivered to those addresses. Hundreds of posts were made before the user was banned and the forums were taken offline 'for maintenance'.

Infowars was ready for the Silk Road techniques to combat spam and bypassed the site's safeguards within minutes. He or she reposted the personal information in every current thread available, amassing hundreds of posts. Many addresses cropped up several times, with different orders attributed to them. Several of the addresses were in Australia.

The natural assumption was that Infowars was a 'bot' (an automated web robot) of some sort. But then came a post from the offender stating, 'I'm not a bot.' Apparently enjoying the havoc they were wreaking, a few minutes later the spamming dox-bot followed this up with a post saying, 'Maybe a bot.'

Although both times forum administrators were alert and removed the offending posts within twenty minutes or so, forum regulars were naturally concerned. Who would do such a thing? A rogue vendor who retained customer addresses and decided to post them? Were vendors selling their clients' personal information? Was it the result of phishing a seller's account? Was the competition posting it to create fear in the Silk Road community? Law enforcement spreading 'FUD' (fear, uncertainty, doubt)? Or was it just one big hoax?

There was no doubt the addresses were real street addresses. Many were Australian addresses that led to private homes, though at least some of the names used were fictitious. The purported orders were nearly all personal amounts of MDMA, with delivery addresses in the USA, UK and Australia.

One of the addresses that featured several times over was in an upmarket suburb in Melbourne. Several 5-gram MDMA orders had allegedly been made under a variety of names of famous people. One of the false names was that of Andrew Johns, a former National Rugby League captain who had revealed live on TV's *The Footy Show* that he had regularly taken ecstasy during his playing career (it helped him deal with the high level of pressure associated with being an elite sportsman, he explained). Another was that of deceased billionaire Richard Pratt. But even if law enforcement had visited the address, proving anything would be difficult. Such was the demographic of Silk Road's userbase, they could easily question an eighteen-year-old who answered the door, only to discover the ecstasy users were her parents. Or the house could have been used as a drop address for another local who knew that the occupants were always away when the mail arrived.

A random list of names and addresses on a black market's discussion board proved nothing, but it certainly gave people a scare. Nobody whose address had been posted admitted to it in the forums, so nobody was able to verify whether the addresses really were of Silk Road customers.

After wreaking more havoc than any poster had ever done, Infowars disappeared as abruptly as they had appeared. Nobody knew whether they had simply become bored with their game, or whether Dread Pirate Roberts had found a way to deal with them.

In March 2013 a poster named 'Whistleblower' told the forums that the cocaine vendors on Silk Road were forming a cartel of sorts. Whistleblower advised that the cocaine sellers had agreed to fix the price of cocaine at above-market level. Any vendors trying to undercut the cartel prices would be subject to false purchases and negative feedback, ruining their reputation and making them unable to compete.

Leading the pack was vendor 'Nod With The Bitchin Tar', or 'Nod'. 'In my experience we as vendors are pretty competitive,' he said in the Vendors' Roundtable. 'I think this is a bad thing, when we compete all we can do is take one another's business and drive prices down. There's a ton more money to be made cooperating than by competing.'

Most of the cocaine buyers were upset at this revelation and expected the site administration to take a stand against it. They were disappointed by the reaction from Dread Pirate Roberts, who dismissed their concerns and said he would not do anything to stop the vendors from forming cartels:

Cartels are nearly impossible to maintain without the use of violence, especially in an environment as competitive as Silk Road. There is also nothing morally wrong with them. If a cartel were to form I would not attempt to break it up unless its members were breaking other rules. If you want an explanation for why cartels are nearly impossible to maintain in a free market environment, please read *Man, Economy and State*, chapter 10, part 2 section D.

And indeed it seemed Nod's cartel suggestion did not go very far. Nod was later raided by the FBI after being investigated for over a year. They found a kilogram of heroin, 500 grams of methamphetamine and 500 grams of cocaine. The raid had nothing to do with

Silk Road, but authorities discovered the connection during their subsequent investigation.

One of the greatest thorns in Silk Road's side was a figure who went by hundreds of names but was best known as 'Coachella', 'DealerofDrugs' and 'Hallucinating Horse'. As a vendor, Coachella reportedly scammed thousands of dollars out of buyers with a basic FE (finalise early) scam. Unlike the others who had disappeared, leaving members wondering what had happened, Coachella came on to the forum with a belligerent 'fuck you' attitude and told everyone they wouldn't be getting their money.

But that wasn't the end of this character. Coachella seemed to have endless time to harass Silk Road and Dread Pirate Roberts, creating an insane number of new identities and spreading rumours and FUD throughout the forums and on the Silk Road sub-Reddit. He would create stories about scams or busts using an authoritative tone, claiming some sort of insider knowledge. There were always people who took the anonymous rantings at face value, and panic and wild rumours would ensue.

Coachella claimed he had sent SWAT teams to the addresses supplied by buyers who gave him bad reviews. He repeatedly posted the names and details of people whom he claimed were Silk Road moderators or major vendors (the details were of real people, but there was no evidence they were connected to the usernames he claimed). He impersonated successful vendors in the hope of damaging their reputation, and posted from dozens of shill, or sock-puppet, accounts to trash other vendors and agree with himself.

Eventually one Silk Road member got so annoyed with Coachella's antics that he turned himself into an investigative journalist. Using the name 'Raoul Duke', a nod to Hunter S. Thompson, he spent a week delving into Coachella's history, allegedly uncovering his name and address. Coachella, he said, was a child pornographer and habitual scammer. He was also mentally challenged, according to Duke. This did not stop Duke from naming not only the person he thought was Coachella, but also his family members. 'He's a fat, 23-year-old kid in San Antonio Texas with a trashy Mom who had her nursing license taken away for "endangering public health with impaired nursing" and is forbidden to practice nursing in the state of Texas,' he said.

Doxing was not tolerated in any form on Silk Road, even if the information was readily available elsewhere. The Silk Road moderators removed Raoul Duke's posts as quickly as he put them up, but he posted the story on a pastebin (a simple website where anyone can upload blocks of text) and put the links on Reddit and other forums. Debate raged about whether he had done the right thing.

'That's fucked up. Buyers and vendors knew he was going to dox a SR member and did nothing to stop it?' wrote Reddit user 'snoggleberries'. 'Holy shit. It only takes one leak to start sinking a ship. The captain is having enough trouble plugging holes and bailing water. Raoul should be walking the plank.'

'The dipshit has stolen thousands of dollars and fucked over dozens if not hundreds of buyers. There's no shame in outing someone like that,' retaliated 'badgrl2'.

Silk Road responded by banning Raoul Duke and blocking any attempts to post links to the pastebin. No reputable news wire picked up the story. But Coachella stopped trolling the forums.

The anonymity provided by the dark web makes it a hotbed for scams and rip-offs. Silk Road was in no way immune to these scams, and those who tried to nab a bargain outside of escrow were given no sympathy.

It's been over two years and Silk Road is still here. We've had setbacks here and there, but I'm happy to say that mostly we've thrived. Everyone who's taken their security seriously, and many who haven't remain free and prosperous despite the wishes of the powerful law enforcement agencies that target us. It is easy to start feeling confident, invincible, even cocky.

I encourage you to look for this in yourself and refrain from acting on it. A thread was recently started in this forum publishing the personal information of LE agents that users had a particular grudge with. Let me make this abundantly clear:

We are not strong enough to attack our enemies directly!

If we start organizing attacks from this forum against LE agents, it will become exponentially harder to resist their attacks and keep Silk Road alive. This task is hard enough as it is, please don't make it any harder!

– Dread Pirate Roberts, 'Caution against confidence',

5 June 2013

Enter Atlantis

By the beginning of 2013, Silk Road was not the only online black market in town, but it was certainly the market leader. And as happens when one entity is taking all the glory – not to mention the money – someone is going to notice and come in to take some market share for themselves.

A new marketplace calling itself 'Atlantis' did just that in March 2013. It rumbled in, blatantly advertising on the Silk Road forums and recruiting Silk Road's best dealers by offering enticements and deals on seller accounts. Any verified Silk Road vendor became an instant 'Verified Seller' on Atlantis, providing them with the badge of trust that would usually take a minimum of fifty flawless transactions to acquire.

This was the first time an illegal market had been so aggressive with its marketing campaign. Atlantis not only tried to poach Silk Road's customers, but the owners were determined to lure new clientele on to Tor and into the world of online drug dealing.

They set up a presence on the clearweb, advertising their wares and services on Reddit and in cryptocurrency forums. They had a culture of being responsive to member suggestions and requests and were proactive in messaging members about scams. One Silk Road member said, 'The admins over at Atlantis are very flexible, and they have implemented almost all the reasonable suggestions that people have made to the admins here. I think in a year's time the road will either adapt, or die.'

Instead of bitcoin, Atlantis initially accepted only litecoin, a new form of cryptocurrency. It was odd that the site didn't accept bitcoin, which by now had become widely used not only on the black markets but increasingly for legitimate purposes. Small retailers, online stores, activist groups and charities were all hopping on board to accept bitcoin for payment for their goods and services and for donations. The decision to accept only litecoin led to some speculation that Atlantis had a vested interest in the alternative cryptocurrency. One of the founders fuelled that suspicion when they said, 'Litecoin has a much smaller market share than bitcoin, so we needed to do something drastic to bring attention to the currency and to Atlantis as a way of jump starting the community.' But pressure from the drug-using community soon forced Atlantis to accept bitcoin as well, as people were wary enough trying a new market, let alone an untested currency.

Despite the slick marketing to Silk Road's customers through Reddit and the Silk Road forums, their Facebook and Twitter presence, a better customer-response team and a smoother interface than Silk Road, Atlantis struggled to draw customers. The site had no problem attracting vendors, offering a lower commission structure and special treatment for Silk Road's finest, but the buyers did not follow. Making inroads into the black-market share was not coming easy. 'You need to give customers a good reason to move from their existing market,' an Atlantis representative said in an interview. 'We do this in several different ways: usability, security, cheaper rates (for vendor accounts AND commission), website speed, customer support and feedback implementation. Other markets would need to improve on all of these aspects to make an impact. We welcome the challenge.'

The unrelenting marketing push worked against Atlantis to a large extent. People thought it was indicative of a police sting operation to trap and expose Silk Road's largest vendors. Vendors were generally better protected than buyers in online black markets. They didn't need to supply any identifying information at all, while buyers had to at least supply an address at which they would take delivery of the drugs. But the theory was that law enforcement could harvest addresses and other information from those who did not manually encrypt communications. They could work with postal services to triangulate exit points of that particular profile of mail and then use the profile with socially engineered telling details of vendors to bust the major sellers.

Despite keeping a high profile, Atlantis struggled. Then, in mid-March 2013, they started courting journalists, hoping to score stories in a mainstream environment such as Silk Road had been getting without asking. They also wanted to place advertisements on alternative sites, including my blog, All Things Vice – a request that had to be politely declined.

Atlantis made it clear they wanted not only to take market share from Silk Road, but also to bring recreational drug-dealing websites to a mainstream audience. They were the first black-market operator to grant a real-time interview on Cryptocat, a secure (or supposedly secure, as later discovered) web-based chat application.

In the interview, 'Loera' and 'Vladimir' claimed to be two of the founders of Atlantis, all of whom came from different backgrounds – business, IT and drug dealing, though the latter was apparently the least important trait.

'Vladimir and I represent the board,' Loera said. 'We make up a larger group of about five technical team members.'

It was mind-blowing that the operation had a 'board'. How many other drug-dealing businesses could lay claim to a formal business structure? The two spoke like any business owners keen to give a good impression of their company to the media. Loera admitted to never having been involved in the drug trade prior to establishing Atlantis.

The two remained upbeat and positive throughout the interview, insisting they weren't worried about the sluggishness of customer uptake, denying it was even true. 'For a community that has only been live for just over six weeks, with over 10,000 user signups I think we're doing rather impressively,' said Loera, revealing they had taken in $70,000 so far. 'We've already seen some of the top 1 per cent and 2 per cent vendors making a move to cover more ground.'

They also denied trying to poach Silk Road's customers. 'People are attracted to our lower commission rates and our rapid development cycle. We are also the first to offer support for multiple currencies. We began by offering three months commission-free to vendors on the Road to jump-start the community.'

Loera said he thought it natural that people were sceptical, but that the scepticism had started to fade. This didn't really seem to accord with the facts at the time. Everything Atlantis did they got hammered for. For example, having determined that most people didn't bother to learn PGP, Atlantis offered automatic PGP encryption – which security experts said would lull the foolish into a false sense of security. Many users of black markets who simply wanted to buy drugs and not go to the hassle of learning encryption may have been reassured by the claim the site would do it all for them and so they would hand over a plaintext (unencrypted) address or other details.

'We don't force our users to use any of these "convenience" features,' said Loera. 'They're simply there to add a bit of extra functionality to the website for those who wish to use them.'

Atlantis used standard forum software that included, as part of the terms of service:

> The owners of this forum also reserve the right to reveal your identity (or any other related information collected on this service) in the event of a formal complaint or legal action arising from any situation caused by your use of this forum.
>
> Please note that with each post, your IP address is recorded, in the event that you need to be banned from this forum or your ISP contacted. This will only happen in the event of a major violation of this agreement.

It was obvious that these were the generic terms that came with the software, but Onionland jumped up and down screaming that it was proof that Atlantis was a honeypot, ready to nab everyone in due course. They didn't seem to stop and think that it would hardly be advertised, nor would the user have to agree to it, if that were so.

That interview with the founders of Atlantis was the first of its kind – a world-first proper interview with the new breed of drug lord. In contrast, although Dread Pirate Roberts would respond to every private message sent to him, he was presumably always aware that he could be speaking to law enforcement, and his responses to questions were short and unencrypted. The owner of Black Market Reloaded, 'Backopy', was not interested in media of any type.

The publicity, however, seemed to be for naught. Atlantis was able to attract vendors with its three months commission-free offer and lower commissions thereafter, but buyers stayed away. It was a classic case of FUD that may or may not have been spread deliberately. People continued to believe it was a honeypot, or full of scammers. Buyers, Silk Road members and Reddit users all warned each other to stay away from Atlantis in what essentially became a web-wide game of Chinese whispers.

Most importantly, the Atlantis founders were not Dread Pirate Roberts, who had by now engendered such loyalty and devotion that his acolytes seemed offended by the very idea that anyone would open up a market in competition. Many of the Silk Road community felt they were not just taking drugs, they were part of a movement or revolution. Copycats didn't impress them.

Atlantis continued to put a sunny spin on things, insisting their market was growing. Loera, this time calling himself the Atlantis CEO, did a Reddit AMA ('Ask Me Anything'). Regular customers of the black markets derided Atlantis' publicity and marketing efforts. There is a certain contingent who think that once they have discovered a black market, it should be kept secret. These are the sort of people who quote *Fight Club* and insist that nobody talk about it, despite the fact that they themselves most likely heard about Silk Road through the media or a thread on Reddit. In any event, these customers were not happy about the publicity-hungry stunts of Atlantis.

But Atlantis was determined to take black-market publicity to new heights.

By their very nature, black markets are supposed to be a secret. They are illegal and so their activities should remain underground. But the administrators of Atlantis didn't agree. They maintained their clearweb presence and continued their marketing push.

And then came the commercial.

In one of the boldest and most bizarre moves ever, Atlantis commissioned someone to create a YouTube commercial advertising their site. They advertised on Reddit for a marketing person to attract buyers. 'We're launching videos as our first tactic, targeting buyers directly,' Loera said. And as far as the person they were hiring, 'we are after a person who can make YouTube how-to videos, create forum posts in various communities to increase the exposure to our site'.

The YouTube advertisement was aimed at the general drug-taking public and concentrated just on the purchase of marijuana – even Atlantis knew they would put too many people offside if they mentioned the ease with which someone could purchase heroin or crystal meth. But they wanted to reach people who had not yet taken the step into the dark web. 'We don't want to preach to the choir,' 'JK' said. 'Most of the general population have never even heard of Silk Road, let alone Atlantis.'

Two different commercials were created (somewhat amusingly, the person who won the contract to do so claimed to be a customer of Silk Road, not Atlantis). One was to introduce the concept of buying drugs online and the second, to run later, provided step-by-step instructions to getting on to Atlantis and making a purchase. The production values were not particularly sophisticated, but it was intriguing to see where they went with it.

The one-minute commercial, unleashed on YouTube on 26 June 2013, was done with cheesy animation and even cheesier background music. 'Meet Charlie,' the flashcards said over a cartoon dude. 'He's a stoner. Recently his job made him move cities, and he can't find any dank buds.' Luckily Charlie was turned on to Atlantis, 'the world's best anonymous online drug marketplace'. After determining it was free to sign up, there were no fees for purchases and he would get next-day delivery, good old Charlie had those buds mailed to him, making him 'high as a kite' and very happy. 'Don't you want what Charlie wants? What are you waiting for?' the video asked. 'Try it now.'

The Atlantis founders were well aware that their ad would be short-lived. The video amassed nearly 100,000 hits before YouTube removed it for violating its terms of service. But it had the desired effect of creating attention. News services worldwide picked it up. Forums and blogs exploded with theories of whether it was a hoax. Atlantis would go on to do a few more interviews, but they soon replaced Loera and Vladimir with someone calling themselves 'Heisenberg2.0', named after the lead character's alter ego in the TV series *Breaking Bad*. Heisenberg was hired to be the public face of Atlantis, and Loera and Vladimir, although still active as administrators of the site, stopped doing media. Subsequent interviews were all done with Heisenberg, who was their PR representative and not someone who knew the founders at all. He appeared on Channel Ten's *The Project* by way of TV voice-changing technology over the telephone.

Atlantis had arrived.

I don't often express my opinion here on the forums, but I've had enough time to stew on this one and no one else seems to be saying it, so here goes:

If you take someone's invention, tweak one little thing, and then go around telling everyone that you are 'better', you get zero respect from me.

– Dread Pirate Roberts forum post, 'What's the Deal with copycats?', 1 July 2013

Black Market Reloaded and Co.

Although Atlantis arrived with much fanfare, they were by no means the only competition to Silk Road. After the turbulence Silk Road had experienced in late 2012 and early 2013, its members started to look at the alternatives lest it happen again. By this time they had several to choose from.

Many of the markets would offer preferential treatment to any prominent Silk Road vendors who could prove who they were and were willing to sell their wares under the same username on the new market. The administrators would provide high-calibre vendors with vendor accounts with no setup fees and full support in the hope of raking in commissions from customers who would follow their favourites to the new markets. Silk Road customers found they could purchase exactly the same goods from their favourite vendor at a lower price from the alternative sites.

With the media ramping up reports that internet drug dealing was on the rise, it was no great surprise that new marketplaces started popping up wanting a piece of the action. Most of them turned out to be wannabes with no real hope of making a dent into the big boys' market share. Atlantis continued to struggle to find buyers but slowly moved to a respectable 2500 listings. They maintained their marketing push, which continued to alienate many of the black-market regulars.

Black Market Reloaded (BMR) grew steadily and quietly in the background. By early 2013, BMR was reporting $400,000 in sales per month from its 4000 drug listings – nothing near that of Silk Road, but perfectly respectable and reasonably profitable for its owner, Backopy. BMR was the one site that had been around for almost as long as Silk Road. Its owner was always happy to let Silk Road and, later, Atlantis, take the limelight while it maintained steady sales and a loyal following without attracting attention.

Many drug users refused to use BMR for ethical reasons. Unlike Silk Road, which claimed the 'high moral ground' when it came to what it would sell, BMR sold not only drugs, but poisons, firearms and explosives, stolen Paypal accounts and credit-card numbers, and online banking account numbers and passwords. The site stopped its contract killing listings after eighteen months – not for any moral reason, but because they were deemed to all be scammers.

BMR, the second-largest of the dark markets, also somehow managed to maintain a profitable weapons section. In 2013 VICE Media produced a documentary about buying guns on the dark web in which they interviewed a German gun dealer. Judging from the screen shots, the dealer sold weapons over BMR and spoke at length about sales and distribution, and about the ease and reliability of the online black-market system.

Over time BMR managed a steady growth, and picked up a number of new customers when Silk Road experienced outages due to DDoS attacks and technical issues. BMR responded to its growth by implementing several changes in an effort to fight scammers and lift sales, but the site never touted for new members or made grandiose statements. Despite the VICE documentary, it managed to stay under the radar and avoid demands from the public that it be shut down. The limelight was firmly focused on Silk Road.

A lot of users reported finding Backopy more down to earth, practical and responsive than Dread Pirate Roberts. Backopy made it a point to avoid discussing philosophy or politics and was also more approachable by site users than DPR, who would not often reply directly to members' questions but would respond through his employees or by writing a catch-all post.

Sheep Marketplace arrived to little fanfare in mid-February, but struggled at a mere thirty-two drug listings and forty-four registered forum members two months later. The administrator remained hopeful, though, posting in early April: 'Since the launch of Sheep, thirty-five days have passed . . . We have over 5000 registered people and some sinner who received permanent BAN.' The marketplace was run out of an Eastern European country, most likely the Czech Republic. It seemed an unlikely contender at its inception, but managed to survive and grow with a small band of loyal customers. It was the only new marketplace other than Atlantis to be discussed often on Silk Road, with several members reporting successful and smooth purchases.

RAMP – the Russian Anonymous Marketplace – was consistently active throughout 2013. But its being in Russian made it difficult for most people to understand what was going on there, even with the assistance of Google Translate. What was clear was that it was busy and thriving, servicing the Russian market.

Other black-market sites selling drugs were so far behind Silk Road in size and turnover that they barely rated a mention in any of the forums related to the dark markets. One of these, the BlackBox market, operated differently. Rather than a marketplace that displayed its wares, it operated more like a security deposit box to which you could give anyone the key. A vendor would rent a 'black box', then do their sales and marketing elsewhere – in real life, on regular clearweb sites or in non-sale forums. Once they had an eager buyer, they would provide them with an ID number and a password to view the items for sale. From there the buyer could make a purchase on any terms the buyer and seller agreed to, whether inside or outside of escrow. As all sales were completely private, it was difficult to discern how well used this market was. 'We have no key to read the sale and no party can identify another. Even forensic examination of our servers will reveal nothing. All payments are made through an anonymous bitcoin structure provided by us,' the site claimed.

Another odd little site was BuyItNow, which came complete with a peculiar code of conduct that included such rules as 'Never serve any government' and 'Never hold significant assets in countries known to sieze [sic] assets'. The administrator seemed to put a great deal of effort into the creation of the site, but it never made much of a splash.

Dread Pirate Roberts responded to a query about his competition without seeming too concerned. 'Competition is healthy and I welcome it,' he said, 'so long as it is friendly.'

For the most part, despite some temporary defections during Silk Road's outages and downtime, vendors and sellers alike seemed happy to stick with the status quo. Devotees of Silk Road were quick to forgive any issues and many staunchly defended the Road against any potential competitors.

As one disciple put it, 'Don't bother looking for a better version of the Silk Road . . . You'll never find what doesn't exist.'

Let me make this clear. The bar is set HIGH for SR vendors. You can be great in many ways, but you are expected to follow the few rules I put into place. Honoring and respecting your customer is in the Seller's Guide, and I take that seriously.

– Dread Pirate Roberts forum post, 31 July 2013

Nice Guys Finish First

Vendors on Silk Road came and went, some disappearing with their customers' money and drugs, and several of them going because they got busted. But occasionally, there would be those who got in, did well, made people happy, made some money and got out.

UK vendor 'JesusOfRave', who started selling on the Road in September 2012, was one of those who finished their Silk Road stint on their own terms. JesusOfRave had climbed the ranks to become Silk Road's number-one seller of MDMA, LSD, hash, ketamine and 2C psychedelics. A typical customer review was: 'The level of customer care you go to often makes me forget that this is an illegal drug market. You guys are a credit to humanity! Thank you for your hard work.'

In July 2013 JesusOfRave announced they were shutting up shop. They provided customers with plenty of notice so they could make their final orders and finalise any outstanding payments.

The reason, they said, was that they had made enough money and decided to get out before they were forced out:

> Hey we have brought the date forward to the 24th . . . We will close the shop at the end of the day . . . GMT.
> <WHY>
> There is nothing that we can see that increases the risk at this time. It is not out of concerns on that front – though too long in the limelight can make you sweat a little.
> We'll use an analogy, which we heard – somewhere – and this is a butchered paraphrased version:
> Sometimes you can be riding a raging horse, clinging on for dear life, doing everything you can to hold on and to not fall off. You become absorbed with how to stay on the horse. You do not necessarily know where this horse is going, but you cling on anyway.
> Sometimes you can choose to fall off the horse and walk somewhere else of your own choosing . . .

A representative of JesusOfRave provided a few insights into their time on the Road. He didn't provide a name, so I'll call him 'Joseph'.

Before Silk Road, Joseph and a few friends made extra money selling party drugs – mostly ecstasy and LSD – to people they knew. 'We were people interested in experimentation,' he said. The group soon gained a reputation among their peers as 'honest and awesome' dealers. The one problem with dealing to friends and acquaintances was 'it can confuse social relations'.

Like many, Joseph first heard about Silk Road from the June 2011 Gawker feature, but he didn't act on it right away. A year later, the name Silk Road had popped up a few times in the media. Intrigued, he co-opted some trusted friends and the group spent time reading and setting up their infrastructure. In September 2012, they introduced themselves on the forum as new vendors 'JesusOfRave', selling LSD, ecstasy, MDMA, ketamine, hash and marijuana.

To get business rolling, JesusOfRave sent out more than £600 worth of free drugs to trusted site members in exchange for their reviews. Not surprisingly, 'We became very popular very quickly,' Joseph said. 'We had more than 300 orders within the first two weeks.' Within two months they were the number-one seller.

Unlike what could be expected with drug dealers on the streets, Joseph was pleasantly surprised by the amount of cooperation and skill sharing among vendors on Silk Road. 'There are more buyers than sellers can stock. There was no sense of competition for us, during our time on SR,' he said.

Nor did JesusOfRave experience problems with any of their customers. 'Of tens of thousands of orders, no nightmares come to mind. By and large you are dealing with nice people,' Joseph said. He added a caveat, though: 'We understand the scene for crack, coke and H has a slightly different crowd than we were communicating with.'

JesusOfRave did not start selling on Silk Road only because it was a new means of doing what they were already doing – selling drugs at a profit – but because the team fully subscribed to the philosophy of the site.

'When I was growing up I asked a lot of questions,' Joseph said. 'Why can't we have a tick-box system where you only pay taxes towards those things that you agree with? Hospitals, roads, schools: tick. Bombs, wars, expensive politicians, queens: no tick.'

Dread Pirate Roberts had once written: 'This is the beauty of libertarianism. The people are free to choose what system they want. No need for one size fits all government solutions. If you want to use a debt based inflationary monetary system, go right ahead, doesn't affect me so long as you don't try to force me to use it as well.' Silk Road's philosophy, Joseph felt, fit in with his and his team's values.

Although they listed on a couple of other black markets – Atlantis and Black Market Reloaded – JesusOfRave's loyalty remained with Silk Road. 'This has a large part to do with DPR's writings. We feel we share complementary ethics,' Joseph said.

Closing up shop was not an easy decision, but it was the right one for them. 'For a team of our size, it was unsustainable,' he said. 'Our team was fewer than five people. We were all working 14–17 hour days . . . so something needed to change.'

Joseph was cagey when asked if JesusOfRave had earned enough to be set up for life. 'You could earn enough on SR to rival Tony Blair – or any head of state who wanders through the revolving doors between state and big business,' he said. 'The main difference being you can do it without exploiting or harming anyone against their wishes. We procured high-quality substances such as LSD and MDMA, direct from the source. We then listed them, processed orders and sent them through the mail to people who wanted them.'

He was proud of the way JesusOfRave left Silk Road, with the same integrity and values as he felt they had operated with during their year or so of online dealing. 'By the time we left we had the most fans on the site and had established ourselves as honest and friendly with the highest quality LSD and MDMA with some of the lowest prices.'

He credited Dread Pirate Roberts with the success of the Road. 'We have a lot of admiration for DPR and those working on this project behind the scenes.'

DPR has no issue with threatening people . . . He doesn't have my ID. He does, however, have the ID of SSBD and Libertas.
— ex-Silk Road staff member, 7 July 2013

A Changed DPR?

By mid-2013, suspicions were rising that there was more than one Dread Pirate Roberts and that the person posting in the Silk Road forums under that moniker was not the original founder of the site. It seemed either a long handover had been, and perhaps still was, taking place, or that the founder had outsourced his public face.

The original Dread Pirate Roberts was the DPR of legend, the one who wrote passionate missives about his philosophies and the Silk Road community, who had developed a cult-like following and convinced his customers they were part of a revolution. That DPR either gave 'no comment' responses to media or provided one- or two-line answers to specific questions. He was always polite, always responded to private messages, but was also careful not to give too much away. He preferred to speak directly to his audience in his own words, on his own forum. He would engage with other members on matters of business, but also wrote long posts sharing

255

his philosophies and thoughts on life. He would often remind his membership how much he loved them.

But from around October 2012, when there was a lengthy unexplained downtime of the site and the sudden demotion of longstanding moderators, the usually loquacious Pirate's posts dwindled to a trickle. Queries were handled by the new team of moderators and administrators, most notably 'Libertas', 'Inigo' and Australia's own Samesamebutdifferent (SSBD). DPR posted that he would be changing his writing style to fool the authorities. His posts became infrequent and brief, and regulars lamented his lack of presence on the forums. They wanted their leader telling them what was going on, not his appointed staff.

Some of the few posts made by DPR during early 2013 didn't read like they came from him at all: they had different capitalisation styles or different quirks of punctuation. But there were a couple of posts made under the DPR handle that were reminiscent of the old Pirate. Was part of the handover an agreement by the outgoing DPR to write up a few missives for misdirection purposes? That would certainly make sense and would be part of a well-thought-out plan to obfuscate the change.

Then suddenly, in July and August of 2013, Dread Pirate Roberts returned with a bang. He was highly engaged, posted frequently, gave interviews to media and interacted in the forums like an excited member. He opened a Twitter account. He quoted posts by other members in his signature (albeit a most worthy member; the formidable DoctorX). Although friendly and helpful, the posts he, she or they made were not remotely similar to the DPR of old. For one thing, emotion and irritability often crept in, something that had rarely happened in the past, when posts had seemed highly measured. Even more tellingly, DPR repeatedly spelled the word 'withdrawals' as 'withdraws'. It clearly wasn't a typo and he had never made this error before – a search of his old posts confirmed that he'd had no problem with the spelling. Of course, it could have been an example of the change of writing style, but this seemed doubtful.

Questions were asked directly of the Pirate, 'How many people have access to the DPR account? And do they all have access to the PGP key to digitally sign messages?'

'Hmmm . . .' he responded. 'I think I like this one being a mystery.'

The change in style went hand in hand with a bunch of changes and improvements to Silk Road, including the ability to browse in dozens of currencies, more accurate bitcoin exchange rates and more detailed purchasing statistics visible to vendors. The site went offline for server maintenance frequently.

Had ownership changed hands, or had Silk Road simply appointed a publicity officer, outsourcing the 'public face' of the site as Atlantis had done? Many of the changes to the site met with resistance from its vendors and customers. Security-conscious members were quick to point out flaws in updates as they were rolled out and many were irritated that those measures hadn't been considered pre-change. And a lot of members didn't like the idea of DPR, who had once shared himself only with his membership, courting the media and tweeting.

The most notable example of the new, engaged and publicity-seeking DPR came in September 2013. The previously taciturn Roberts granted an extensive interview to Andy Greenberg of *Forbes* magazine. Roberts claimed as fact what many people considered to be Silk Road's worst-kept secret – that the person now posting as Dread Pirate Roberts and steering the ship was not the same person who had founded Silk Road.

'I didn't start the Silk Road, my predecessor did,' he said, but declined to confirm when the site changed hands.

'It was his idea to pass the torch, in fact,' Roberts told *Forbes*. 'He was well compensated.'

He seemed confident in his security measures. 'Only I have access to the private keys corresponding to the Silk Road and forum URLs for example as well as my public PGP key,' he told Greenberg. 'I'm also the only one with access to the wallets that back the accounts and escrow on Silk Road, so there is no possibility of a rogue member of my team running off with the funds.'

DPR praised bitcoin for its role in making his dream of an independent market for the peaceful sale of drugs a reality. And he threw out some less-than-subtle boasts about the success of his venture: 'As far as my monetary net-worth is concerned, the future value of Silk Road as an organization dwarfs its and my liquid assets. At this point I wouldn't sell out for less than 10 figures, maybe 11. Whether someone would buy it for that much is another question, but at some point you're going to have to put Dread Pirate Roberts on that list you all keep over at Forbes. ;)'

Some of the turns of phrase in the *Forbes* interview sounded vaguely familiar. But they didn't necessarily sound like the Dread Pirate Roberts, who, by now, his membership felt they had come to know.

JTAN provides tools for law abiding people to go about their lives on the net without being logged and tagged. We let good guys reach the parts of the net that they want to reach without fear of exploitation.

– Homepage of JTAN.com, a small internet hosting company
in Pennsylvania, USA

On 26 July 2013, US Homeland Security knocked on the door of an address on 15th Avenue in San Francisco, California. Earlier that month, in a routine inspection of inbound mail from Canada on the US–Canada border, they had intercepted a package of false identification documents. The IDs for the US, Australia, Canada and the UK had nine different names but all had a photograph that matched the man who answered the door, who identified himself as Ross Ulbricht.

Ulbricht denied knowing anything about the documents. After all, he told the agents, hypothetically anyone could go on to a website named 'Silk Road' on Tor and purchase any drugs or fake identity documents the person wanted.

Ulbricht wasn't charged and he went about his business.

The Homeland Security agents also interviewed one of the young man's housemates. The housemate knew Ulbricht as 'Josh'. Josh was a nice guy, quiet. He was always home in his room on the computer.

. . . it is likely that the TARGET SERVER *contains records of user activity on the Silk Road website spanning a much longer date range than the data kept on the Silk Road Web Server . . .*

– Extract from search warrant served on JTAN.com on

9 September 2013

Exit Atlantis

On 20 September 2013 an abrupt announcement was made on the Atlantis website: 'Warning. Atlantis will be closing down over the next few days. Please see the forums for further information.'

The 'further information' was posted on the Atlantis forums by an administrator:

Dear all users

We have some terrible news. Regrettably it has come time for Atlantis to close its doors. Due to security reasons outside of our control we have no choice but to cease operation of the Atlantis Market marketplace. Believe us when we say we wouldn't be doing this if it weren't 100% necessary.

Due to the urgency we are allowing all users to withdraw all their coins for one week before the site, and forum, are shut down permanently. Please remove all of your coins, these will not be recoverable after one week from now. Anything remaining in your accounts will be donated to a drug related charity of our choosing.

We wish to thank all of you for making Atlantis a great and memorable place to trade on. We wish you all the best in your future endeavors.

Best wishes,

The Atlantis team

That was the last anyone ever heard from those with the keys to the Atlantis marketplace. Nothing from Loera, nothing from Vlad. They simply disappeared.

Moderators 'Cicero' and Heisenberg2.0 (who was also the spokesperson for the site) wrote farewell messages in which they made it clear they had no more knowledge than any of the site's members. 'I had no idea the site was going to shut down, and I was not warned ahead of time. Nor were any vendors to my knowledge,' said Cicero.

The claims that members could cash out appeared a week later to be simply a mechanism for buying time. Members were soon complaining on Reddit and the Silk Road forums that they could not withdraw from the site. There was no report of any substantial donation to a drug-related charity. Reports poured in from people who had lost money, from a few hundred dollars to one member claiming he or she had lost over $3000 in cryptocurrency.

But did the owners of Atlantis simply run off with the money? It certainly seemed they weren't making the income they had hoped for – but why would they have posted a warning on their main page if that was the intention? Were they a honeypot after all and it simply didn't work?

The Atlantis closure was a hot topic of conversation, with theories ranging from the mundane (they closed because they weren't profitable enough) to the conspiratorial (they had planned the long con from the beginning). One of Silk Road's most trusted security experts, 'Astor', thought it was the former:

> I don't know if that was their fatal error, but it was one of many bone-headed mistakes. Like . . . suggesting CryptoCat as a place to chat with reporters, when CryptoCat's encryption was broken up until a couple of months ago (why not use an in-house messaging system that you can control and secure rather than a third party service with a long history of security vulnerabilities?). Or the lack of a tumbler (how were coins transferred safely from buyers to sellers?). Or their media blitz, which brought way more unwanted attention on them than they needed, especially considering their size.
>
> The real reason for the shut down may be far more mundane than these speculations about security problems, though. Quite simply, they weren't profitable so they closed their business.
>
> They may have planned it all along. If the media blitz didn't bring in enough customers, they were going to quit. It was a hail mary and it didn't work. They got a decent number of sign ups, or so they claimed, but that didn't convert to sales, as is demonstrated by the fact that most listings have no reviews.

Astor also had some insights into why, despite doing everything right and having a robust business model, Atlantis had been unable to make any impact on Silk Road's market. Silk Road, in business terms, had 'first-mover advantage'; the advantage of the initial significant player in a market segment:

> The reason the media blitz didn't work and they lost in the competition against SR is not because of any security issues, since most people don't know anything about those issues and that was not a part of their decision making process. They lost because they couldn't beat the network effect on SR.
>
> How likely is Facebook to be replaced by another social network at this point? Any new social network will be a wasteland. If you sign up, you will have no friends there. But if you sign up on Facebook, half the people you know will already be on it, creating a better experience. SR's biggest asset is the people who are already using it. A new buyer can get instant access to 1200+ vendors, while a new vendor can get instant access to tens of thousands of buyers.
>
> Another aspect of it is the psychology of brand loyalty. SR has proven to be a trusted platform. People like and trust DPR (they don't merely put up [with] him like Mark Zuckerberg, for example). People are rightfully suspicious of others in the drug world, because there are a lot of scammers and assholes, but SR works for the vast majority of people. It has proven itself. People stick with what works, rather than take risks with new products (or markets) even if they are theoretically a better alternative.

The general consensus was that Atlantis had shot itself in the foot. Drug users had become accustomed to being part of a secret society, making clandestine assignations and keeping their indulgences, habits or addictions, as the case may be, from wider society.

Atlantis thumbed its nose at that, trying to bring drug dealing to the mainstream.

After a while few people seemed to believe Atlantis had been a honeypot, one of the favoured conspiracy theories upon the closure announcement. Nor did they believe the 'security issue'. Now everyone felt it had just been a failed business venture. Atlantis couldn't attract the buyers, who maintained their loyalty to Silk Road. Its owners closed up shop practically six months to the day they had opened – they simply hadn't made the profits they needed.

Dread Pirate Roberts wrote a gracious post lamenting the loss:

Some thoughts on Atlantis closing

Atlantis was good for Silk Road and the community at large and I am sad to see it go. Yes they were a bit cocky and aggressive, but they never crossed the line and did anything unethical, and they served their customers well. They reminded us in the Silk Road administration that to stay #1, we have to be constantly thinking of our users and how to serve them best and can not take for granted your loyalty.

There has been more than one occasion where I have wanted to quit as well. Without going into details, the stress of being DPR is sometimes overwhelming. What keeps me going is the understanding that what we are doing here is more important than my insignificant little life. I believe what we are doing will have rippling effects for generations to come and could be part of a monumental shift in how human beings organize and relate to one another.

I have gone through the mental exercise of spending a lifetime in prison and of dying for this cause. I have let the fear pass through me and with clarity commit myself fully to the mission and values outlined in the Silk Road charter. If you haven't read it yet, please do. Here is the link: silkroadvb5piz3r. onion/silkroad/charter

The bottom line is . . . Silk Road is here to stay so long as there is breath in my lungs, a spark in my mind, and fire in my heart. I know many of you in this community feel the same way and [it] is an honor to stand beside you here.

Lastly, to anyone considering opening another market, you WILL face unexpected challenges one way or another, and if you don't have the conviction to overcome them then your efforts will likely be in vain. And please open up a dialogue with me if you do open another site. Even competitors can talk from time to time on friendly terms. :)

Atlantis admins, if you are reading this, I hope you stick around and contribute as you are able.

A couple of weeks later, Atlantis' claims of security concerns became far more plausible.

Security is a bit like religion . . . some things have to be taken on faith. Where security differs from religion is that security is NOT retroactive. Unlike Christianity, where you can come to Jesus, be 'saved' and have all your sins washed away, with security you can adopt Tails [a privacy device] or PGP, and be secure from that point forward, but rest assured that your previous sins (security failings) WILL come back to haunt you and bite you in the ass.

The original DPR is the poster child for that, right now.

– Nightcrawler's forum signature on Silk Road 2

Part Three
The Fall

A Series of Unfortunate Events

On 3 October 2013 came news that rocked Onionland: Silk Road had been seized and Dread Pirate Roberts had been arrested. Thousands of Silk Road faithful around the world read with mounting disbelief the breaking story of 29-year-old Ross William Ulbricht, arrested not only on drugs, money-laundering and hacking charges, but also murder-for-hire and conspiracy to commit torture. Reports said he was the Dread Pirate Roberts, the enigmatic, peace-seeking libertarian and founder of Silk Road.

Ulbricht, casually dressed in jeans and T-shirt, had been chatting online, taking advantage of the free wi-fi of a local library in Glen Park, San Francisco. The library was a small, single-room affair, and the desk next to the sci-fi section – a rack on the wall, no wider than an average adult arm-span – was the most coveted in the library. Here a patron could sit with sunshine on their back, and a view to anyone approaching.

In typical IT-nerd style, Ulbricht had several windows open on his computer so he could easily flick between tasks, messages and chats. He must have been startled when a woman charged at him, screaming, 'I'm so sick of you!' He never had a chance to log out of the sites or activate any kill switch he might have had on his laptop when the woman and several other 'patrons' grabbed hold of him.

He was pushed up against the wall and all his technology seized, experienced FBI officers ensuring that what was on his computer was preserved for evidence. This included 144,336 bitcoins in a wallet on the hardware, worth a little over $20 million at the time. The wallet, they believed, was Ulbricht's personal account.

What the authorities claim to have found on his computer, and the details from the various court documents that were released after Ulbricht's arrest, would require a suspension of disbelief if they were in a movie or detective novel. If they are to be believed, Dread Pirate Roberts was a violent, bumbling, overconfident and sloppy fool with little technical knowledge and even less common sense, who should have been caught within a week of creating Silk Road.

According to the various public documents, the FBI had found clues leading to Ulbricht by combing clearweb sites. They found the early posts by altoid advertising Silk Road on Shroomery and touting the new marketplace on the Bitcointalk forum. They saw a link to Ulbricht's email address in altoid's advertisement for an IT pro. They had also noted a March 2013 question on technical website Stack Overflow about connecting to a hidden Tor site using computer language Curl, suggesting someone who was programming a hidden site. A minute after posting the question the user changed their name from 'Ross Ulbricht' to 'frosty'.

And they'd had undercover agents on the inside for over a year.

Ulbricht, who had an advanced degree in chemical engineering and who had allegedly developed a cult-like following among the Silk Road users as Dread Pirate Roberts, a supposed criminal mastermind, was apparently caught in a public place logged into every incriminating site he had access to.

This was the same Ross Ulbricht who had been visited by Homeland Security in July 2013 in relation to the package containing multiple counterfeit identification documents all bearing his photo. This had occurred at the same time that DPR was known to have been seeking such documents on Silk Road.

This criminal mastermind, who had built an empire the turn-over of which the FBI valued at $1.2 billion, didn't seem to think that perhaps the Homeland Security visit might be the catalyst for him to take a long overseas trip to a non-extradition country (though he had started an application for citizenship to the Dominican Republic). Instead, he continued frequenting a public place where he would log into the master control panel of the Silk Road website.

And he kept a journal on his computer, in which he wrote the equivalent of 'Dear Diary, today the illicit drugs market I founded reached record turnover and I commissioned a hit on somebody.' Not that the journal mattered, because apparently he didn't bother with PGP encryption when discussing sensitive matters in private messages online.

He also conveniently recorded a to-do list in case anything frightening happened (more frightening than a visit from Homeland Security, presumably). Headed 'Emergency', the list read like some-thing a junior scriptwriter might submit for their very first action film:

– encrypt and backup important files on laptop to memory stick
– destroy laptop hard drive and hide/dispose
– destroy phone and hide/dispose
– hide memory stick
– get new laptop
– go to end of train
– find place to live on craigslist for cash
– create new identity (name, backstory).

The initial reactions of those who had had interactions with the Dread Pirate Roberts over the years was incredulity. As the reports kept rolling in, the allegations of his willingness to use violence to protect his empire were incomprehensible. The benign leader of the peaceful drug users' paradise was, according to the documents, willing to order contract killings of people he'd never met for the most tenuous of reasons.

Somehow, the FBI had managed to track down one of the Silk Road servers in a foreign country, never revealed but widely suspected to be Iceland, on 23 July 2013. However, forensic analysis, while confirming it was indeed the Silk Road web server, determined that data was regularly purged from the databases. This meant that the server image seized by the FBI contained data reflecting only the sixty previous days of user activity.

But the FBI hit gold when forensics revealed backups were being periodically exported to another server, the fees for which were paid in bitcoin. Astonishingly, this server was traced to the US and a small internet hosting company in Pennsylvania called JTAN.com.

Three weeks before the authorities seized Silk Road and arrested its alleged founder, the FBI had served a search warrant on JTAN. This had provided them with copies of all private message logs, including those of the Dread Pirate Roberts. They could also view transaction records dating back to the site's launch.

And what they allegedly found in those logs was far more sinister than an online drug trade. According to details in the FBI's criminal complaint, Dread Pirate Roberts felt that the threats in March 2013 of the person going by the name of FriendlyChemist to expose customers' details warranted torture and murder.

The complaint claimed that after receiving the demand for $500,000 in order to pay off FriendlyChemist's dealers and in return for his silence, Dread Pirate Roberts suggested to the black-mailer that the suppliers contact him so that he could 'work out something' with them. Soon after, a user previously unknown to Roberts using the moniker 'redandwhite' introduced himself: 'I was asked to contact you. We are the people friendlychemist owes money to. What did you want to talk to us about?'

'Red and White' is a common nickname for the Hells Angels, being the colour of their club patches – not the sort of name many people would have the guts to hijack. It's not clear whether DPR was told explicitly that this user was affiliated with the Angels, or if he concluded it himself, but his journal entry on 28 March 2013 read: 'being blackmailed with user info. talking with large distributor (hell's angels)'.

DPR apparently didn't think it odd that the blackmailer put him in touch with one of his suppliers to talk about him behind his back. He started up an unencrypted dialogue with redandwhite, proposing he become a vendor on the site. 'I'm not entirely sure what the best action to take is, but I wanted to be in communication with you to see if we can come to a conclusion that works for everyone. Friendlychemist aside, we should talk about how we can do business. Obviously you have access to illicit substances in quantity, and are having issues with bad distributors. If you don't already sell here on Silk Road, I'd like you to consider becoming a vendor,' DPR wrote.

Redandwhite responded: 'If you can get Friendlychemist to meet up with us, or pay us his debt then I'm sure I would be able to get people in our group to give this online side of the business a try.' This comment seems to suggest that redandwhite did not know FriendlyChemist's true identity, and was new to online drug dealing. It is not clear how redandwhite and FriendlyChemist were carrying out their business, if they had not met, nor were they transacting by computer.

DPR offered the supposed Angels member FriendlyChemist's real name and general location details (White Rock, Canada), along with the titbit that he was married with three children. There is no indication in the complaint of how DPR extracted such personal information from the extortionist. 'FriendlyChemist is a liability and I wouldn't mind if he was executed,' wrote Roberts – again, presumably not using the basic precaution of PGP. Although it seems astonishing, Dread Pirate Roberts never used PGP in his correspondence with journalists, even in response to encrypted messages. This made sense at the time, as he was always guarded in what he said and never provided any sensitive information that could be used by authorities against him. That would be justifiable, but failing to encrypt plans to execute people seems to lack the kind of self-preservation you would expect.

Apparently FriendlyChemist was becoming antsy, not having heard from DPR for nine days, and he delivered an ultimatum:

DPR had seventy-two hours to pay up before '5000 users details and about 2 dozen vendors identities' would be released. 'Wats [sic] it going to be?'

DPR decided that these threats were unforgivable and so, several hours later, on 29 March 2013, he sent a message to redandwhite: 'I would like to put a bounty on his head if it's not too much trouble for you. What would be an adequate amount to motivate you to find him? Necessities like this do happen from time to time for a person in my position.'

Redandwhite responded quoting a price of $150,000 to $300,000 'depending on how you want it done – clean or non-clean', whatever that means – but it doesn't sound very pleasant. Given the higher price quoted, it might mean the latter involved pre-death torture. 'It doesn't have to be clean,' DPR wrote.

But it seemed that the price was a bit high for the Pirate. 'Are the prices you quoted the best you can do? I would like this done asap as he is talking about releasing the info on Monday.'

They eventually agreed on a price of 1670 bitcoins – approximately $150,000 at the time – for the job. A transfer of 1670 bitcoins can be found in the blockchain for that date.

A day later, redandwhite updated DPR, stating: 'Your problem has been taken care of . . . Rest easy though, because he won't be blackmailing anyone again. Ever.'

On 1 April, DPR updated his journal: 'got word that black-mailer was excuted [sic]'. And a few days later, 'received visual confirmation of blackmailers execution'. Ever the sceptic, DPR had demanded a picture of the dead victim with random numbers supplied by him written on a piece of paper next to the body, which redandwhite dutifully supplied.

'I've received the picture and deleted it. Thank you again for your swift action,' DPR wrote.

Redandwhite must have decided this murder-for-hire for the online drugs czar had the potential to be lucrative, because a couple of days later he told DPR that his goons had extracted some interesting information from FriendlyChemist with some not-so-friendly questioning. FriendlyChemist had identified another Canadian who had been working with him on the blackmail scheme as well as running a number of scams for a couple of years.

That individual was Tony76, the vendor responsible for the greatest heist in Silk Road's history. And redandwhite had his real name.

Again, not stopping to wonder where redandwhite had come from or whether he was really who he said he was, DPR ordered another hit. 'I would like to go after [Tony76],' he wrote. 'If he is our man, then he likely has substantial assets to be recovered. Perhaps we can hold him and question him?'

There was a problem, though. Tony76 lived with three other drug dealers, and at least two were always home. 'Ok, let's just hit [Tony76] and leave it at that. Try to recover the funds, but if not, then not.'

Redandwhite was a little more bloodthirsty – either that, or he needed the money. He offered to hit Tony76 alone for $150,000, but said that he would have a better chance of recovering any money if he did all four occupants of the house. 'Anything recovered would be split 50/50 with you,' he said. Redandwhite quoted the bargain price of $500,000 to do all four – practically a 'buy three, get one free' deal. Whether he was nervous or he liked the idea of 50 per cent of recovered earnings, DPR responded later that day: 'hmm . . . ok, I'll defer to your better judgment and hope we can recover some assets from them.'

'Gave angels go ahead to find tony76,' he wrote in his journal, along with a few housekeeping issues about cleaning up unused libraries on the server. He transferred another 3000 bitcoin to redandwhite ('sent payment to angels for hit on tony76 and his 3 associates,' says the journal), an amount which again appears in the blockchain for that day.

A week later, he received confirmation that he had been successful in ordering the murders of four people, three of whom he did not know and had no beef with. 'That problem was dealt with. I'll try to catch you online to give you details,' wrote redandwhite. 'Just wanted to let you know right away so you have one less thing to worry about.'

'Thanks,' said DPR, 'see you on chat.'

Dread Pirate Roberts' apparent nonchalance about ordering hits on five people may be explained by something he wrote when trying to screw redandwhite down on the price. 'Not long ago, I had a clean hit done for $80K,' he'd written. Redandwhite probably considered this bluster for bargaining, but Roberts was referring to a hit he had apparently taken out on former administrator Chronicpain, the Silk Road employee who had brokered a deal for a kilogram of cocaine between seller Nob and Silk Road member Googleyed1.

When DPR got word that Chronicpain – real name Curtis Clark Green – had been arrested on drugs charges, he panicked, knowing that Green had access to sensitive information about the Silk Road website. This was also at a time when somebody – and

DPR suspected that somebody was Green – had stolen funds from Silk Road vendors' accounts, which Roberts was obliged to repay.

He turned to his friend Nob, whom he'd decided was a bit of a badass and would probably have the contacts to rough up Green, a grandfather who lived with his wife and daughter, and force him to return the money.

'I'd like him beat up, then forced to send the bitcoins he stole back, like sit him down at his computer and make him do it,' he wrote. But before the command could take place, DPR had a change of heart. 'Can you change the order to execute rather than torture?' he asked. He'd had a chance to think about it and realised that Chronicpain had had access to inside information for some time and, having been arrested, might give up some of that info in return for a reduced sentence. 'I've never killed a man or had one killed before, but it is the right move in this case,' he said.

DPR was right about Nob being the kind of guy who could make things happen. The two brokered a deal whereby Nob would arrange the hit on Green and DPR would pay him $80,000 – half up-front and the other half upon confirmation that Green was no longer a potential problem. Nob assured him that his guys were pros: 'as soon as 40 lands the guys will go out.'

For reasons unknown, rather than use bitcoin, Roberts transferred the down payment of a contract killing in a more easily traceable form: from Technocash Limited in Australia to a bank account at Capital One Bank in Washington, DC.

Warming to his new role in murder-for-hire, Roberts said he would need proof of death – preferably video, but pictures would do – before he would send the second instalment. 'They should probably just give him the note, let him use his computer to send the coins back, and then kill him,' DPR suggested. 'I'm more concerned about silencing him than getting that money back.'

Nob assured him that once the wife and kid were out of the house, he would torture Green, get the money back, then kill him. And in due course he reported that he had him, 'still alive but being tortured'. He sent DPR photographic proof of the torture.

Green must have been tougher about giving up information than DPR gave him credit for, though, because it wasn't until a week later Nob reported that he died from 'asphyxiation/heart rupture' while being tortured. Roberts was certainly going to get his $80K worth from Nob. How Dread Pirate Roberts had characterised this hit as 'clean' is a mystery.

'I'm pissed I had to kill him,' DPR said, 'but what's done is done.' It was Chronicpain's own fault, really: 'I just can't believe he was so stupid . . . I just wish more people had some integrity.'

Upon receipt of the photograph of Green's dead body, Roberts admitted to being 'a little disturbed, but I'm ok . . . I'm new to this kind of thing is all.' He wired the balance of what he owed, as agreed. 'I don't think I've done the wrong thing,' he said. 'I'm sure I will call on you again at some point, though I hope I won't have to.'

Just two weeks later, Roberts started to get blackmailed by FriendlyChemist. But by the time he next had cause to have someone bumped off, he'd apparently become buddies with what-ever chapter of the Hells Angels it is that carries out contract killings. It seemed Nob was on the outer, despite being so much cheaper.

Who knew that a softy could lead an international narcotics organization? Behind my wall of anonymity, I don't have to intimidate, thankfully. But yea, I love you guys. Thank you for being here. Thank you for being my comrades. Thank you for being yourselves and bringing your unique perspectives and energy. And on a personal note, thank you for giving me the best job in the world. I've never had so much fun! I know we've been at it for over a year now, but really, we are JUST getting started.

I'm so excited and anxious for our future I could burst.

– Dread Pirate Roberts forum post, 22 September 2012

Sting or Scam?

While DPR may have felt pleased he'd successfully removed his enemies, the joke was on him. Apparently there were never any murders.

Chronicpain/Curtis Green had, it seemed, been cooperating with police after his arrest, including an undercover Maryland agent who was calling himself Nob.

Back in April 2012 the undercover agent had started grooming Roberts, claiming to be a drug smuggler who specialised in moving large quantities of illegal drugs. By December that year, Roberts trusted him enough to try to organise a deal for the massive quantities Nob wanted to move, which was where Chronicpain came in.

Unknown to Roberts, Chronicpain had taken it upon himself to act as a middleman, providing his own home address to Nob for the drop of a kilogram of cocaine, which he would then pass on to Googleyed1, the buyer. On 17 January 2013, undercover federal agents delivered the cocaine to Chronicpain and allowed him time to confirm delivery to Googleyed1 before arresting him. Upon hearing that DPR had ordered his murder, Chronicpain agreed to stage photographs of himself being tortured and killed.

DPR had paid $80,000 for some special effects, and the State of Maryland had earned itself a tidy little sum.

As for the other five murders, of Tony76 and his associates and FriendlyChemist, according to the court documents the FBI and Canadian authorities compared notes and could find no homicides matching the names or any other details of the alleged victims. No law enforcement agency laid claim to having an undercover agent calling himself 'redandwhite'.

It is unlikely this was another sting by the authorities. The most probable explanation was that redandwhite and FriendlyChemist were the same person – maybe even Tony76 – carrying out an elaborate scam. FriendlyChemist had started blackmailing Silk Road around the same time as Lucydrop – whom many thought was Tony76 – had absconded with thousands of dollars worth of members' bitcoin.

This time, it seemed DPR had paid around $650,000 to a slick-talking shyster. Ross Ulbricht was facing charges of conspiracy to commit six murders that apparently had never taken place, and Dread Pirate Roberts may have paid all the money to Tony76.

If it was as it appeared, Tony76 first robbed hundreds of Silk Road customers to the tune of six figures in April 2012, scammed them again for a similar amount under the name LucyDrop a few months later, then attempted to blackmail Dread Pirate Roberts with customers' addresses he had gathered while selling as Tony76 and LucyDrop. When that failed, he extracted the money out of

Silk Road by pretending to be a hit man, carrying out the murders of himself and his alter egos.

It must surely rate as one of the most epic cons in history. And it netted the con man over a million dollars – several million if he delayed cashing out until bitcoin reached its peak – from behind his computer screen.

I want to use economic theory as a means to abolish the use of coercion and agression [sic] amongst mankind. Just as slavery has been abolished most everywhere, I believe violence, coercion and all forms of force by one person over another can come to an end. The most widespread and systemic use of force is amongst institutions and governments, so this is my current point of effort. The best way to change a government is to change the minds of the governed, however. To that end, I am creating an economic simulation to give people a first-hand experience of what it would be like to live in a world without the systemic use of force.

– Ross Ulbricht's LinkedIn profile

An administrator of the Silk Road website, Curtis Green, a/k/a 'Flush', and 'chronicpain', age 47, of Utah, pleaded guilty today to conspiracy to distribute and possess with attempt to distribute cocaine.

...

According to his plea agreement, beginning in November 2012, Green worked for the creator and operator of Silk Road, Ross Ulbricht, whom Green only knew by his alias, 'Dread Pirate Roberts.' Silk Road was an online, international marketplace that allowed users to anonymously buy and sell illegal drugs, false identifications, and other contraband over the internet. Ulbricht collected a fee for each transaction on the website.

Green's responsibilities included responding to questions and complaints from buyers and sellers, resolving disputes between buyers and sellers, and investigating possible law enforcement activity on Silk Road. As part of his role as an administrator, Green had the ability to see messages Silk Road users sent to each other, to see the details of each transaction on Silk Road, and to see the accounts – including financial information – of Silk Road users, including the accounts of Ulbricht.

– Press release, District of Maryland US Attorney's Office,
7 November 2013

Shutdown

The initial reaction of the Silk Road community to the take-down of the site and the bust of Dread Pirate Roberts was that it was a joke. A seizure notice was displayed on the Silk Road website when members tried to log in, which stated 'This hidden site has been seized' and displayed the badges of the various agencies involved in the operation. But, as several people pointed out, the seizure notice was emblazoned with a watermark of the Silk Road green camel logo. Surely it was some sort of bizarre practical joke?

'The image was created by SR staff to be used in a dead man's switch,' theorised one member on the Silk Road forums, which were still running despite the market being seized and shuttered. 'DPR probably slipped up somewhere, aware that the FBI were on to him, sends a command to the server that SR runs on, and "boom" all data is wiped, placing that image as a warning to it's [sic] users.'

But within a couple of days, nobody could deny the server had been seized and an arrest had been made. The news made headlines in every major media outlet around the world, and the website remained offline. Previously sealed official documents from law enforcement were released to the media.

Over the ensuing weeks and months, a more complete picture of how Ross Ulbricht had been arrested emerged as more official documents were made public. It appeared that parallel investigations were being carried out by several agencies, including the FBI, Homeland Security, the DEA and local authorities in New York and Maryland.

The State of Maryland had lodged a sealed indictment in May 2013 for 'John Doe aka Dread Pirate Roberts' alleging the plot to murder Chronicpain, as well as running an international drug empire. It's not clear whether at that stage Ulbricht was on their radar.

A New York–based agent involved in the investigation had found the January 2011 references to Silk Road by somebody calling himself altoid attempting to promote the site in its beginning. Sifting through altoid's postings on Bitcointalk, the agent had found the Gmail address of Ulbricht.

Once law enforcement had connected Ulbricht to altoid, which connected them to Silk Road, they built a case that he was the site's founder, Dread Pirate Roberts. Most of the evidence was circumstantial. Ulbricht's GooglePlus page and YouTube profile both referenced the Mises Institute website, which DPR linked to within his signature on the Silk Road forums. Ulbricht posted under his own name on tech site Stack Overflow, inquiring about how to use Curl/PHP on Tor (technology that would be used for

Silk Road), before changing his username to 'frosty' a moment later.

The court records are hazy on how the authorities managed to seize the Silk Road web server, but they made an image of a complete copy on 23 July 2013 under the Mutual Legal Assistance Treaty. It included user account and transaction information, and at least sixty days' worth of messages, including those from administrators and Dread Pirate Roberts. It also provided the FBI with the lead to the server in the US that stored transaction records dating back to the site's launch.

In what had turned out to be a most fortuitous 'routine border inspection' in history, multiple false identification documents were intercepted by US Customs & Border Patrol. Each carried a photograph of Ulbricht with a false name and details. This occurred a couple of weeks after Dread Pirate Roberts had told another Silk Road user that he was looking for fake IDs in order to rent a new stock of servers for the site. When questioned by Homeland Security about the fake IDs, Ulbricht mentioned Silk Road as the sort of place where anyone could purchase such things.

Ulbricht was renting a room in the San Francisco house to which the IDs were addressed. He paid his rent in cash, using a false name. Logs from the servers seized and imaged by the FBI showed that someone logged on to the Silk Road administration panel from San Francisco. Subpoenaed records from Comcast showed the IP address belonged to an internet cafe in San Francisco, 150 metres away from the home of a friend of Ulbricht, which he used, according to Google records, to regularly log into his Gmail account.

The New York criminal complaint against Ulbricht also said that Special Agent Christopher Tarbell of the FBI and several other undercover agents had infiltrated the site as members. Law enforce-ment had made over 100 drug purchases, including ecstasy, cocaine, heroin, LSD and other substances. Laboratory tests of the samples typically returned high purity levels of the drug in question.

From 6 February 2011 to 23 July 2013, sales of just over 9.5 million bitcoin brought in commissions of 614,000 bitcoin to Dread Pirate Roberts from 1,229,465 transactions and just under a million registered users. The FBI valued the revenue at $1.2 billion and commissions at $79.8 million, although the former figure, at least, was erroneous and likely significantly less. To arrive at that figure, the FBI had multiplied the number of bitcoin seized by the current exchange rate. But the value of a bitcoin had fluctuated from $0.67 to $214.67 during Silk Road's lifetime. The rate at the time of calcu-lation was around $126. So if a gram of MDMA was worth a steady $50, purchasing a gram of MDMA in February 2011, when bitcoin reached parity, would have cost 50 bitcoin. The same gram a couple of years later would have cost 0.5 bitcoin. This meant 50.5 bitcoin would have actually been spent to purchase the two grams for $100, but the FBI would have valued it at around $6363.

DPR's personal stash – the commissions figure – could be correct, however. If he had not cashed out his bitcoin, its value would have grown exponentially over the lifetime of the website.

The seized data showed that, of the site's users, 30 per cent were from the US, 27 per cent were 'undeclared' and the remainder, in descending order of prevalence, were from the UK, Australia, Germany, Canada, Sweden, France, Russia, Italy and the Netherlands.

The FBI believed DPR to be the sole owner and operator of Silk Road. Aside from delegating non-sensitive tasks to a team of administrators and moderators, he handled all aspects of the site himself.

The FBI's version of events was greeted with considerable scepticism by the Silk Road community. Had the criminal mastermind really made that many basic security mistakes? Hadn't the visit by Homeland Security holding the smoking gun of nine fake IDs been a signal that maybe DPR should get out of the US? And most of all, how could their beloved leader, with his peace-loving reputation, order the murders of six individuals, some of whom he had never met and had not done him any harm?

Conspiracy theories and explanations surfaced on Reddit and the Silk Road forums. The fact that the forums were still operating was itself a source of speculation. Many thought it was because the forums were on a different server that had not been seized, others that it was because the forums in and of themselves were not illegal. The tinfoil-hat brigade, of course, assumed it was because law enforcement had taken over the forums to gather intelligence on the Silk Road user base.

A YouTube video surfaced of Ulbricht talking with a friend for whom he had relocated to San Francisco and from whose home Google records showed several logins to the rossulbricht Gmail account. Some felt that the friend had more of the personality of DPR and had set Ulbricht up for the fall right from the beginning. Others thought they might be in it together and would provide each other's reasonable doubt. 'Ulbricht was a fall guy, quite possibly paid to take the fall. Some sort of loyalty to the group. This is no one-man operation,' they said.

Then there was the theory that the whole thing was an ingenious ruse that was going to plan so that double jeopardy laws could be invoked later: 'I think it's all some AMAZINGLY CLEVER game being played by DPR and Co, where there [sic] suddenly numerous "DPR's" are somehow (mis)identified, and in the end it's such a massive clusterfuck that the prosecution wont be able to build a solid case or find a fair jury for many reasons already about!' said one proponent of this theory. 'We could be in for one hell of a show.'

Of course, many thought it was a setup by law enforcement so the authorities could be seen to have done something. Much of the coincidental nature of the evidence – the world's luckiest 'random inspection' of mail, for example – lent itself to accusations that the authorities were engaged in 'parallel construction' (i.e. building a second evidentiary basis for a case to explain discoveries that were obtained illegally). Many found the official line hard to swallow.

A slightly odd occurrence just after the arrest of Ulbricht was the resurrection of the long-deleted thread 'Silk Road anonymous marketplace: feedback requested', which had been started by the defunct user 'silkroad' on the Bitcointalk forum. At some time between the last post made in that thread, on 15 June 2011, and Ulbricht's arrest, all traces of silkroad had been obliterated from the forum other than a single instance of another user's post in an unrelated thread in which they quoted silkroad.

The Bitcointalk forum went down shortly after the arrest of Ulbricht, with reports saying they had been hacked by a group calling itself the Hole Seekers. When Bitcointalk came back online, user silkroad made a reappearance, as did the thread introducing the Silk Road marketplace. Resurrection of long-deleted users and threads might have been a result of the restoration process, but the timing was incredibly coincidental. Of course, the forum owner may have decided that in light of recent events it would be good 'clickbait' to restore the posts of the now-notorious former member.

But what it did was effectively sever the direct link drawn by the FBI between the Dread Pirate Roberts who had written 'I started a thread on the Bitcoin forum' and Ross Ulbricht. Previously, the only visible thread started on the Bitcointalk forum was by altoid, with whom Ulbricht was connected. The reinstated posts pointed to DPR talking about the thread started by the user silkroad, who did not appear to have any connection with Ulbricht.

The court documents provided only the detail necessary for an indictment and omitted classified details of the law enforcement procedures used to track Ulbricht and shut down the site, so many people felt they weren't getting the complete picture. The lucky coincidences, the lax security practised by one of the most hunted fugitives in the world and the murder-for-hire allegations all seemed to belong in an action movie. None of what was emerging fit the image Silk Road users had of the ideological leader of the world's most successful online black market. This was the man who had publicly admonished members who wanted to reveal private information relating to suspected law enforcement infiltrators of Silk Road and who preached peace.

But as more official documents were released, the case against the Dread Pirate Roberts began to look more and more damning.

Worldwide Silk Road arrests came thick and fast. Some, like a UK arrest of three men, were hailed as Silk Road arrests but yielded little detail. On 7 November 2013, Curtis Clark Green, aka Chronicpain, pleaded guilty to drug conspiracy charges. He was facing up to forty years in prison, but at the time of writing had not been sentenced.

Steve Lloyd Sadler, aka Silk Road vendor Nod, a top-ranked heroin, meth and cocaine dealer – he of the cocaine price-fixing cartel – had been arrested on 31 July 2013, unbeknown to the community, as his account remained active for a good two months after his arrest. His arrest was related to his real-life activities rather than his online dealings and, according to court documents revealed by whistleblowing website The Smoking Gun, he had been under surveillance for a year or more prior to being busted. After his arrest, it was alleged, he turned informant, providing the authorities with information on Silk Road.

Nod later told Patrick O'Neill, now working for *The Daily Dot*, that the charges were true. He admitted to O'Neill that he had been working with Homeland Security to track down Dread Pirate Roberts, and that he had an 'unspoken agreement' that his assistance would reduce the charges against him. But when the FBI arrested Ulbricht in an unrelated investigation, Homeland Security no longer had any use for him and he was arrested and put on bond to await trial.

A group of people who formed 'Hammertime' – a vendor who had allegedly sold over $600,000 worth of meth through Silk Road over a one-year period – were arrested in the US. Among their 3200 transactions were sales totalling 17.5 grams of meth sent to undercover federal agents in Maryland. Deputies also seized methamphetamine, computers and firearms in that raid.

Blake of AussieDomesticDrugs posted his thoughts on the shutdown:

Fuck. The damage was going to be considerable, I had a lot in escrow on all of my buying and selling accounts. Once I had calculated the damage it was over $60,000 worth of BTC. A lot less than I had made in the time I'd been selling there but a considerable loss regardless.

I cleaned my house, searching for anything incriminating. Paperwork, USB sticks and removable media were burned, laptops all formatted with DBAN [a program designed to securely erase a hard disk] for good measure and I mentally went through every message I could remember exchanging on the site to make sure I could account for all loose ends.

I spent the day driving around and checked every single drop I had. I grabbed all the orders that had arrived and then abandoned all of the drops after that, never to be checked again.

Then I went out and got royally drunk with my business partner. We toasted DPR and all the money he had made us and wished for his health and security, and that things would somehow work out for him.

When SR shut down I lost just over $60,000 that was held in escrow with 2 European vendors as well as in escrow on my vending accounts, however I still did quite well financially from Silk Road.

I feel I have done extremely well in my time here because on top of saving up so much money I have also spent a great deal of money and lived a very nice lifestyle.

The road might be down but this is only a temporary setback. DPR has shown us the ease with which dealers can now amass large fortunes without fear of being brought down by informants, who are the main source of information police use to arrest street dealers. Dealers can now safely sell to anyone they like, even the police themselves and be safe as long as they follow simple security precautions. At the same time sellers can buy from dealers without the risk of violence or extortion, and they can compare reviews from other buyers to make sure they are getting exactly what they paid for and not something potentially harmful. Best of all though, the person running the operation can become a multi-millionare [sic] doing nothing more than maintaining a marketplace and providing a trusted escrow service for the buyers and sellers. It's a win/win/win situation for everyone except law enforcement and people have seen the light. Now that Silk Road is down it's not like everyone is going to go back to the street and start again. We know this model works and the financial incentives are there for the next person to take over the reigns [sic] where DPR left off, start a second Silk Road or a similar marketplace and get just as rich as he did. I would love to do it myself but I lack the technical knowledge.

It is very sad what happened to DPR, he was an inspiration to me personally and I really came to respect him. It is my belief that he was in over his head when it came to computer security though. He studied physics and engineering at university and was a very bright guy but when it came to setting up a secure website he had no formal training, qualifications or relevant experience and this is what let him down as he made so many rookie errors. He was learning as he went along and because he couldn't have known at the start how popular his idea would become he initially underestimated the resources of the opponents he was facing. The authorities chasing him could make a thousand mistakes but he only had to make one tiny slip up and it could be his downfall.

I am really interested to see what happens next!

Interests: trading, economics, physics, virtual worlds, liberty.
                    – Ross Ulbricht's LinkedIn profile

Meet Ross Ulbricht

At his bail hearing in November 2013, Ross Ulbricht's lawyers submitted a total of sixty-three letters from family, friends and others attesting to his character and integrity. They described his reputation for charity and generosity and praised his gentle and peace-loving nature. Bail was denied, however, when the authorities countered with four more murder-for-hire charges to add to the two that had already been laid.

'We found it interesting timing that four new murder-for-hire accusations were revealed only that day,' wrote his mother in her blog. 'Ross's attorney received this information only the evening before, making it impossible for him to discuss it with Ross and challenge it at the hearing. Of course, as with the first two, there are no bodies connected to these new allegations, and we are certain there never will be.'

On 16 January 2014, the US government received permission from US District Judge J. Paul Oetken to sell off the

29,655 bitcoins seized from Silk Road and valued at around $25 million – but not the 144,366 bitcoins that had been found on Ulbricht's laptop. Ulbricht filed a civil forfeiture action, asserting that he was the owner of the bitcoins found on his computer hardware – by this time worth well over $100 million – and disputing their forfeiture. Cryptocurrency, being mere data, was not subject to civil forfeiture, he contested. He may well have needed access to the funds to pay his newly appointed lawyer, Joshua Dratel, who was known for his defence work in high-profile terrorism cases.

On 4 February 2014, Ulbricht was indicted in the US District Court for the Southern District of New York on four counts: narcotics conspiracy, engaging in a continuing criminal enterprise (sometimes called the 'kingpin' charge), conspiracy to commit computer hacking, and money-laundering conspiracy.

Notably absent was any mention of the murder-for-hire allegations. As these were the most sensational accusations against Dread Pirate Roberts, some thought this was an indication that DPR had been the victim of entrapment or fabricated evidence. 'I didn't really believe the murder charges at first,' said one forum member. 'Now it's 100% bullshit, fucking pigs.'

Others believed he did it, but was justified. 'I believe DPR ordered the two killings, from careful reading of the documents available,' said one member. 'I believe his actions were moral. In a just world, his right to property would be protected by the government, and he would have recourse to the police, court system, and prisons . . . Without access to those institutions, and with no ability to incarcerate those guilty of non-capital crimes, DPR chose the only available option.'

Another theory was that there really had been more than one person with access to the Dread Pirate Roberts account, and the DPR who had ordered the hits was a different person from the DPR who ran the site. But most people were appalled and said they would withdraw all support for DPR if he had ordered the murders. 'The unsealed complaint leaves absolutely no doubt that he payed [sic] money in exchange for murder. No one but a fanatic or a syco-phant would dispute this,' Silk Road forum member 'cRandom' wrote. 'He did something illegal and now you're all crying the blues because he got arrested for it? People go into this line of business understanding the risks. They don't do it and cry about how unfair it is when they get caught . . . Just realise your god was nothing more than a suburban white boy with someone else's itchy trigger finger. Nothing more. Stop defending him, it's pathetic.'

Ulbricht pleaded not guilty to all charges.

'Who is Ross Ulbricht? (Really): Eagle Scout, academic honors student, scholarship recipient, beloved son, grandson and brother, friend of many,' said the Twitter feed set up by his family, @Free_Ross.

Many publications worked hard to unearth details of Ulbricht, most notably *Rolling Stone*, which published a lengthy piece by David Kushner. According to the various articles, Ross Ulbricht – a handsome Robert Pattinson lookalike – told anyone who asked that he was a foreign currency trader and described himself on his LinkedIn profile as an 'Investment Adviser and Entrepreneur'. He lived simply, paying $1200 a month in cash to sublet a room in a house he shared with two other men, who knew him as Josh Terrey. His housemates told *Forbes* that he was quiet and tidy and kept to himself, spending most of the day on his computer. He was a nature-loving former Eagle Scout and academic high achiever who had earned multiple scholarships to the University of Texas at Dallas for Academic Excellence, Engineering and Science, as well as a Graduate Fellowship at Pennsylvania State University.

'For those of us who know Ross, the accusations would be laughable if they were not so serious,' wrote his mother, Lyn Ulbricht, on a fundraising page the family set up to help with Ulbricht's defence costs. 'Ross is an honorable, caring person who is loved and admired by countless friends and, of course, his family.' His family included his sister Cally, with whom he had lived in her Bondi home for six months in 2011, when Silk Road was in its infancy.

Ulbricht's family and friends found it just as incomprehensible that he was the Dread Pirate Roberts as DPR's supporters found the murder-for-hire allegations.

'As I've told Ross himself many times, I look to him as a role model for how to live life and be as a person,' one testimonial said. 'I haven't met anybody who has met him and doesn't love him.'

'The quality that stands out the most is his integrity. Ross is deeply loyal and caring about his friends and family and would never deliberately hurt or cheat another human being (or animal for that matter),' said another.

Family and friends put their life savings on the line in bail pledges. 'I trust Ross completely: So much so, we are putting up our house toward his bail. I would never consider jeopardizing the roof over our heads if I didn't think Ross was completely trustworthy,' said his aunt.

Online, stories began to emerge from sources other than the FBI that Dread Pirate Roberts might not have been quite the peace-loving revolutionary everyone thought he was. In particular, ex-staff members from Silk Road started coming out of the woodwork to call him out as a control freak and even as frightening.

The person who claimed to be original moderator, Nomad Bloodbath, had been scathing of DPR in the time prior to Bloodbath's departure: 'He didn't care about members' safety he didn't care about the rampant scams,' he wrote. 'SR had mutated to [a] not so pleasant place to spend your waking hours and id seen many things I didn't support and never signed on for.'

Another former moderator wrote in the forums after Ulbricht's arrest:

The DPR I had interactions with more closely resembles the profile painted by the prosecution than the picture of a warm, caring individual painted by his family.

To make a long story short, let me just say that I was the person who was first offered the job that ended up being taken by Curtis Green a.k.a. Chronicpain/Flush. I wasn't using this pseudonym (obviously) but another one that became known for expertise in security and encryption. DPR offered me the 'customer service' position, but I refused it on the basis that my time was spoken for. As I explained to DPR at the time, I was dealing with an extremely ill relative, and there was simply no way that I could devote the time to the job that it would have required.

DPR's reaction to that polite refusal was cold, even callous. What he said was that if I did decide to take the position Silk Road would have to be my TOP priority. Normally, if I have an interaction with someone that mentions that they are looking after an extremely ill relative, my first reaction would [be] to express my sympathies for their situation. I would express my best wishes for their relative's recovery. To do so is not only polite, it expresses empathy for the circumstances another human being is currently undergoing.

NONE of this was evident in DPR's response to me. All that he apparently cared about were his wants, his needs, and his desires. I thought then (and I think now) that such self-absorption, not to mention a complete lack of empathy, borders on the sociopathic. Even if I had not already been predisposed not to accept this offer, this would have torpedoed the matter right then and there.

. . .

To put it mildly, communications with DPR was [sic] spotty, at best. He might take days to reply to a PM. If you asked him half a dozen questions, he might reply to one, if you got any reply at all.

Some time later DPR again came down on me hard, again accusing me of 'abusing my authority'. I was told, point blank, if I repeated my actions, I would be stripped of my moderator privileges. Now you might be led to wonder what high crime had I committed to earn this all-too-stern rebuke?

My high crime consisted of stickying [ensuring the post appeared at the top of the forum] a security-related post. It was not long after that DPR stripped all the moderators of their privileges, without so much as a by your leave. Apparently the efforts of those who had donated their time and skills to help support the site were unworthy of even so much as a simple 'Thank You.' (Nevermind an explanation.)

Shortly after that, I bailed from the site. deleting all my posts, and never returned.

The picture emerging of the man once hailed as a hero, a visionary and a revolutionary was very unflattering indeed.

But was it Ross Ulbricht?

Aftermath

The seizure of Silk Road and the arrest of the man the FBI claimed was the Dread Pirate Roberts were a boon for Silk Road's two remaining competitors, Black Market Reloaded and Sheep Marketplace.

On the Silk Road forums, members held confabs about what to do next. Threads started to spring up advising that a vendor had moved: 'XXX vendor now on BMR and Sheep! Same great product, same great prices!' Those who assumed the Silk Road forums had been compromised used Reddit to discuss the alternatives. What was clear was that the closure of Silk Road was no more likely to prevent people from buying drugs online than the closure of Napster had prevented people from illegally downloading audio files.

The vendors on Silk Road were ready for the sudden closure of the site. Backups of their contact details had been collated and stored offsite by StExo, and buyers were able to verify their vendors by using PGP keys previously supplied. If you sent someone an encrypted message and they were able to read it, you could be pretty confident they were the same person. Ulbricht's indictment admitted that the quality and purity of drugs obtained from Silk Road were far superior to those of the drugs generally available on the street, so it should have come as no surprise to the authorities that people would search for a new online source.

BMR and Sheep, both websites that had contentedly remained in the background until Silk Road's closure, were suddenly inundated with vendors and customers alike. BMR, which had been around for at least two years, was almost as old as Silk Road. The alternative marketplace was so swamped with new members that its owner, Backopy, had to close the site to new registrations every few hours. 'SR grew that much over two years, getting the same load in a couple of days isn't easy to adjust,' said Backopy. He urged members to split themselves between his site and Sheep: 'Too much for a single site would put a spotlight on it.'

But some members expressed reservations about transferring their business to BMR because the site did not subscribe to Silk Road's philosophy of not listing anything the intent or purpose of which was to harm or defraud others. Black Market Reloaded's willingness to list weapons, poisons, stolen goods and credit card and bank account details did not sit well with the moral high ground drug users.

It was a confusing time. Opportunists were taking advantage of the situation by setting up accounts on the alternative websites under the names of trusted Silk Road vendors. Savvy customers were switched on to this, though, and were able to verify their vendors either by using their PGP key or by contacting them via the still-active Silk Road forums.

Then there was the spread of FUD on all of the forums. Some was no doubt the result of genuine fear, uncertainty and doubt on the part of the spreader. But a lot of it was by trolls and probably some by law enforcement. The various reports that had been leaked over the internet over the years had, after all, reiterated several times that undermining user trust and social engineering were law enforcement's best weapons in fighting Silk Road.

Australian users interviewed for *The Age* about what the takedown of Silk Road meant for them suggested their response would not be to reduce or eliminate their drug use. Stacey Long decided she would sit back and wait for a while, though she was pretty sure that wouldn't be too long.

'I went and checked out BMR and Sheep right away,' she said. 'I signed up for both, but none of my favourite vendors were there.' This had been a theme with Stacey. She built up trust with certain vendors and found it really hard to move on. Moving to a whole new website was much scarier.

'If Ivory or Symbiosis [her preferred vendors] were there and I could verify them, I'd be on it straight away,' she admitted.

'Paul', a heroin addict, wrote about where the bust left him:

The arrest of DPR and the consequences to Silk Road as result have hit me hard and those just like me, and I feel that by telling my story I truly speak for the vast majority of people in the same boat as me.

I've been a Heroin addict for 5 years now and I've done pretty much every drug you can think of and SR seriously was nothing short of a God-send for myself (and those just like me). Now that SR is gone I (and countless others just like me) got to go back to scoring from my real life street sources and when you're talking about Heroin it's not like going and scoring a ten pack of eckies for a festival on the weekend. It's a whole different world, a much seedier more crime-orientated world.

Now if [sic] got to go back to associating with criminals and the dregs of society to get my drug of choice. And if that's not bad enough the quality of the H that I get IRL [in real life] is sub-par to the stuff I was getting on SR and the prices are pretty much the same. This is a sad day for everybody involved indeed.

It was an opportunity for Black Market Reloaded and Sheep Marketplace to step into the void. BMR provided Silk Road refugees with their own forum to regroup and reconnect with their favourite vendors, while former Silk Road vendors went through a verification process and were given a badge to prove they were the same seller.

Sheep Marketplace had previously languished behind the other markets, with few listings or customers. But once Silk Road was seized they were inundated with new customers who did not want to go to Black Market Reloaded or wanted further options. Sheep was happy to take in the new customers:

Greetings to all,
Unfortunately, today it was announced that site owner Silkroad was arrested. Silkroad pages are gone. It [sic] irreparable damage to all who took advantage of Silkroad. For us Silkroad not only competition but the main inspiration.

We believe that replace Silkroad will not be easy. But we want our plan to continue.

For a start, we have increased many times server performance. If you have any questions feel free to ask or write to technical support.

Kind regards

SheepSupport

But the competition was short-lived. A little over a month later, Sheep Marketplace claimed that it had been hacked by one of its vendors, who had stolen around $7 million worth of bitcoin. 'We are sorry to say, but we were robbed on Saturday 11/21/2013 by vendor EBOOK101. This vendor found a bug in the system and stole 5400 BTC – your money, our provisions, all was stolen,' Sheep said. Its response to this was to shut up shop and take off with whatever bitcoin was still sitting in users' accounts.

For a while a frenzy of internet sleuths believed they were following the blockchain trail of the rest of Sheep's funds, on which they were putting a figure of $100 million – an astonishing number when for all intents and purposes the site had been operating for only a short time. The cryptocurrency detectives followed the transfers through tumblers and wallets, eschewing sleep and occasionally making a minuscule donation of 0.00666 of a bitcoin, hoping to freak out the thieves as they saw these unexplained amounts enter the accounts they believed were laundering their bitcoin.

It all became a bit embarrassing when someone who had been following the detectives pointed out they were actually following the internal transfers of BTC-E, a legitimate bitcoin currency exchange. By that time, whoever had absconded with the $7 million worth of coin from Sheep had managed to either cash out or thoroughly hide the money.

Black Market Reloaded, on the other hand, never went rogue. Rather, Backopy announced he did not want the responsibility of running the largest market on the web and was going to close down. He did, however, provide ample opportunity for all of BMR's members to complete any transactions in progress and withdraw any bitcoin they had sitting in the marketplace. BMR was also subject to a hack, which took around $200,000 of funds in escrow; Backopy paid this back from his own earnings. The black market most reviled by Silk Road users seemed to be the most honourable when it came to shutting up shop.

But still, it shut. 'Tor can't support any site to be too big,' Backopy explained on the BMR forum.

'Tor is all about community and you just keep anonymous as long as you can blend with the community. Tor isn't a place for big enterprises, and can't hold another wave of refugees,' he said, referring to the waves of new registrations the site received every time one of its competitors shut down.

A representative of long-time trusted vendor The Scurvy Crew expressed frustration at the rapid closure of all the viable online black markets. 'We have lost more money in 5 months than many entire families make in a lifetime,' he said.

It was beginning to look like law enforcement had won the war after all.

Silk Road 2.0

While BMR and Sheep were inundated with Silk Road refugees, the race had already begun to create a new incarnation of Silk Road. The rallying cries were there: 'We won't be taken down! You will never take our freedom!'

A few members of the old forums began building new markets, each with a strained goodwill toward the others, all making passive-aggressive posts pointing out why their new market should be the anointed successor. 'They really were a bunch of illiterate, incompetent nutjobs!' said 'Wicked Words' about the first attempt.

A couple of false starts later, the frontrunners for the new Silk Road emerged when some former moderators and senior members of the seized market took on the job. Libertas, who had been an administrator on the old forum, took charge:

Ladies and gentlemen,

I would like to announce our new home: http://silkroad-5v7dywlc.onion

As I have always stated, even with Silk Road itself, you should act at all times as though any site or marketplace you visit has been compromised from the very beginning. That is the only way to ensure that you do not become lax with your security.

Do not fall into a false sense of security at any time on any site. Do not get comfortable. When you get comfortable you get confident, when you get confident you get cocky, and when you get cocky you get caught.

With the necessary security warnings out of the way, I look forward to seeing you all over on the new site. Let LE waste their time and resources whilst we make a statement to the world that we will not allow jackbooted government thugs [to] trample our freedom.

We are born free, yet moments later we are shackled by the rule of law. It is time, once again, to break free of those shackles.

Libertas

A new Dread Pirate Roberts – whose identity was hotly debated but ultimately kept secret – was appointed and was soon dubbed DPR 2.0. A team started work around the clock to re-create the market: same philosophy, same name, same look but ultimately a new and improved version.

This new captain of the ship was proactive and friendly. Like the DPR of the months leading up to Ulbricht's arrest, he actively courted the media – but went a step further: the new Silk Road provided a special membership for those journalists and writers the administration felt had fairly represented the site in the past. These individuals were bestowed with an avatar that was a different colour from that of the regular members – lime-green boxes under your name instead of yellow. And they had access to a subforum that was invisible to everyone but them and the moderators. The chosen journalists would hear of changes and new market features before anyone else, straight from DPR 2.0 himself.

Silk Road 2.0 officially launched one month and three days after the first Silk Road was shuttered. It was originally set for opening at the poetic time of 4.20 pm on 5 November 2013 ('420' is slang for marijuana and 5 November is Guy Fawkes day, Fawkes' mask being the symbol for Anonymous). A technical glitch pushed the grand opening back twenty-four hours to 6 November, a date on which little of note has ever happened. Silk Road 2.0 was relaunched with a triumphant – if a little dramatic – speech by the new leader on the homepage:

Welcome to the new Silk Road.

As everyone is now aware, the previous Silk Road has fallen. For law enforcement worldwide this was a small victory for them where they would receive a pat on the back from their superiors and maybe a good Christmas bonus coming up for them. However, what law enforcement has failed to understand is the consequences of their actions.

Silk Road is not one man. Silk Road is an idea, and where Silk Road now lies is in the people who made it what it was and it is those people who will, with a little help, bring the idea back to life again under a new name. We are not afraid of our governments, and we never should be. I hope this next phase in the life of the Silk Road is going to be just as interesting, just as productive and just as helpful as the last one was and we will move on from the individual man who started the idea to produce a new site for the free exchange of substances and materials.

Whilst our marketplace is not yet fully developed, I feel it was necessary to release the forums in good time so as to keep the community together. It should not be long until the full market is release[d] and we can all resume trading again and this time, I have taken on board the lessons of the first market. We are designing everything with scalability in mind to ensure the flawless expansion of the market, and will also launch a new awareness campaign of our presence.

This community has some fantastic sellers amongst us, too numerous to name them all individually, but their services are a tribute to the trade and are helping to slowly fix the image the average man and woman on the street picture when they hear of drug dealers. You are professionals in your own right, and I wish you all the very best of luck in your trades for whatever reason you are doing it.

When we launch our new marketplace, I should make all aware that we will also at the time be bringing out some new features which will give us the competitive edge over all other markets, as well as help draw customers in and increase the security of individuals by creating a phishing-proof login method which those competent in PGP will be very pleased to see. In addition to this, our marketing campaign will be wide-spread, we hope to bring in the entire former Silk Road community by reaching out to them on every platform and via every means we have at our disposal. In the mean time, this will also attract new users to our market and help continue our trend of expansion.

Together we will show law enforcement that whilst they may be able to lock up and imprison one man, they can never stop the idea behind it.

As an end to this debut speech, many of you are perhaps wondering who I am because it is only logical that I am not the original Dread Pirate Roberts? I am not him no, I am not 'the original', but I am somebody who was close to him from the very start of his work, right until the very end, and I fully intend to continue what he started as the title is passed to me. I have no doubt one day I will either be caught or pass the title on before that time, but the most important thing we should remember is that no matter who the man is behind Dread Pirate Roberts, you do not serve him – I am here to serve you.

Your new loyal leader,

Dread Pirate Roberts

The new administration recognised the vital role the community had to play in the success of the market and set about rebuilding that community. Many of the former members signed up under their old usernames and reposted their favourite threads. DoctorX was back dispensing advice and spare coins were being handed out to those most deserving.

As well as the new Dread Pirate Roberts and Libertas, there was a behind-the-scenes administrator, 'Defcon', and moderators 'Cirrus' and 'Sarge'. Popular Silk Road veteran and spreader of spare coins and love 'ChemCat' became the 'Newbie Guide' appointed to help new members get the best out of their Silk Road experience.

Spirits were buoyed when ex-administrator Inigo joined the team in his old role. Then former moderator Samesamebutdifferent (SSBD) resurfaced. The team was a mix of old and new names, highly engaged and popular with the community.

The new team advertised for contractors and freelancers to work for the website. Those with the appropriate IT skills were offered 'bounties' of various amounts to complete tasks required by Silk Road but that did not require access to any sensitive information.

Vendors and buyers drifted back to the name they knew. The community grew confident; it seemed that Silk Road had been born again. The team seemed to be working hard to protect its members. In one interview, with Ken Klippenstein of *Ars Technica*, DPR 2.0 claimed he had 'already locked down over 15 law enforcement honeypot vendors' and 'our team is busy fighting off an armada of hackers'.

Silk Road was back. Security was better than ever and staff old and new were invincible. They wouldn't be making the mistakes of their predecessor.

I won't be around that long I am afraid. I can only advise you to buckle up for one rough ride.
– Dread Pirate Roberts 2.0 in response to a request from the author to contribute to this book, 19 December 2013

I believe the data will contain numerous private messages between users of the site that may enable the FBI to identify particular users, potentially including the administrators of the website and the most prominent drug dealers operating on it.

– Extract from search warrant issued on JTAN.com,
9 September 2013

The Sinking Ship

On 19 December 2013, the media reported that Silk Road administrators and moderators Inigo (real name Andrew Jones), Libertas (Gary Davis) and SSBD (Peter Nash) had been arrested in Virginia, Ireland and Brisbane, respectively. Davis and Nash faced deportation to the US on conspiracy charges, which carry a maximum life imprisonment term.

Silk Road members speculated that Ross Ulbricht had provided their names to the authorities in an effort to cooperate, and DPR 2.0 called Ulbricht a 'coward' in a media interview. But given that the FBI had access to all of Dread Pirate Roberts' private correspondence and Ulbricht denied that he was DPR (and so would be unlikely to give up any names of his staff), the more likely explanation was that their details had been found on the server. As everyone now knew, the first DPR had not been fond of encrypting private data.

Arrests went beyond the Silk Road marketplace itself. The vice chairman of the Bitcoin Foundation, Charlie Shrem, was later charged with money laundering related to Silk Road, along with Robert Faiella, who was alleged to be an underground bitcoin exchanger.

Jones and Davis were released on bail almost immediately, but Nash was remanded in a Queensland prison until his extradition hearing in February 2014. Despite his only crime being the moderating of an internet discussion forum – he had no role in the marketplace alleged in the indictment – he was being treated more harshly than some of the worst violent offenders.

DPR 2.0 wrote one final post in the confidential media forum, confirming the arrests, and then disappeared. Sarge quit. The forum mods who were left – Cirrus and ChemCat – and administrator Defcon went into 'emergency mode' and released a dramatic 'contingency plan':

Silk Road Community –
It has now been over 24 hours since we last heard from our Captain. He is most certainly in grave danger. As posted by Cirrus: Do not trust DPR 2.0's PGP keys. Do not trust any communication claiming to be from DPR 2.0.

As his second in command, I have very clear instructions as to what to do in this worst case scenario.

He appointed a successor before he began. You know who you are, and you know what to do. Consider this the signal.

I cannot elaborate on the specifics, but the marketplace is safe and in my hands until the Captain returns or his successor appears.

Given these shocking events, I am delaying Christmas Break for another 12 hours so that you may withdraw your coins if you so desire.

Make no mistake – Silk Road is not dead, the marketplace is not compromised, and it will return after the break regardless of how this plays out.

Meanwhile, a campaign of misinformation and deliberate chaos ensued on the forums. Mysterious members who previously had made few posts surfaced claiming inside information on the identity of the new Dread Pirate Roberts. The forums filled up with reports that he had been arrested, that he was on the run, or that he hadn't gone anywhere and Defcon was him under another name.

One member in particular, 'Oracle', posted frequently that he had 'important news' and 'intel' about Silk Road, including that the new Dread Pirate Roberts was StExo, the money launderer from the original site.

StExo and the new DPR certainly shared some traits – grandiose statements and overdramatic flourishes in their musings, in particular. These were also similar to the posts made by the original DPR in the couple of months before the Ulbricht arrest. And now the administrator Defcon was writing in a similar style.

But then Oracle claimed to have been part of a master plan to spread misinformation to throw off the authorities and give DPR time to get away. Silk Road became farcical as sensational claims of 'opsec', 'master plans' and 'emergency mode' rang through the forums. It sounded like the site had become overrun with wannabe criminal masterminds. The dramatic posts, banning of members and deletion of threads caused enough confusion that many long-time members became exasperated and left.

Silk Road closed for its planned Christmas break, then reopened for 2014. Administrator Defcon had taken the reins. 'This past week our ship suffered major damage,' he wrote. 'Three of our crew were lost, and our Captain was forced into exile.' But, he said, there was a slight problem: 'As contingency plans were engaged, an even graver situation reared its head below deck. Will this be the end of everything we fought for? Will our movement be remembered as a cypherpunk fad, or as an unstoppable force? I'm here to fight. But I recommend that you take a deep breath.'

What had happened? The new Silk Road's bitcoins in escrow were stored offline ('cold storage') to protect against hackers. Cold storage can be either a computer that has never been connected to the internet or a physical piece of paper kept in a safe. In the case of an emergency, Dread Pirate Roberts was to hit a 'killswitch' and Defcon would receive an encrypted message with the keys to the escrow cold storage. 'I am still waiting for it,' Defcon said. 'If you have funds in escrow, you will not be able to access them yet, even once they are released/refunded to you.'

He went on to say: 'I cannot elaborate on the specifics of the killswitch mechanism or the Captain's present situation, as it will cause more harm than good. We do know for a fact that he has not been compromised or detained by our oppressors, and that he does not hold any information which would threaten any within this community.' Defcon said that he and his fellow administrators had committed to repay vendors personally from their commissions over the coming months.

Instead, the escrow bitcoins were mysteriously released by DPR 2.0 and business returned to normal. A few people pointed out that Defcon could have accessed the funds in cold storage only if he had physical access to the offline wallet. The entire process smacked of an elaborate charade. But it seemed to work. Theories were put forth and their merits argued, but Silk Road was soon practically back to normal, and in no time there were more than 13,000 listings of illicit drugs available for sale.

But the site had become a farcical facsimile of its former self, and the dramas continued. In February 2014, Silk Road claimed it had been hacked via the same methods as MtGox had been, with all the money in its wallets stolen.

'I am sweating as I write this,' said Defcon. 'This movement is built on integrity, and I feel obligated to be forthright with you. I held myself to a high standard as your leader, yet now I must utter words all too familiar to this scarred community: We have been hacked.'

He went on to say that the hack had happened at the worst possible time. As the administration of the site had planned on launching a new auto-finalise feature, all of the community's coins had been moved into hot storage. They were all gone.

Few believed the story and the consensus was that Defcon, or whoever was at the helm by this time, had absconded with the money. Long-term members left in droves. Reddit's 'Dark Market' sub-Reddit flagged Silk Road as suspicious, marking it with a prominent warning sign. Other alternative news outlets that had previously been friendly towards Silk Road withdrew their support.

Again the administrators – constantly changing their names and personas, if not the people behind the keyboards – promised all coins would be returned. But there would be changes. Escrow, previously the backbone of the market's business model, was disabled. All transactions were to be made on a 'finalise early' and thus buyer-beware basis. It seemed that the management team was now operating Ponzi-style – repaying the debt with new income.

The discussion forums stopped being a lively, intelligent home of self-styled revolutionaries united in their fight against the war on drugs. Infighting and division became the norm and the site's management became increasingly less visible and engaged, emerging only to provide the occasional update reassuring those who were left that all was fine. Reports of scamming sellers became increasingly frequent, with many accusing the administration of aiding and abetting the scammers.

Silk Road journalist Raoul Duke had been ostracised by the administrators of the website and now retaliated by posting lengthy diatribes in which he admitted to being several of Silk Road's well-known identities. He said he had 'socially engineered' his way into being given vendor status under one identity and journalist status under another, having never sold an item on a black market nor written anything other than amphetamine-fuelled rants on the discussion forums. He claimed DPR 2.0 and other staff of the new Silk Road had co-opted him to engage in 'psyops' (psychological operations) to undermine troublesome vendors and spread uncertainty throughout the community, including slandering marijuana vendor 'Green Machine' over a supposed $30,000 he lost. He accused the new management of self-interest and of protecting known scammers, and named several Silk Road staff members as being complicit in the so-called psyops.

If this was a deliberate attempt to spread confusion and misinformation, it worked. Many theories were floated about the new administration of Silk Road, with the one seeming most likely being that the original Dread Pirate Roberts was either effecting a handover of the business to StExo or had allowed him access to the forum account to become Silk Road's public face, and that it was StExo who had taken over the Dread Pirate Roberts forum account around mid-2013, if not the keys to the marketplace. He had then become DPR 2.0, as well as some other Silk Road 2 staff members. Tellingly, both Defcon and 'DrClu' repeatedly made the same error of using 'withdraws' instead of 'withdrawals' that the post-August DPR had made (and the pre-August DPR had not). However, the suspected connection is by no means confirmed. The team at Silk Road 2.0 continued to spread disinformation designed to confuse. Journalist Ken Klippenstein, who interviewed some of the site's staff members, wrote:

> Defcon, Silk Road's interim leader, is a hacker whom staff describe as more technically capable than his predecessor [DPR 2.0]. Whether or not Defcon will don the black mask of 'Dread Pirate Roberts 3.0' is uncertain, though the site's attitude about free access to drugs remains: 'As you wish.'

Stylometric analysis – a method of identifying anonymous authorship – had long been flagged as a way to catch online criminals. Running several of those 'most likely' through the system (assisted by a professor at the University of Newcastle), the results were inconclusive, but did not rule out the same author being responsible for several reams of text. The strongest connections were between StExo, DPR 2.0 and the Dread Pirate Roberts in the latter part of 2013, the one who had provided numerous media interviews.

And that person is writing his own script as he goes.

DPR 2.0 wrote one last private message to me after warning me to buckle up for a rough ride and after he'd disappeared from the forums:

You're not the only one writing a book, you know.

Satoshi Unmasked?

While Silk Road dominated the headlines, bitcoin continued on its way, its value fluctuating wildly every time it was mentioned in the news – which was increasingly often.

In February 2014, MtGox, the original and largest bitcoin exchange in the world, claimed it had been hacked, with 850,000 bitcoin – around half a billion dollars worth – stolen. The coins were stolen thanks to a security flaw called transaction malleability. Mark Karpeles, the 28-year-old CEO of the Tokyo-based exchange, filed for bankruptcy.

Many did not believe the hack story: elusive, shadowy hackers, they said, had become a convenient way to explain million-dollar thefts. The complex technologies involved meant that truth could be obfuscated, red herrings could be flung about to lead internet sleuths astray, and confusion and conspiracy theories could drown out more strategic investigations. Disgruntled bitcoin owners started class actions against MtGox claiming fraud and conspiracy on the part of its major shareholders, top executives and a Japanese bank.

Somewhat surprisingly, the bitcoin value stabilised and then stayed consistent after this time. The financial pages of major media outlets continued to report on the cryptocurrency, with various experts divided about its relevance and longevity. But it was clear that it no longer relied on the dark markets for its value. What would Satoshi Nakamoto think of his multibillion-dollar invention now?

The hunt for Satoshi had not slowed down. Revered as the genius father of bitcoin, his elusiveness made him all the more interesting.

American IT sociologist and philosopher Ted Nelson had named maths genius Shinichi Mochizuki (male, 44, Japan) in May 2013 in a video he released on YouTube, but, as with earlier 'unmaskings', the evidence was weak. And again, the accused denied it.

In mid-2013, blogger Sergio Lerner uncovered a hoard of about $120 million in bitcoins owned by a single entity. That entity had begun mining right from block one – the so-called 'genesis block'. Evidence pointed to the stash being owned by Nakamoto. That the coins had remained untouched sparked another round of conspiracy theories: that he had died, that the coins were held on a corrupted hard drive and could therefore not be recovered, or that he couldn't cash out without destabilising the currency or revealing his identity.

Satoshi Nakamoto was named *Business Insider*'s most important person of 2013 and was a contender for the title in several other publications, including *The Guardian*.

Journalist Andrew Smith wrote a lengthy piece for the UK's

Sunday Times in late February 2014 about his personal hunt for Satoshi Nakamoto. Smith interviewed the suspects (or at least, those who agreed to speak to him) and found evidence lacking for each. All those who had been 'unmasked' by various publications over the years continued to deny they were the pseudonymous creator.

Smith put forth yet another name – mathematician David Chaum, founder of the International Association for Cryptologic Research. He was unable to contact Chaum, however, and admitted that while the profile fit, the evidence was – as always – circumstantial.

And then *Newsweek* promised the biggest story of the crypto-year. On 7 March 2014, journalist Leah McGrath claimed that Satoshi Nakamoto was . . . Dorian Satoshi Nakamoto, a 64-year-old Japanese-American living a humble life in suburban Los Angeles. In a feature that bordered on harassment of the man (he called the police to support him as he spoke to McGrath), photos of a nondescript, ageing man and his modest house belied the myth. His fortune – the so-called and still untouched 'genesis block' of the first bitcoins mined – by this time would have been worth over $400 million.

'Tacitly acknowledging his role in the bitcoin project, he looks down, staring at the pavement and categorically refuses to answer questions,' wrote McGrath.

'I am no longer involved in that and I cannot discuss it,' Nakamoto allegedly told the reporter. 'It's been turned over to other people. They are in charge of it now. I no longer have any connection.'

With no more words coming from Nakamoto himself, the rest of the story focused on a two-month investigation and conversations

with family and friends. Nakamoto, they said, had worked on classified projects for the government. And he liked model trains. Flimsy
though the evidence was, *Newsweek* decided to post pictures of the
man and his easily identifiable house, along with an estimate of his
net worth, for the world to see.

The story set off a media frenzy and soon reporters and journalists were camped outside the house, jostling for position and
taking pictures through the screen door. In a bizarre and somewhat surreal scene, Nakamoto emerged from his house looking
for a lift to go and buy sushi. 'No, no questions right now. I want
a free lunch. I'm not involved in bitcoin. Wait a minute. I want
free lunch first. I'm going to go with this guy,' he said, indicating a
reporter from Associated Press. Ignoring Nakamoto's own Corolla,
the two took off in the journalist's car, with all the less-favoured
following in a slow chase that was duly photographed and tweeted
as it happened.

Investigative journalists used the lunch break to track down
early online musings of the man enjoying his sushi. They had
absolutely no similarity to the carefully crafted writings of Satoshi
Nakamoto.

At the lunch, Dorian Nakamoto emphatically denied having any
involvement in bitcoin. He'd misunderstood the *Newsweek* reporter,
he said, English being his second language. The sole quote they
had got out of him – 'I am no longer involved in that' – was a reference to his work as an engineer on classified government projects.
He claimed he hadn't even heard of bitcoin before *Newsweek*
contacted him.

Later on the day of the sushi lunch came another bizarre twist.
A post appeared by 'Satoshi Nakamoto' on the P2P Foundation

website, where the real Nakamoto had unleashed his creation in 2009 and engaged in robust discussions about his 2008 white paper. The account that made the post was confirmed by the administrators of the site as being the same as that used by Satoshi Nakamoto, creator of bitcoin. It had been dormant since 2010. The author took pains to mask his IP address when posting.

The message was short and to the point. 'I am not Dorian Nakamoto,' the post said.

Once Associated Press had its interview and it became clear that Dorian Satoshi Nakamoto was less likely than any of the other candidates to be the creator of bitcoin, the media harassment stopped. Enthusiasts raised around $28,000 in bitcoin, joking that it was to provide Mr Nakamoto with free sushi for a year, but hoping it would help with his medical bills – Mr Nakamoto had apparently suffered a stroke and had battled prostate cancer.

Was the post on the P2P Foundation website a red herring or joke by the administrators of the site, who would be able to hijack an account on their forum by performing a password reset? Had hackers managed to crack Satoshi's password? Or had the real Satoshi Nakamoto come out of the woodwork to stop the harassment of the innocent Dorian?

It's likely we will never know. The post has since disappeared, and Satoshi Nakamoto is as much a ghost as he ever was. Perhaps he has simply 'gone on to other things'.

My primary motivation is not personal wealth, but making a difference. As corny as it sounds, I just want to look back on my life and know that I did something worthwhile that helped people.

– Dread Pirate Roberts forum post, 23 September 2012

Marketplaces are no longer being run by men with some form of integrity. They're being run as get rich quick schemes.
             – Oracle, posting to Silk Road 2, 28 June 2014

The Hydra

As Ross Ulbricht sat in prison awaiting his November 2014 trial, unable to access the $100 million worth of bitcoin stored on his computer, his mother tirelessly rallied to raise funds for his legal defence. The murder-for-hire allegations never made it into the formal charges of the indictment, but he still faced several life imprisonment terms. Supporters, including so-called 'Bitcoin Jesus' Roger Ver, raised over $200,000 in bitcoin donations to support his legal fund.

Efforts by Ulbricht's lawyer to have the remaining charges dropped – most notably the money-laundering charges, running the argument that bitcoin was deemed not to be money by the IRS – were unsuccessful. Ulbricht released a photograph of himself in prison garb and sent a message to the attendees of Porcfest, an annual gathering of the Free State Project, a libertarian movement:

Hi Porcfest, this is Ross.

The first thing they tell you when they arrest you is that what you say will be used against you, and they mean it. So I have to keep this brief. I'd just like to thank you for giving my Mom, Lyn, the chance to tell you about the situation I'm in and why the outcome of this legal battle will have a lasting impact on you and the rules you live under in this country.

One thing I've learned since beginning my tour of the federal criminal justice system is that these guys are not all-powerful. They can be beaten and precedent can be set that will limit their ability to infringe on our rights.

I urge you to stand by me and do what you can to turn this horrible situation into a win.

I wish I could be there with you, but of course I can't. With your help though, I'll see you at Porcfest 2015!

Peter Nash, allegedly forum moderator Samesamebutdifferent, decided not to fight extradition and was deported to the US in June 2014. In Brisbane, he had been placed in protective custody when a local newspaper revealed he had worked in a prison (albeit as a prison psychologist, not as a guard), and after his deportation he alleged he had been bashed by riot squad officers while he was locked up. The conspiracy charges he faces in the United States could see him in prison for life.

Andrew Jones, alleged to be Silk Road administrator Inigo, was released on a reported $1 million bail and was placed under 24/7 house arrest. One of his bail conditions was that he was not allowed access to any internet-enabled devices.

At the time of writing, Gary Davis, the man the authorities say was administrator Libertas, is awaiting the outcome of his extradition hearings in Ireland.

The 30,000 bitcoins seized from Silk Road were auctioned off by the US Marshal's office and purchased for an undisclosed amount by US-based venture capitalist Tim Draper. The 144,336 bitcoins (worth just shy of $100 million in June 2014) stored on Ulbricht's personal computer, however, remain the subject of a civil forfeiture claim.

Silk Road managed to continue to trade on its name as newcomers drifted to the only market that had made headlines. At its peak, it boasted more than 16,000 listings – 3000 more than the original Silk Road ever had, before subsiding to just under 13,000 at the time of writing. The administration, still headed by Defcon, appeared to be trying to do the right thing by its members, repaying coins they claimed had been stolen and trying to keep their sinking ship afloat.

But the community that had made Silk Road so successful was a shadow of its former self and those who had supported it for years moved to the less high-profile alternatives.

Although the rest of the major markets – Black Market Reloaded, Atlantis, Sheep Marketplace – had closed their virtual doors for good, dozens more sprang up in their place. These marketplaces operated on a smaller scale, sharing the heat and providing vendors with several outlets for their wares. Should one fail, customers knew where to find others.

Reddit became the main source for determining which dark markets could be trusted, and a new discussion forum in Onionland, The Hub, provided black-market users with a single home to discuss the various shops and make private arrangements with their favourite drug dealers. A new dark web search engine,

'Grams', was developed to work like an airline or hotel site aggre-
gator. Using an interface and design that mimicked Google, a
purchaser could input the name of their drug of choice and the
search engine would provide details of the most popular sellers
across all of the dark markets.

Some markets were short-lived, being seized by authorities
almost as soon as they opened for business. Others were scams
from the start. But little by little 'legitimate' black markets picked
up the Silk Road refugees and quietly did a roaring trade.

Many of Silk Road's largest vendors were arrested and
charged. Twenty-two-year-old Dutchman Cornelis Jan Slomp, aka
Supertrips, who had once boasted that 1 per cent of all bitcoin in
circulation had gone through his account, could have been right.
He was arrested during a trip to Miami and police estimated he
had taken in the equivalent of $170 million through Silk Road.
'Xanax King', a prolific supplier of prescription drugs, was a six-
person consortium; they were arrested in California. Bitcoin seller
'BTCKing' fell foul of an IRS investigation. Others, like The Scurvy
Crew, granted in-person interviews to journalists in an effort to
explain – and probably drum up – their business.

Although it seemed in the short term the authorities had won,
hundreds of thousands of people had accessed the various black
markets and made contacts they would not have been able to make
otherwise. Once the markets started getting seized, these same
people made private arrangements with their trusted vendors to
continue buying drugs on a one-on-one basis, using encrypted
private emails. It would be impossible for law enforcement to make
any sort of dent in the millions of single transactions that would
now be taking place through thousands of email accounts.

According to a report released on 30 April 2014 by Digital Citizens Alliance, a group of 'individuals, organizations and businesses dedicated to making the Internet safer and crime-free', the darknet drug economy as a whole contained 75 per cent more listings for drugs than it had at the time of the Silk Road seizure. A couple of months later, BBC reported that the number of drug deals available from dark web sites had doubled in less than a year, with 43,175 listings across twenty-three markets. Like the Hydra of Greek mythology, once one head was cut off, five more sprang up in its place. Silk Road remained the market leader, with nearly double the drug listings of its nearest competitor, newcomer Agora, closely followed by another new marketplace, Pandora. But none of the markets had the tight-knit, interactive community of the original Silk Road.

The moniker Dread Pirate Roberts may have been designed to be passed on from successor to successor, but it seemed nobody could fill the shoes of the revolutionary who had started the movement.

But perhaps Silk Road had done its job. Drug users around the world knew there was an alternative to buying from the streets. Connections had been made, business relationships had been forged and details of how to make online purchases could be found openly on the clearweb. The new markets made no pretence of trying to change the world; they were purely commercial enterprises.

The battle may have been won, but the war on drugs has been comprehensively lost. And Silk Road will go down in history as having changed the face of illicit drug dealing forever.

In one of the last interviews with Dread Pirate Roberts on the first Silk Road, a couple of months before the server was seized and

Ulbricht was arrested, the final question put to him was whether there was anything else he'd like to say about his business or the philosophy that underpinned it.

'Don't fight the future!' was his reply.

Sources

Aldridge, Judith and Décary-Hétu, David, 'Not an "eBay for drugs": The cryptomarket "Silk Road" as a paradigm shifting criminal innovation', 13 May 2014. Available at SSRN: http://ssrn.com/abstract=2436643 or http://dx.doi.org/10.2139/ssrn.2436643.

Australian Crime Commission, *Illicit Drug Data Report*, 2011–2012.

Barratt, M. J., 'Silk Road: eBay for drugs', *Addiction* 107(3), 2012.

Barratt, M. J., Ferris, J. A., & Winstock, A. R., 'Use of Silk Road, the online drug marketplace, in the United Kingdom, Australia and the United States', *Addiction* 109(5), 2014.

Bell, James, 'Assassination Politics', *Infowars*, 3 April 1997

Chen, Adrian, 'Please join me in welcoming myself', *Gawker*, 9 November 2009.

Chen, Adrian, 'The underground website where you can buy any drug imaginable', *Gawker*, 1 June 2011.

Chen, Adrian, 'Now you can buy guns on the online underground marketplace', *Gawker*, 27 January 2012.

SOURCES

Christin, Nicolas, 'Traveling the Silk Road: A measurement analysis of a large anonymous online marketplace', July 2012, arXiv:1207.7139 [cs.CY].

Crawford, Angus, 'Dark net drugs adverts double in less than a year', BBC News, 31 July 2014.

Davis, Joshua, 'Bitcoin and its mysterious inventor', *The New Yorker*, 10 October 2011.

Digital Citizens Alliance, 'Busted, but not broken: The state of Silk Road and the darknet marketplaces', 30 April 2014.

Dratel, Joshua L., law offices of, PC letter of support for bail application for Ross Ulbricht, 19 November 2013.

Federal Bureau of Investigation, Unclassified FBI Intelligence Assessment. 'Bitcoin virtual currency: Unique features present distinct challenges for deterring illicit activity', 24 April 2012.

Greenberg, Andy, 'Collected quotations of the Dread Pirate Roberts, founder of underground drug site Silk Road and radical libertarian', *Forbes*, 29 April 2013.

Greenberg, Andy, 'Meet the Dread Pirate Roberts, the man behind booming black market drug website Silk Road', *Forbes*, 2 September 2013.

Hanrahan, Jake, 'My Top Secret Meeting with One of the Silk Road's Biggest Drug Lords', *Vice Magazine*, 14 April 2014. http://www.vice.com/en_uk/tag/The+Scurvy+Crew.

Klippenstein, Ken, 'Dread Pirate Roberts 2.0: An interview with Silk Road's new boss', *Ars Technica*, 6 February 2014.

Klippenstein, Ken, 'What it's like to work for the pirate king of Silk Road' *Wired*, 9 June 2014.

Krebs, Brian, 'The world has no room for cowards', *Krebs on Security*, 13 March 2013.

Kushner, David, 'Dead end on Silk Road: Internet crime kingpin Ross Ulbricht's big fall', *Rolling Stone*, 4 March 2014.

McClintock, Alex, 'Silk Road and the fast-changing world of online drug shopping', *The Monthly*, June 2013.

McGrath, Leah, 'The face behind Bitcoin', *Newsweek*, 6 March 2014.

Meiklejohn, Sarah, Pomarole, Marjori, Jordan, Grant, Levchenko, Kirill, McCoy, Damon, Voelker, Geoffrey M. & Savage, Stefan, 'A fistful of bitcoins: Characterizing payments among men with no names', University of California, San Diego, 2013.

Nakamoto, Satoshi, 'Bitcoin: A peer-to-peer electronic cash system', www.bitcoin.org.

Nelson, Ted 'I think I know who Satoshi is', YouTube, 13 May 2013.

O'Neill, Patrick, 'Ambition has no rest: The long education of a Silk Road money launderer', *Weirder Web*, 10 June 2013.

O'Neill, Patrick, 'The final confessions of a Silk Road kingpin', *The Daily Dot*, 22 January 2014.

Pauli, Darren, 'Police struggle with online drug networks', *IT News*, 11 September 2012.

Penenberg, Adam L. 'The bitcoin crypto-currency mystery reopened', *Fast Company*, 11 October 2011.

Schumer, Charles E. & Manchin, Joe, 'Manchin urges federal law enforcement to shut down online black market for illegal drugs', press release, 6 June 2011.

Smith, Andrew, 'Desperately seeking Satoshi', *The Sunday Times*, 2 March 2014.

The Smoking Gun, 'Top Silk Road Drug Dealer Was Flipped By Feds', 21 October 2013.

United Nations Office on Drugs and Crime, *World Drug Report 2012*, June 2012.

United States Department of Justice, United States Attorney,
Southern District of New York letter to Judge Fox opposing bail
of Ross William Ulbricht, 20 November 2013

United States District Court for the District of Maryland, indictment of 'John Doe' aka Dread Pirate Roberts, 1 May 2013.

United States District Court for the District of Maryland, indictment of Ross William Ulbricht, 1 October 2013.

United States District Court for the Eastern District of Pennsylvania,
Search and Seizure Warrant on JTAN.com.

United States District Court Southern District of New York, United
States Of America vs Ross William Ulbricht, a/k/a 'Dread Pirate
Roberts', Criminal Complaint, 27 September 2013.

United States District Court Southern District of New York, indictment of Ross William Ulbricht, 4 February 2014.

Van Buskirk, J., Roxburgh, A., Bruno, R. & Burns, L., *Drugs and the
Internet*, National Drug and Alcohol Research Centre, Sydney,
1 August 2013.

Websites

Silk Road Tales and Archives at www.antilop.cc
The Silk Road at www.gwern.net
All Things Vice at www.allthingsvice.com

Forums

Silk Road forums at various .onion addresses
Reddit's Silk Road sub-Reddit at www.reddit.com
Shroomery at www.shroomery.org
Bitcoin forums at www.bitcointalk.org
Black Market Reloaded forums at various .onion addresses
The Hub forums at http://thehub7dnl5nmcz5.onion

Acknowledgements

I could never have produced this book without the support of my wonderful family and friends, and especially my partner, Cam, who was always in my corner and provided me with a fabulous country retreat to work from.

Thanks to my agent, Lyn Tranter, and Tom Gilliatt, who commissioned the book. To Angus Fontaine, my publisher, and to my hardworking editors Samantha Sainsbury, Foong Ling Kong, Deonie Fiford and Katie Purvis, thank you for your patience, ideas, feedback and faith in the manuscript.

To Graham Reilly, features editor at *The Age*, for giving me my first break in journalism, thank you for taking a chance on an unknown, unpublished writer and for your subsequent enthusiasm and encouragement.

To the many drug reform advocates who supported my work, in particular Dr Monica Barratt, who was always available to share her thoughts in interviews, I hope your efforts to apply evidence and reason to the drug debate help bring about long-overdue reforms.

To my fellow journalists who were not afraid to report on Silk Road accurately and without hysteria, I salute you but am afraid to name you all because I know I will miss some. And to the pseudonymous heroes Gwern of gwern.net and LaMoustache of antilop.cc, your websites are astonishing resources for those interested in the history of Silk Road.

Finally, to all the Silk Road users who allowed me into their world, especially the moderators, administrators and every incarnation of the Dread Pirate Roberts, thanks for your stories, information and insights into a world few people understand.